Financial Analysis of Mergers and Acquisitions

"This book is the first and most comprehensive book that covers the financial analysis of M&A transactions. The book is rigorous but also very practical. Anyone with a serious interest in making good decisions in M&A transactions should read this book".

—Professor Florin P. Vasvari, *London Business School, London, UK*

"This book should be regarded as the encyclopaedia of accounting issues related to mergers and acquisitions (M&A) and inter-company holdings. The text tackles complex issues with clear and simple-to-understand exposition. A notable strength is the rich set of examples, cases and illustrations accompanied by detailed explanations. Another strength is that the coverage of both US GAAP and International Financial Reporting Standards. This book is a must for accounting and finance academics, students, and M&A specialists".

—Professor Gilad Livne, *University of Exeter Business School, Streatham Court, Rennes Drive, Exeter, UK*

"Amir and Ghitti provide a rigorous, yet accessible, discussion of M&A accounting, how it affects the financial statements, and therefore how it must inform the analysis of deals. They also examine other important aspects of M&A transactions, such as tax consequences, financing, and deal structure, and illustrate the book's concepts with a series of real-life cases. The book will be a valuable resource to students interested in working in M&A, as well as to practitioners who are already doing so".

—Professor Leonard Soffer, *University of Chicago Booth School of Business, Chicago, IL*

"The book provides the reader with a comprehensive tool kit for analyzing all aspects of business combinations. It not only describes the accounting treatments and financial analysis of different transactions but also includes a large collection of real-life cases. The authors have managed to discuss a challenging topic in an easy-to-understand way. I have been teaching M&A accounting in MBA classes for two decades and will certainly take this book to my course materials".

—Professor Juha-Pekka Kallunki, *Oulu Business School, University of Oulu*

"This textbook covers a topic missing from the literature: the financial analysis of M&A transactions. As such, it will be extremely useful to students and practitioners of accounting and finance. It combines breadth and depth and clearly explains the M&A related accounting rules with many examples. A set of interesting real-life cases complement the text and make the concepts and techniques more understandable. It is difficult for me to envision a financial statement analysis course without reference to this book".

—Professor Theodore Sougiannis, *University of Illinois at Urbana Champaign, Champaign, IL*

Eli Amir · Marco Ghitti

Financial Analysis of Mergers and Acquisitions

Understanding Financial Statements and Accounting Rules with Case Studies

palgrave
macmillan

Eli Amir
Coller School of Management
Tel Aviv University
Tel Aviv, Israel

Marco Ghitti
SKEMA Business School
Paris, France

ISBN 978-3-030-61768-4 ISBN 978-3-030-61769-1 (eBook)
https://doi.org/10.1007/978-3-030-61769-1

Image credit: BAIVECTOR

This Palgrave Macmillan imprint is published by the registered company Springer Nature Switzerland AG
The registered company address is: Gewerbestrasse 11, 6330 Cham, Switzerland

To Irit Amir, Tal Amir, Adi Amir and Gal Amir
and
To Elisa, Anna and Aurora
and
In memory of Yehuda Amir and Franco Ghitti

Foreword

Most companies, over their life, go through business combinations and major restructurings. Surprisingly, while there are many handbooks on financial statement analysis, the effects of mergers and acquisitions and corporate restructurings on financial analysis is virtually ignored by most manuals.

This book fills a gap in the current knowledge on business combinations and is an essential reading for all those who intend to understand and analyze real financial statements.

Acquisitions and divestitures, spin-offs and equity carve-outs, leverage buyouts and recapitalizations are company-defining moments, and the accounting treatment of these deals, as well as the related corporate disclosures, call for detailed elucidation. As most publicly listed companies issue consolidated financial statements, it is very important to understand the financial consequences of M&A transactions and other major restructurings. M&A transactions clearly "shock" the consolidated balance sheet, income statement, and cash flow statement. Analyzing financial statements without reference to M&A transactions is incomplete at best. Understanding the accounting rules for inter-corporate investments in general and the rules for M&A transactions in particular, is, therefore, key to understanding the business and economics of the reporting company. All the more so in the presence of different types of deal structures managers put in place to achieve a specific corporate objective. Furthermore, as deal volume, both within and across borders, increase, accounting and reporting of M&A transactions become crucial in analyzing financial statements.

This book is a road map to successfully analyzing M&A transactions based on financial statements and digging into real-life landmark deals.

The reader stands to benefit from this book for many reasons. First, because of the invaluable experience the authors developed through many years in the M&A world, both in academia and in the advisory profession. Second, because of the authors' ability to break down the major components of this subject into concrete steps, enabling the reader to walk through the varieties of accounting rules for M&A transactions using a detailed and comprehensive roadmap, enriched by many examples. The book is useful because it is a practical, hands-on, and a user-friendly guide rather than a general and theoretical essay. In addition, the real-life case studies provided in the second part of the book are truly gems that illustrate, step-by-step, all the different aspects behind the financial interpretation and reporting of M&A deals.

There is a strong demand among business students and practitioners for a manual that provides a comprehensive framework for using financial statement data in order to analyze and evaluate M&A transactions. This book definitely provides such a framework.

Annalisa Prencipe
Bocconi University
Milan, Italy

Preface

Mergers and acquisitions (M&A) reshape the corporate landscape helping companies expand market share and gain a strategic advantage. Therefore, the ability to initiate, analyze, and complete M&A transactions is valuable. We contribute to the overall understanding of M&As by focusing on one particular area: financial analysis. Being able to analyze M&As using financial information is clearly useful to those who engage in M&A transactions.

There are many different aspects of M&A transactions, which are often discussed in detail in other textbooks. These aspects include legal ground for M&As, optimal deal structure, strategic issues, negotiations in M&A deals, taxation, and valuations of target companies. However, as far as we know, there is no textbook focusing on financial analysis of M&A transactions. Our book attempts to fill in the gap by looking at the impact of M&A transactions on the balance sheet, income statement, and the cash flow statement, and how management can exercise discretion in accounting for these transactions. For instance, whenever a leveraged buyout (LBO) is being effected, where will the debt show up? On the target company's balance sheet or on the sponsoring entity's? Is there going to be some goodwill arising from the transaction? If so, how should it be measured and what would that imply for the post-deal performances of the firms involved? Also, are there any differences between IFRS and US GAAP regarding LBOs and recapitalization and what is push-down accounting? Throughout this book, we aim at providing answers to these and many other questions related to the accounting and financial reporting of M&A transactions and the assessment of such deals using financial statements. Our goal is indeed to improve the ability of users of financial information to understand M&As by retrieving and analyzing information provided in financial statements. Therefore, we will focus on understanding the link between underlying economic events and the information in financial statements, and on how this link affects our assessment of the firms involved in the transaction.

We will extensively cover accounting and reporting—under both IAS/IFRS and US GAAP—of consolidation methods, goodwill, noncontrolling interests, step acquisitions and disposals, spin-offs and equity carve-outs, joint ventures, leveraged buyouts, special purpose entities, and tax issues related to M&A deals. The first part of the book includes a description of the accounting rules governing M&A transactions. In this part, we use many simple examples to demonstrate the accounting treatment. Without a basic understanding of the accounting rules, it is virtually impossible to evaluate a mergers and acquisition transaction. The second part includes real cases of M&A transactions. Each case focuses on a different element of M&A transactions and it is accompanied by a detailed teaching note of the case.

This book is particularly useful for students in master's programs in finance and accounting. MBA students specializing in finance could also find this book very useful. Owing in part to the real cases, this book could also be very useful for financial analysts CFOs and other practitioners who are involved with M&A transactions.

Tel Aviv, Israel Eli Amir
Paris, France Marco Ghitti

Acknowledgments

Financial statement analysis of mergers and acquisitions is a dynamic area as accounting rules keep changing. In addition, there are differences between accounting rules under US GAAP and IFRS, which makes writing the text and cases more challenging. This book is the result of the authors, colleagues, reviewers, and editorial and production staff working together as a team to publish the best possible book. We are deeply indebted to everyone who participated in bringing this book to publication.

Several of the cases included in this book started as a project with Master's of Finance students at London Business School under the supervision of Eli Amir. The Kraft and Cadbury Part I and Part II were originally written by Chemi Wieder and Hwangman Kim. Joan Esteve Manasanch wrote the first draft of the Ensign Group case. The Nokia-Siemens Case was originally written by Arik Parizer and Awais Raoof. Melisa Gonzales originally wrote the Bank of Hope case as a project. We owe special thanks to all these remarkable students. These cases, including the corresponding teaching notes, were later revised by the authors; the authors alone are responsible for any remaining errors.

We owe thanks to many who provided us with comments, guidance, and advice. In particular, we would like to thank: Ronny Barnes (formerly at London Business School), Mary Barth (Stanford's Graduate School of Business), Chris Higson (London Business School), Yael Gerasi and Moshe Peretz (PWC in Israel), Gilad Livne (University of Exeter Business School), Gregory Miller (University of Michigan), Steven Monahan (INSEAD), Tomer Regev (Morgan Stanley), Florin Vasvari (London Business School), Oktay Urcan (University of Illinois at Urbana Champaign), Danny Vitan (KPMG in Israel), Michele Casò (Bocconi University), Raluca Sandu (Skema Business School), and anonymous reviewers. We deeply regret if we forgot to mention someone.

In addition, we would like to thank those who wrote some of the end-of-chapter exercises. Some of these exercises have been written by others, who may have served in other academic institutions, but we unfortunately lost their identity with the passage of time. Special and warm thanks go to Ronny Zappella (Bocconi University and SGA) for his invaluable contribution in revising and editing the book.

Finally, we thank our wives, Irit and Elisa for their endless support during periods of writing, revising, and editing this book. We also thank our children, Tal, Adi, Gal, Anna, and Aurora for providing meaning to our lives before, during, and after this project.

Contents

Part II Case Studies

About the Authors

Professor Eli Amir, CPA (Israel) is currently a Professor of Accounting at the Coller School of Management at Tel Aviv University and a visiting professor at London Business School. Amir received his B.A. degree in Accounting and Economics from Tel Aviv University (1986) and his Ph.D. in Business Administration from the University of California, Berkeley (1991). From 1991 until 2000, Amir was a faculty member at Columbia University's Graduate School of Business. From 2000 to 2003 Amir served as the Chairman of the Israel Accounting Standards Board where is initiated the adoption of international accounting standards in Israel. From 2003 until 2012, Amir was a professor of accounting at London Business School and from 2012 to 2018 he was a part time faculty member at Cass Business School, City University of London. In addition, Amir was associated with the University of Oulu in Finland teaching and working with faculty. Amir is also a Certified Public Accountant in Israel since 1987. Amir teaches undergraduate and graduate courses in financial accounting, financial statement analysis, financial analysis of mergers and acquisitions, and empirical research in accounting. Amir's research concentrates on the role of financial information in capital markets. His recent research projects examined the capital market effects of cyber-attacks, the association between the precision of information and the cost of equity capital, the differential precision of positive and negative information, the economic consequences of business corruption, the association between criminal convictions and risk taking by auditors and senior corporate executives, and pension asset allocation. He has published many articles in leading academic journals such as the *Accounting Review*, *Review of Accounting Studies*, *Journal of Accounting and Economics* and the *Journal of Accounting Research*, and won prestigious awards for his research. Amir also holds an Honorary Doctorate from the University of Oulu, Finland.

Professor Marco Ghitti, CPA (Italy) is Assistant Professor of Accounting and Finance at SKEMA Business School—Université Côte d'Azur (Paris Campus). He received an M.Sc. in Law and Business Administration from Bocconi University (2006), a Master's in Finance from London Business School (2010) and a Ph.D. in Finance from Edhec Business School (2016). He has moved between academia and the advisory world. In 2008, Marco became partner and head of the Corporate Finance advisory team of Studio Ghitti & Associati (SGA), an independent advisory boutique involved in corporate finance, accounting, tax, and legal advisory. In

2011, Marco joined the Bocconi University Accounting Department, in Milan, as teaching fellow. From 2015 to 2018, he also lectured for Edhec Business School Finance Department in Nice. His research interests are law and economics, corporate governance, and bankruptcy.

List of Figures

List of Tables

Part I
Accounting and Financial Reporting

Introduction to Accounting for Inter-corporate Investments

1

1.1 Introduction

Corporations often invest in equity and debt securities of other corporations. This chapter focuses on the accounting for and financial reporting of investments in equity securities, and in particular, investments in ordinary shares that grant the investor voting rights in the investee. Depending on how many securities are acquired, the investor may have little or no influence over the investee, significant influence over the investee, and even control of the investee. The accounting methods discussed here reflect the level of influence the investor has over the investee (no significant influence, significant influence, or control).

The level of influence an investor has over an investee is often determined by the ownership level. The rebuttable presumption is that ownership of less than 20% of the voting rights gives the investor no significant influence over the investee. Ownership of between 20% and 50% of the voting rights means that the investor has significant influence over the investee, and an ownership of more than 50% of the voting rights constitutes control over the investee. Ownership of more than 50% of the voting rights is not the only way to achieve control. Control over an investee can be achieved by other means; for instance, by convertible securities (e.g., options, convertible preferred shares, convertible bonds), or contractual arrangements. Furthermore, ownership of more than 50% of the voting rights does not automatically grant control over an investee. For example, involvement of a company in bankruptcy procedures, government regulations, or restrictions on cross-border dividend payments, may prevent an investor from effectively exercising control.

For investments without significant influence (ownership of up to 20% of the voting rights), the accounting method is Fair Value Accounting, if fair value

---

Electronic supplementary material The online version of this chapter (https://doi.org/10.1007/978-3-030-61769-1_1) contains supplementary material, which is available to authorized users.

E. Amir and M. Ghitti, *Financial Analysis of Mergers and Acquisitions*,
https://doi.org/10.1007/978-3-030-61769-1_1

can be determined reliably. If fair value cannot be determined reliable, the Cost method should be used. Normally, an investment in equity securities of publicly listed companies is recognized on the investor's balance sheet at fair value and investments in private corporations will most likely be presented on the investor's balance sheet at cost. For investments with significant influence (20%–50% of the voting rights), the accounting method is the Equity method, which is discussed later in Sect. 1.3. For controlled investments (above 50% of the voting rights), the accounting method is full consolidation under the Purchase Method of Accounting, which is discussed in Sect. 1.4.

There are two additional accounting methods for investments in equity. The first one is the Proportionate Consolidation, which was applied in cases where more than one entity jointly control another entity. The second one is the Pooling of Interests method, which was applied in certain mergers. To date, both methods are not normally applied in practice. We will describe these methods to highlight certain features of accounting for consolidations in Sects. 1.5 and 1.6.

Next, we will briefly discuss each method, by describing the balance sheet recognition and the recognition of gains and losses in the income statement (profit and loss account). We will also briefly discuss investments in debt securities.

1.2 Passive Investments in Equity and Debt Securities—Fair Value Accounting

When an investor holds less than 20% of an investee's voting shares, the presumption is that there is no significant influence over the investee's operating, investing, and financing activities ("passive investment"). By their nature, investments in debt securities do not provide the investor with significant influence over the investee, hence these are also passive investments. Both International Financial Reporting Standards (IFRS) and US GAAP provide detailed guidance for investments in financial assets (IFRS 9 and ASC 320 / ASC 321).

Under IFRS 9, financial assets can be measured either at:

- amortized cost (for debt securities only);
- fair value through other comprehensive income (FVOCI);
- fair value through profit or loss (FVPL).

The measurement varies according to both:

- the investor's business model for each category of financial assets (hold to collect *versus* hold to collect *and* sell); and
- the contractual cash flows originated by each category of financial assets (solely payments of principal and interest on the principal amount outstanding, or else).

Under IFRS, the presumption is that passive investments in equity securities are held for trading. That is, the investor holds these shares primarily for price appreciation and/or dividend income. The accounting rule for these investments is to present them on the balance sheet at fair value and to recognize unrealized gains and losses (that is, changes in the value of the investment) in the income statements (fair value through profit and loss—FVPL). In addition, all realized gains and losses, as well as dividend income, are recognized in the income statement.

In some cases, though, the investor holds equity securities for purposes other than trading. For example, a company may be required to hold a stake in the investee to gain access to certain markets or because of regulatory requirements. In these cases, recognition of unrealized gains and losses in the income statement may distort the company's reported profitability because management has no intention to trade the investment. These investments may be classified as non-trading investment in equity securities (or, available for sale securities), and unrealized gains and losses would then be recognized in other comprehensive income (OCI), which is part of shareholders' equity (fair value through other comprehensive income—FVOCI). Essentially, these unrealized gains and losses bypass the income statement and are recognized directly in shareholders' equity.

According to US GAAP, the required accounting method for investments in publicly listed equity securities is to recognize unrealized gains/losses in the income statement (trading securities). That is, under US GAAP, investments in publicly listed equity securities may not be classified as available for sale securities, although investments in debt securities may.

Classification of investments in publicly listed equity securities as FVPL is also the default accounting treatment under IFRS; nonetheless, the reporting entity can use the alternative classification as FVOCI, if it actively classifies the investment as non-trading. Irrespective of the classification as trading (FVPL) or non-trading (FVOCI) securities, disposal of these investments will normally result in recognition of gains or losses on the income statement.[1]

As for investments in debt securities, there are three alternative methods. These investments may be presented at FVPL, FVOCI, or Held-to-Maturity (Amortized Cost method). To be classified as Held-to-Maturity, the investor must have a positive intent and ability to hold the investment in the debt security until its maturity.

Example starts

Tal Company Ltd. was founded on January 1, 2019. At that time, the company had £100,000 in cash and £100,000 of ordinary shareholders' equity. The company

[1]Under US GAAP, the accounting rules for trading securities are substantially the same as those described for IFRS. Notwithstanding, in case of equity securities with easily determinable market values, they must be classified at FVPL.

presents financial statements for December 31 of each year. Assume the tax rate is 25%. On January 2, 2019, the company made the following investments:

(a) no. 1,000 ordinary shares of Red Company for £20 a share;
(b) no. 600, 5% preferred shares, £50 par, of Green Company for £25,000;
(c) £30,000 par value of 10% convertible bonds of Blue Company for £30,000;
(d) no. 2,500 ordinary shares of Gray Company for £10 a share.

During 2019, the company received, in cash, interest on convertible bonds of Blue Company, and dividends on preferred stock of Green Company. Realized gains (interest and dividends) are taxable at 25% while taxation on unrealized gains and losses is deferred until the security is effectively sold. There is no other investment income.

The market values of the investments and their accounting classifications as of December 31, 2019 are as follows:

Investment	Cost	Market value	Accounting classification
Red Company	£20,000	£24,000	Trading equity security
Green Company	£25,000	£30,000	Trading equity security
Blue Company	£30,000	£28,000	Held-to-Maturity debt security
Gray Company	£25,000	£22,000	Non-trading equity security

Required:

Present the income statement and balance sheet for Tal Company as of December 31, 2019.

Solution:

Income statement	£	Comments
Dividend income on preferred shares	1,500	600 × £50 × 0.05
Interest income on bonds	3,000	£30,000 × 0.10
Unrealized gains on trading securities[a]	9,000	(24,000+30,000) – (20,000+25,000)[b]
Income before tax	**13,500**	
Income tax expense	3,375	
Net income	**10,125**	
Other comprehensive income	**£**	**Comments**
Unrealized loss on non-trading security	(3,000)	Gray Company
Tax benefit (deferred)	750	
Net unrealized loss	**(2,250)**	

[a]Note that for Held-to-Maturity security, unrealized gain and losses are not recognized
[b]Red and Green Company

Balance sheet	£	Comments
Cash	4,500	Dividend and interest income
Investment in trading securities	76,000	Market value of equity securities
Investment in bonds held-to-maturity	30,000	Bonds at amortized cost
Deferred tax asset on unrealized loss	750	£3,000 × 0.25
Total assets	**111,250**	
Tax payable on dividends and interests	1,125	4,500 × 0.25
Deferred taxes on unrealized gains	2,250	(4,000+5,000) × 0.25
Total liabilities	**3,375**	
Common shares	100,000	
Retained earnings	10,125	
Other comprehensive losses	(2,250)	
Total shareholders' equity	**107,875**	
Total liabilities and equity	**111,250**	

Example ends

1.3 Investments with Significant Influence—The Equity Method

Companies often acquire a significant, but not controlling, interest in the equity of another company (the investee). Companies may also, at times, sell a controlled subsidiary, but retain a significant investment in it. These investments may be in the form of common stocks, preferred stocks, or other in-substance equity interests.

The investor should apply the equity method of accounting (IAS 28/ASC 323) if the equity investment provides the investor with significant influence over the investee. This is often the case when an investor holds 20% of the voting common stocks (or equivalent) of an investee, but does not have a controlling financial interest. However, ownership levels of as little as 3%–5% may also require application of the equity method in certain circumstances, such as with investments in limited partnerships.

An investor should also apply the equity method to an investment in a joint venture that the investor jointly controls with other investors. "Joint Venture" is a term that is loosely used in practice, but is defined in both IFRS (see IFRS 11) and US GAAP (see ASC 323). The definition of a joint venture (and Joint Arrangement) may have important accounting consequences.

Equity method investments are recorded initially at cost (including transaction costs). Any differences between the cost to the investor and the underlying equity in net assets of the investee at the date of investment (basis differences) should be identified and treated by the investor as in the case of consolidated subsidiaries. Notwithstanding, nothing will appear on the investor's balance sheet other than a single line item showing the carrying amount of the investment: this one-line item includes both the share of the investee's net assets at fair value, as measured on initial recognition, and goodwill, if any.

After the initial recognition, an equity method investment is adjusted to recognize the investor's share of earnings, losses, and/or changes in equity of the investee after the acquisition date. When an investor provides other forms of financial support, such as loans, loan guarantees, or preferred stocks, investee's losses may need to be recorded even after the common stocks investment has been reduced to zero. Anyway, when the investor's share of losses of the investee equals or exceeds its interest in the investee, the investor will usually discontinue recognizing its share of further losses, unless the investor bears an unlimited liability.

Dividends received from the investee generally reduce the carrying amount of the investment on the balance sheet and are not recognized on the investor's income statement. Equity method investments are assessed for other-than-temporary impairment. The existence of basis differences will often result in adjustments to the investor's share in the investee's net income, including impairments. Disposal of equity method investments will normally result in recognition of gains and losses on the investor's income statement.

Example starts

On January 1, 2019, Eli Ltd. acquired 30% of the ordinary shares of Amir Ltd. for £750,000. At that time, the fair values of Amir's assets and liabilities were properly assessed. Tax rate is 30%. Both Eli and Amir issue financial statements as of December 31 of each year. Here are the details:

Amir Ltd. (£)	Carrying amousnt	Fair value
Fixed assets, net	1,500,000	1,600,000
Patents	100,000	150,000
Inventory	400,000	400,000
Long-term receivables	320,000	320,000
Cash	300,000	300,000
Total assets	**2,620,000**	**2,770,000**
Bonds payable (6%)	600,000	600,000
Contingent liability	–	50,000
Shareholders' equity	2,020,000	2,120,000
Total liabilities and equity	**2,620,000**	**2,770,000**

During 2019, Amir reported net income of £200,000 and distributed dividends on ordinary shares of £100,000. The remaining useful life of fixed assets and patents is 5 and 10 years, respectively. Inventory is sold by the end of fiscal 2019. The contingent liability will not be settled prior to December 31, 2021. During 2019, Amir's goodwill lost 10% of its value. Impairment of goodwill is not tax-deductible (i.e., it is treated as a permanent difference for accounting purposes).

Required:

a. Calculate the amount of goodwill purchased.
b. Calculate the amount of Eli's share in Amir's net income.
c. Present a reconciliation of the "Investment in Amir" account during fiscal 2019.

Solution:

Part (a)

Amir Ltd. (£)	Carrying amount	Fair value	Δ	30% of Δ	Amortization
Fixed assets, net	1,500,000	1,600,000	100,000	30,000	6,000
Patents	100,000	150,000	50,000	15,000	1,500
Inventory	400,000	400,000			
Long term receivables	320,000	320,000			
Cash	300,000	300,000			
Total assets	**2,620,000**	**2,770,000**			
Bonds payable (6%)	600,000	600,000			
Contingent liability	–	50,000	(50,000)	(15,000)	–
Shareholders' equity	2,020,000	2,120,000			
Total liabilities and equity	**2,620,000**	**2,770,000**			
Asset write-up				30,000	
Deferred taxes				(9,000)	
Asset write-up, net of tax				**21,000**	
Share in book value[a]				606,000	
Goodwill purchased[b]				**123,000**	
Total payment				750,000	

[a]£2,020,000 × 0.3
[b]£750,000 – £606,000 – £21,000

Part (b)

Share in net income	£
Share in reported income	60,000
Amortization of fixed assets	(6,000)
Amortization of patents	(1,500)
Deferred tax on amortization	2,250
Reduction in goodwill	(12,300)
Share in net income	**42,450**

Part (c)

Investment account	£
Investment January 1, 2019	750,000
Share in net income	42,450
Share in dividends	(30,000)
Investment December 31, 2019	**762,450**

Example ends

1.4 Consolidation—Controlling Interests

When an investor holds a controlling interest in the investee, the investor will present consolidated financial statements.[2] Several international accounting standards prescribe the rules for consolidations. IFRS 10 establishes principles for the presentation and preparation of consolidated financial statements, when an entity controls one or more other entities.

The basic rule is that if you control another entity, you consolidate it; if you do not control that entity, you do not consolidate it. IFRS 10 is more specific in its definition of control, with the aim of ensuring that all entities that should be consolidated are indeed so. Consolidation techniques are detailed in IFRS 3. The disclosure requirements for interests in subsidiaries are specified in IFRS 12. IFRS 9 does not apply to interests in subsidiaries that are consolidated. When instruments containing potential voting rights (see further) give access to the returns associated with an ownership interest in a subsidiary, the instruments are not subject to the requirements of IFRS 9.

When an investor controls an investee, the investor will normally present consolidated financial statements. An investor controls an investee when it is exposed, or has rights, to variable returns from its involvement with the investee and has the ability to affect those returns through its power over the investee. The three elements of control thus are:

- power over the investee;
- exposure, or rights, to variable returns from involvement with the investee;
- the ability to use power over the investee to affect the amount of the investor's returns.

IFRS 10 requires an investor to reassess whether it controls an investee if facts and circumstances indicate that there are changes to one, or more, of the three elements of control.

Consolidation shall begin from the date the investor obtains control of the investee. It ceases when the investor loses control of the investee. When preparing

[2]See IFRS 10, IFRS 3, ASC 810, and ASC 805.

consolidated financial statements, the parent uses uniform accounting policies for both itself and its subsidiaries and it must make appropriate adjustments to achieve conformity.

Consolidated financial statements:

- combine like items of assets, liabilities, equity, income, expenses, and cash flows of the parent with those of its subsidiaries, after making uniform accounting standards and policies adopted by the entities falling within the consolidation area;
- offset (eliminate) the carrying amount of the parent's investment in each subsidiary and the parent's portion of equity of each subsidiary (goodwill, if any, is accounted for according to IFRS 3);
- eliminate in full intragroup assets and liabilities, equity, income, revenues, expenses, and cash flows relating to transactions between entities of the group (profits or losses resulting from intragroup transactions that are recorded in assets, such as inventory and fixed assets, are eliminated in full).[3] IAS 12 applies to temporary differences that arise from the elimination of profits and losses resulting from intragroup transactions. Revenues and expenses of the subsidiary are based on the amounts of the assets and liabilities recorded in the consolidated financial statements at the acquisition date. For example, depreciation expenses recorded in the consolidated income statement after the acquisition date are based on the fair values of the related depreciable assets recorded in the consolidated financial statements at the acquisition date.

When consolidating, there are several aspects which need to be taken into consideration. Some of them are the following:

- potential voting rights;
- reporting date;
- goodwill;
- non-controlling interests;
- loss of control.

Potential voting rights:

To assess control, an entity should consider potential voting rights. When potential voting rights (or derivatives containing potential voting rights) exist, profits, losses and changes in equity allocated to the parent and non-controlling interests in preparing consolidated financial statements are determined solely on the basis of existing ownership interests and do not reflect the possible exercise, or conversion, of potential voting rights and other derivatives.

[3]Intragroup losses may indicate an impairment that requires recognition in the consolidated financial statements.

Example starts
Many offshore companies are set up for a specific purpose, such as securitizations. For legal and tax purposes, local directors (such as lawyers and accountants) manage such companies. The onshore unit wishes to avoid being seen as managing the offshore unit. The onshore investing company may enter contracts with the offshore unit for specific services that the offshore unit provides. Such contracts virtually run the offshore unit and transactions are executed automatically. These transactions often include receiving funds from specific operators and remitting these funds to the onshore company. The role of the directors is to administer the contract. The ownership of the offshore unit is irrelevant, as the offshore unit is governed by the contract. Therefore, the onshore company should consolidate the offshore unit in its accounts.
Example ends

Reporting date:

The financial statements of the parent and its subsidiaries shall have the same reporting date. Otherwise, the subsidiary prepares, for consolidation purposes, additional financial statements as of the same date as the financial statements of the parent. If it is impracticable for a particular subsidiary to prepare its financial statements as of the same date as its parent, the parent shall consolidate the financial information of the subsidiary using the most recent financial statements of the subsidiary, adjusted for the effects of significant transactions, or events occurring between the date of those financial statements and the date of the consolidated financial statements. The difference between the date of the subsidiary's financial statements and that of the consolidated financial statements shall be no more than three months, and the length of the reporting periods and any difference between the dates of the financial statements shall be the same from period to period.

Goodwill:

Under the purchase method of accounting, the purchase price paid by the parent is allocated to the net identifiable assets of the subsidiary on a fair value basis (this process is known as Purchase Price Allocation). After completion of such process, any residual constitutes goodwill, which is reported as a non-current intangible asset on the consolidated balance sheet. Under IFRS, goodwill can be calculated in two alternative methods:

- as the difference between the fair value of the whole subsidiary and the fair value of its net identifiable assets (Full Goodwill method); or
- as the difference between the purchase price and the fair value of net assets acquired by the parent (the share of the subsidiary's net identifiable assets acquired by the parent). This method is called the Partial Goodwill method.

Under US GAAP, only the full goodwill method is allowed.

Example starts
On January 1, 2019, Parent acquires a 75% interest in the equity of Subsidiary by paying a cash consideration of $1,500. At that date, the fair value of Subsidiary's net identifiable assets is estimated to be $1,000 and the fair value of the remaining 25% of Subsidiary is estimated to be $450.

Based on these details, under the full goodwill method, goodwill will be equal to ($1,500 + $450 − $1,000 =) $950. Under the partial goodwill method, goodwill will be equal to ($1,500 − 75% × $1,000 =) $750.

The key difference between the two procedures is that:

- under the full goodwill method, both the parent's and the non-controlling interests' share of goodwill will be recognized on the consolidated balance sheet; whereas,
- under the partial goodwill method, only the parent's share of goodwill will be recognized on the consolidated balance sheet.

To see this, consider what Parent paid to get its share of Subsidiary's net identifiable assets and what non-controlling interests "paid" to get their share of Subsidiary's net identifiable assets:

- Parent paid $1,500 to get 75% of $1,000 (Subsidiary's net identifiable assets on a fair value basis), resulting in a goodwill of $750;
- non-controlling interests "paid" $450 to get 25% of $1,000 (Subsidiary's net identifiable assets on a fair value basis), resulting in a goodwill of $200.

The sum of the two figures above ($750 + $200) represents the amount of goodwill recognized under the full goodwill method ($950).

Example ends

Non-controlling interests (NCIs):

Whenever a parent gains control over an investee, it will have to report 100% of the investee's assets, liabilities, revenues, expenses, and cash flows, irrespective of the actual level of ownership held. When a parent owns less than 100% of a subsidiary, therefore, it is necessary to recognize non-controlling interests (formerly known as "minority interests") to account for the proportionate share of the investee's (or, rather, subsidiary) net assets not owned by the parent.

This non-controlling interests account is shown in the consolidated balance sheet within shareholders' equity, separately from the equity of parent's owners. These are external owners of shares in the subsidiaries of the parent company.

The parent should attribute the net income and the components of other comprehensive income to the owners of the parent and to the non-controlling interests, even if this results in the non-controlling interests having a deficit balance.

If a subsidiary has outstanding cumulative preferred shares classified as equity and they are held by non-controlling interests, the parent should compute its share of net income after adjusting for the dividends on such shares, whether or not such dividends have been declared.

Purchases and sales of shares in subsidiaries between the parent and the non-controlling interests increase, and decrease, their accounts in equity, while control is maintained. Profits, or losses, on these transactions are recorded in the equity of the parent, usually as additional paid-in capital but not in the income statement (see Chapter 3).

There are two alternative accounting methods for non-controlling interests: the full method and the partial method. These methods correspond to the two alternative methods for measuring goodwill. Consider the previous example: under the Full Method, non-controlling interests are $450, whereas under the Partial Method, they are equal to $200.

Loss of control:

If a parent loses control of a subsidiary, the parent should immediately:

- derecognize the assets and liabilities of the former subsidiary from the consolidated balance sheet;
- recognize any investment retained in the former subsidiary at its fair value when control is lost, and subsequently account for it in accordance with relevant accounting standards (passive investment, equity method, or a joint venture);
- record the gain, or loss, associated with the loss of control attributable to the former controlling interest.

Example starts

On January 1, 2007, Entity A buys 100% of Entity T for €500,000, when Entity T's fair value is €400,000. On acquisition, goodwill is thus €100,000 (€500,000 – €400,000).

On December 31, 2019, Entity A sells 60% of Entity T for €675,000. At that date:

- the fair value of the residual stake held by Entity A in Entity T (40%), including goodwill, is equal to €420,000;
- Entity A's book value of net assets is €800,000, while goodwill is €50,000.

Following the transaction, Entity A loses control of Entity T, but retains an investment in an associate (40% of Entity T). The investment retained in Entity T will be recognized at fair value at the day of disposal and, subsequently, recorded using the equity method of accounting.

The gain associated with the loss of control is computed as the:

- fair value of the consideration received; *plus*
- fair value of any investment retained in the former subsidiary; *minus*
- book value of the net assets (including goodwill) derecognized; *plus*
- book value of NCI, if any.

The gain is thus equal to (€675,000+€420,000 – €800,000 – €50,000=) €245,000.

At disposal, the journal entries on Entity A's books will be the following:

€	Dr.	Cr.
Consideration received	675,000	
Investment in associate (including goodwill)	420,000	
Net assets derecognized		800,000
Goodwill derecognized		50,000
Gain from disposal		245,000

Example ends

Example starts

Below are the balance sheets and income statements for Acquire and Target for the years ended on December 31, 2019 and December 31, 2018. Consider the following scenarios:

1. Acquire buys 100% of Target's voting shares for £400 in cash on 31 December 2018;
2. Acquire buys 100% of Target's voting shares for £500 in cash on 31 December 2018;
3. Acquire buys 60% of Target's voting shares for £500 in cash on 31 December 2018.

Balance sheet (£)	Acquire		Target	
	31/12/18	31/12/19	31/12/18	31/12/19
Tangible fixed assets	700	1,000	350	400
Cash	600	500	100	125
Other current assets	300	500	150	250
Current liabilities	(300)	(400)	(200)	(250)
Net assets	**1,300**	**1,600**	**400**	**525**
Share capital	100	100	50	50
Retained profits	1,200	1,500	350	475
Shareholders' equity	**1,300**	**1,600**	**400**	**525**

Income statements (£)	Acquire		Target	
	31/12/18	31/12/19	31/12/18	31/12/19
Sales	600	900	250	400
Cost of sales	(200)	(300)	(100)	(150)
Operating expenses	(100)	(200)	(50)	(100)
Net income	**300**	**400**	**100**	**150**
Dividends paid	(100)	(100)	–	(25)
Retained profit	200	300	100	125
Retained profits beginning balance	1,000	1,200	250	350
Retained profits closing balance	**1,200**	**1,500**	**350**	**475**

The balance sheet for Acquire assumes no investment in Target even at December 31, 2019. So, you should consider cash effects deriving from the investment separately.

Case 1: £400 cash for 100% of shares

Balance sheet (£)	Acquire		Target		Acquire		Acquire	
	31/12/18	31/12/19	31/12/18	31/12/19	31/12/18	31/12/19	31/12/18	31/12/19
					Equity	Equity	Purchase	Purchase
Tangible fixed assets	700	1,000	350	400	700	1,000	1,050	1,400
Investment in Target					400	525	–	–
Cash	600	500	100	125	200	125[a]	300	250
Other current assets	300	500	150	250	300	500	450	750
Current liabilities	(300)	(400)	(200)	(250)	(300)	(400)	(500)	(650)
Net assets	**1,300**	**1,600**	**400**	**525**	**1,300**	**1,750**	**1,300**	**1,750**
Share capital	100	100	50	50	100	100	100	100
Retained profits	1,200	1,500	350	475	1,200	1,650	1,200	1,650
Shareholders' equity	**1,300**	**1,600**	**400**	**525**	**1,300**	**1,750**	**1,300**	**1,750**

[a]Acquire's cash balance at December 31, 2019 is computed as: beginning cash (£200), less dividends paid (£100), plus dividend received from Target (£25). For simplicity, we do not show the dividends paid by Target in the Acquire's income statement, although in reality they would be there

Income statement (£)	Acquire		Target		Acquire		Acquire	
	31/12/18	31/12/19	31/12/18	31/12/19	31/12/18	31/12/19	31/12/18	31/12/19
					Equity	Equity	Purchase	Purchase
Sales	600	900	250	400	600	900	600	1,300
Cost of sales	(200)	(300)	(100)	(150)	(200)	(300)	(200)	(450)
Operating expenses	(100)	(200)	(50)	(100)	(100)	(200)	(100)	(300)
Share of Target's income					–	150	–	–
Net income	**300**	**400**	**100**	**150**	**300**	**550**	**300**	**550**
Dividends paid	(100)	(100)	–	(25)	(100)	(100)	(100)	(100)
Retained profit	200	300	100	125	200	450	200	450
Retained profits begin	1,000	1,200	250	350	1,000	1,200	1,000	1,200
Retained profits closing	**1,200**	**1,500**	**350**	**475**	**1,200**	**1,650**	**1,200**	**1,650**

Case 2: £500 cash for 100% of shares

Balance sheet (£)	Acquire		Target		Acquire		Acquire	
	31/12/18	31/12/19	31/12/18	31/12/19	31/12/18	31/12/19	31/12/18	31/12/19
					Equity	Equity	Purchase	Purchase
Tangible fixed assets	700	1,000	350	400	700	1,000	1,050	1,400
Intangible fixed assets							**100**	**100**[a]
Investment in Target					**500**	**625**	–	–
Cash	600	500	100	125	**100**	**25**	**200**	**150**
Other current assets	300	500	150	250	300	500	450	750
Current liabilities	(300)	(400)	(200)	(250)	(300)	(400)	(500)	(650)
Net assets	**1,300**	**1,600**	**400**	**525**	**1,300**	**1,750**	**1,300**	**1,750**
Share capital	100	100	50	50	100	100	100	100
Retained profits	1,200	1,500	350	475	1,200	1,650	1,200	1,650
Shareholders' equity	**1,300**	**1,600**	**400**	**525**	**1,300**	**1,750**	**1,300**	**1,750**

[a]Same as in 2018 because goodwill is not amortized

Income statement (£)	Acquire		Target		Acquire		Acquire	
	31/12/18	31/12/19	31/12/18	31/12/19	31/12/18	31/12/19	31/12/18	31/12/19
					Equity	Equity	Purchase	Purchase
Sales	600	900	250	400	600	900	600	1,300
Cost of sales	(200)	(300)	(100)	(150)	(200)	(300)	(200)	(450)
Operating expenses	(100)	(200)	(50)	(100)	(100)	(200)	(100)	(300)
Share of Target's income					–	**150**	–	–
Net income	**300**	**400**	**100**	**150**	**300**	**550**	**300**	**550**[a]
Dividends paid	(100)	(100)	–	(25)	(100)	(100)	(100)	(100)
Retained profit	200	300	100	125	200	450	200	450
Retained profits begin	1,000	1,200	250	350	1,000	1,200	1,000	1,200
Retained profits closing	**1,200**	**1,500**	**350**	**475**	**1,200**	**1,650**	**1,200**	**1,650**

[a]Same as in Case 1 only because goodwill is not amortized

Case 3: £500 cash for 60% of shares

Balance sheet (£)	Acquire		Target		Acquire		Acquire	
	31/12/18	31/12/19	31/12/18	31/12/19	31/12/18	31/12/19	31/12/18	31/12/19
					Equity	Equity	Purchase	Purchase
Tangible fixed assets	700	1,000	350	400	700	1,000	1,050	1,400
Intangible fixed assets							260	260

Balance sheet (£)	Acquire		Target		Acquire		Acquire	
	31/12/18	31/12/19	31/12/18	31/12/19	31/12/18	31/12/19	31/12/18	31/12/19
					Equity	Equity	Purchase	Purchase
Investment in Target					500	575	–	–
Cash	600	500	100	125	100	15	200	140
Other current assets	300	500	150	250	300	500	450	750
Current liabilities	(300)	(400)	(200)	(250)	(300)	(400)	(500)	(650)
Net assets	**1,300**	**1,600**	**400**	**525**	**1,300**	**1,690**	**1,460**	**1,900**
Minority interests					–	–	160	210
Share capital	100	100	50	50	100	100	100	100
Retained profits	1,200	1,500	350	475	1,200	1,590	1,200	1,590
Shareholders' equity	**1,300**	**1,600**	**400**	**525**	**1,300**	**1,690**	**1,460**	**1,900**

Income statement (£)	Acquire		Target		Acquire		Acquire	
	31/12/18	31/12/19	31/12/18	31/12/19	31/12/18	31/12/19	31/12/18	31/12/19
					Equity	Equity	Purchase	Purchase
Sales	600	900	250	400	600	900	600	1,300
Cost of sales	(200)	(300)	(100)	(150)	(200)	(300)	(200)	(450)
Operating expenses	(100)	(200)	(50)	(100)	(100)	(200)	(100)	(300)
Share of Target's income						90	–	–
Minority interests						–	–	(60)
Net income	**300**	**400**	**100**	**150**	**300**	**490**	**300**	**490**
Dividends paid	(100)	(100)	–	(25)	(100)	(100)	(100)	(100)
Retained profit	200	300	100	125	200	390	200	390
Retained profits begin	1,000	1,200	250	350	1,000	1,200	1,000	1,200
Retained profits closing	**1,200**	**1,500**	**350**	**475**	**1,200**	**1,590**	**1,200**	**1,590**

Example ends

1.5 Joint Control

When two or more investors jointly control an investee, none of them has control on its own. Two or more investors jointly control an investee when they must act together to direct the investee's relevant activities. As no investor can direct the activities without the co-operation of the other(s), no investor individually controls the investee; hence, no investor consolidates the investee. Each investor accounts for its interest in the investee in accordance with the relevant IFRS/US GAAP depending on the specific circumstances; for example, the equity method, or the fair value method.

Normally, the investors will use the equity method in case of joint control. In rare cases (which will be discussed later on), the proportionate consolidation method may be applied under IFRS only, but not under US GAAP.

Under proportionate consolidation, the parent recognizes on its balance sheet the share in the assets, liabilities, revenues, and expenses. The share in the assets and liabilities is based on fair values at the time of acquisition, including recognition of goodwill, intangibles, and other fair value adjustments. Note, however, that under proportionate consolidation there are no non-controlling interests.

1.6 Pooling of Interests

While the pooling of interests method is not currently applied, it is important to understand the difference between consolidation under the purchase method and consolidation under pooling. The pooling of interests method was discontinued in the US in 2001, and under IFRS in 2004.

The pooling method was used for merger and acquisition transactions under certain conditions. For example, the deal was based only on exchange of shares and the two merging companies were similar to each other in terms of size. The pooling method involves consolidating the balance sheets of the two companies based on book value and not on fair value as in the purchase method. This is followed by the restatement of historical financial statements as if the two companies were one for many years. Upon consolidation, this method excludes fair value adjustments such as intangible assets and goodwill unless they are already recognized on the balance sheet of one of the merging companies. As such, no goodwill is reported as a consequence of the acquisition or merger.

Certain sectors preferred using the pooling method for business combinations before its discontinuation. The use of the method peaked during 1998, when it comprised 52% of all deal volume. In dollar terms, this equaled $852 billion. Large technology companies used the pooling method, because they were able to avoid recording the related acquisition costs. Earnings were higher because there were no amortization and impairment of goodwill and other fair value adjustments.

Example starts

Consider the balance sheets and income statements for Acquire and Target for the years ended on December 31, 2019 and 2018 as in the previous example. Consider the following scenarios: (i) Acquire buys 60% of Target for £500 in cash and uses the proportionate consolidation method; (ii) Acquire issues 75 shares (at par value) for 100% of the shares of Target and uses the pooling of interests method. Assume the investment is made on December 31, 2016.

Scenarios: (i) Proportionate consolidation for 60%; (ii) Pooling of interests assuming 100% for 75 shares

Balance sheet (£)	Acquire		Target		Acquire		Acquire	
	31/12/16	31/12/17	31/12/16	31/12/17	31/12/16	31/12/17	31/12/16	31/12/17
					Prop.	Prop.	Pooling	Pooling
Tangible fixed assets	700	1,000	350	400	910	1,240	1,050	1,400
Intangible fixed assets					260	260	–	–
Cash	600	500	100	125	160	90	700	650
Other current assets	300	500	150	250	390	650	450	750
Current liabilities	(300)	(400)	(200)	(250)	(420)	(550)	(500)	(650)
Net assets	**1,300**	**1,600**	**400**	**525**	**1,300**	**1,690**	**1,700**	**2,150**
Minority interests					–	–	–	–
Share capital	100	100	50	50	100	100	175	175
Retained profits	1,200	1,500	350	475	1,200	1,590	1,525	1,975
Shareholders' equity	**1,300**	**1,600**	**400**	**525**	**1,300**	**1,690**	**1,700**	**2,150**

Income statement (£)	Acquire		Target		Acquire		Acquire	
	31/12/16	31/12/17	31/12/16	31/12/17	31/12/16	31/12/17	31/12/16	31/12/17
					Prop.	Prop.	Pooling	Pooling
Sales	600	900	250	400	600	1,140	850	1,300
Cost of sales	(200)	(300)	(100)	(150)	(200)	(390)	(300)	(450)
Operating expenses	(100)	(200)	(50)	(100)	(100)	(260)	(150)	(300)
Minority interests					–	–	–	–
Net income	**300**	**400**	**100**	**150**	**300**	**490**	**400**	**550**
Dividends paid	(100)	(100)	–	(25)	(100)	(100)	(100)	(100)
Retained profit	200	300	100	125	200	390	300	450
Retained profits begin	1,000	1,200	250	350	1,000	1,200	1,225	1,525
Retained profits closing	**1,200**	**1,500**	**350**	**475**	**1,200**	**1,590**	**1,525**	**1,975**

Example ends

Example starts

On January 1, 2019, Acquire Ltd. purchased 50% of Target Ltd. for £2,000. At that time, the fair values of Target were properly assessed. Tax rate is 40%. Here are the details:

(£)	Acquire carrying amount	Target carrying amount	Target fair value	Notes
January 1, 2019				
Fixed assets, net	5,000	1,750	2,000	Depreciable life 6 years
Patents	400	100	120	Depreciable life 6 years
Inventory	1,250	400	450	Inventory will be sold in 2019
Long-term receivables	450	200	200	
Cash	2,760	500	500	
Total assets	**9,860**	**2,950**	**3,270**	
Bonds payable	3,750	400	420	Premium amortized over 10 years
Contingent liability	–	–	50	Unrecognized legal claim
Shareholders' equity	6,110	2,550	2,800	
Total liabilities & equity	**9,860**	**2,950**	**3,270**	
December 31, 2019				
Revenues	22,000	4,500		
Cost of goods sold	(16,500)	(2,400)		
Gross profit	**5,500**	**2,100**		
Expenses	(2,350)	(1,400)		
Pretax income	**3,150**	**700**		
Income tax expenses	(1,260)	(280)		
Income before associates	**1,890**	**420**		
Equity in associates	?	–		
Net income	?	**420**		
Dividends paid	750	300		

Required:

a. present the balance sheet of Acquire for January 1, 2019 (immediately following the investment, under proportionate consolidation;
b. present the investment account in Target for the fiscal year ended on December 31, 2019 under the equity method;
c. complete Acquire's income statement for fiscal 2019 under the equity method.

Solution:

(£)	Acquire carrying amount	Target carrying amount	Target fair value	Prop. Cons.
January 1, 2019				
Fixed assets, net	5,000	1,750	2,000	6,000
Patents	400	100	120	460
Goodwill	–	–	–	650
Investment in Target	2,000	–	–	–
Inventory	1,250	400	450	1,475
Long-term receivables	450	200	200	550
Cash (after investment)	760	500	500	1010
Total assets	**9,860**	**2,950**	**3,270**	**10,145**
Bonds payable	3,750	400	420	3,960
Contingent liability	–	–	50	25
Deferred Taxes	–	–	–	50
Shareholders' equity	6,110	2,550	2,800	6,110
Total liabilities and equity	**9,860**	**2,950**	**3,270**	**10,145**
Investment Account (50%)				
Share in Target's equity		1,275		
Fixed assets write-up		125		
Patents write-up		10		
Inventory write-up		25		
Bonds valuation		(10)		
Contingent liability		(25)		
		1,400		
Deferred taxes (40% x w. ups)		(50)		
Goodwill		650		
		2,000		
Income in 2019				
Share in Target's net income		210		
Amortization of fixed assets		(20.833)		
Amortization of patents (6 y.)		(1.667)		
Cost of inventory sold		(25)		
Amortization of bonds (10 y.)		1		
Contingent claim (not settled)		–		
Amortization of goodwill		–		
Deferred taxes		19		

(£)	Acquire carrying amount	Target carrying amount	Target fair value	Prop. Cons.
		182		
Dividends		(150)		
Investment balance 31/12/2019		**2,032**		
Acquire's income statement 2019				
Income before associates		1,890		
Equity in net income of associates		182		
Net income		**2,072**		

Example ends

1.7 Summary

In this chapter, we introduce the accounting methods used in inter-corporate investments, focusing on transactions where one company invests in the voting shares of another company. As described above, the accounting methods reflect the degree of influence the investor exerts over the investee. We start with the accounting method used to account for passive investments without significant influence. The two methods used to account for passive investments are either cost of fair value. The cost method, which is used primarily for investments in private shares, presents the cost of the investment on the balance sheet and recognizes dividends received in the income statement. The fair value method, which is used primarily for investments in listed shares, presents the fair value of the investment on the balance sheet; if the investment is classified as "fair value through profit and loss", unrealized gains and losses are recognized in the income statement. However, if the investment is classified as "fair value through comprehensive income" (only under IFRS for equity instruments), unrealized gains and losses are recognized directly in equity. Note that realized gains and losses are always recognized in profit and loss.

If the investor has significant influence over the investee, for example, if the investor holds between 20% and 50% of the investee's voting shares, the equity method is used. Under this method, the investment is recorded initially at cost and it increases with the investor's share in the investee's profits and decreases with the share in the investee's dividends.

If the investor controls the investee, for example, if the investor holds more than 50% of the voting shares, the purchase method (also called acquisition method) must be used, and the investor presents consolidated financial statements. We also discussed the measurement of goodwill and non-controlling interests (NCI). Finally, we highlighted two additional methods for inter-corporate investments—the Pooling of Interests Method and Proportionate Consolidation; which are less frequently applied in practice.

References

Financial Accounting Standards Board (FASB), *ASC 320 Investments—Debt and Equity Securities*, as updated lastly in 2018.

Financial Accounting Standards Board (FASB), *ASC 321 Investments—Equity Securities*, as updated lastly in 2020.

Financial Accounting Standards Board (FASB), *ASC 323 Investments—Equity Method and Joint Ventures*, as updated lastly in 2020.

Financial Accounting Standards Board (FASB), *ASC 805 Business Combinations*, as updated lastly in 2019.

Financial Accounting Standards Board (FASB), *ASC 810 Consolidation*, as updated lastly in 2018.

International Accounting Standards Board (IASB), *IAS 12 Income Taxes*, as amended lastly in 2017.

International Accounting Standards Board (IASB), *IAS 28 Investment in Associates and Joint Ventures*, as amended lastly in 2017.

International Accounting Standards Board (IASB), *IFRS 3 Business Combinations*, as amended lastly in 2020.

International Accounting Standards Board (IASB), *IFRS 9 Financial Instruments*, as amended lastly in 2020.

International Accounting Standards Board (IASB), *IFRS 10 Consolidated Financial Statements*, as amended lastly in 2015.

International Accounting Standards Board (IASB), *IFRS 11 Joint Arrangements*, as amended lastly in 2017.

International Accounting Standards Board (IASB), *IFRS 12 Disclosure of Interests in Other Entities*, as amended lastly in 2016.

2 Main Issues in Purchase Accounting

2.1 Introduction

Under IFRS 3 (and similarly under US GAAP, ASC 805), each business combination must be accounted for by applying the acquisition (or purchase) method. Applying this method requires the following steps:

1. identification of the acquirer;
2. determination of the acquisition date;
3. recognition and measurement of:
   - net identifiable assets acquired;
   - non-controlling interests in the acquiree, if any (in case of acquisition of less than 100% of the target company);
4. recognition and measurement of goodwill (or gain from a bargain purchase).

Throughout this chapter, we will cover the main issues pertaining to each of the four steps highlighted above. We will focus on IFRS pointing out the main differences between IFRS and US GAAP.

2.2 Identifying the Acquirer

The first step in applying the acquisition method is the identification of the acquirer. IFRS 3 requires that for each business combination, one of the combining entities must be identified as the acquirer, that is, the entity that obtains control of the acquiree. It is always possible to identify the acquirer, even in mergers of

---

Electronic supplementary material The online version of this chapter (https://doi.org/10.1007/978-3-030-61769-1_2) contains supplementary material, which is available to authorized users.

E. Amir and M. Ghitti, *Financial Analysis of Mergers and Acquisitions*,
https://doi.org/10.1007/978-3-030-61769-1_2

"equals", although the identification may not be straightforward. The identification of the acquirer and the acquiree is a result of applying IFRS 10's/ASC 810's guidance regarding the concept of control. If such an identification cannot be achieved by this analysis, application guidance in IFRS 3 provides additional assistance.

Though control is generally presumed to exist when the acquirer owns, directly or indirectly, more than 50% of the voting shares of the acquiree, its existence must be ascertained considering the amount of influence that the acquirer can effectively exercise over the acquiree, rather than by simply looking at the ownership structure. Actually, control is clearly defined under IFRS 10. An investor controls an investee when: "*it is exposed, or has rights, to variable returns from its involvement with the investee and has the ability to affect those returns through its power over the investee.*" Hence, there are three conditions for control to exist:

- exposure or rights to variable returns of the entity;
- ability to affect those returns;
- effective influence on those returns granted by the power over the acquiree.

The definition of control in IFRS 10 extends beyond the legal involvement of the acquirer with the acquiree, focusing instead on the economic relationship between them. To have power over an acquiree, an acquirer must have existing rights (typically in the form of voting rights) giving it the current ability to direct the relevant activities of the acquiree.[1] While assessing whether control exists, it is important to consider not only existing rights but also potential rights (e.g., rights from ownership of convertible securities or derivative contracts). As anticipated, where application of IFRS 10 does not clearly indicate which of the combining entities is the acquirer, a number of additional factors for consideration are set out in IFRS 3 as follows (Table 2.1).

In addition, in case of a share exchange, other relevant facts and circumstances are as follows (Table 2.2).

Where a new Entity (A) is formed to realize a combination between two or more entities, say B and C, Entity A is not necessarily the acquirer (Fig. 2.1).

In fact, there could be two distinct scenarios:

- Entity A issues equity instruments in itself in exchange for equity instruments in B and C; then, either B or C should be identified as the acquirer by applying the guidance in IFRS 3 and 10;
- Entity A transfers cash (or other assets) in exchange for equity instruments in B and C (e.g., from the proceeds of a debt issue to new investors or to existing investors holding a minority interest in B or C); then, Entity A may be identified as the acquirer.

[1]Relevant activities are those that significantly affect a company's returns or economic performances (e.g., selecting, acquiring or disposing of assets, R&D of new products or processes, determining a funding structure or obtaining funding, appointing key management personnel, etc.).

Table 2.1 IFRS 3 guidance

Factor	Acquirer (usually) is
Consideration primarily in cash, other assets, or incurring liabilities	The entity that transfers cash or other assets, or incurs the liabilities
Consideration primarily in equity interests	The entity that issues its equity interests. However, in a reverse acquisition, the acquiree may issue equity interests
Relative size	The entity whose relative size (in terms of assets, revenues, …) is significantly greater than that of the other combining entities
More than two combining entities	Consider which entity initiated the combination (as well as relative sizes)
New entity formed which issues equity interests	One of the combining entities that existed before the combination, identified by applying the guidance in other paragraphs
New entity formed which transfers cash, other assets or incurs liabilities	New entity may be the acquirer

Table 2.2 IFRS 3 guidance (follows)

Factor	Acquirer (usually) is
Relative voting rights in the combined entity after the combination	The entity whose owners as a group retain or receive the largest portion in the combined voting rights after considering the existence of any unusual or special voting arrangements and options, warrants, and convertible notes
No majority interest in the combined entity, but single large minority interest	The entity whose single owner or group of voters holds the largest minority voting interest in the combined entity
Composition of the governing body of the combined entity	The entity whose owners have the ability to elect or appoint a majority of the members in the governing body
Senior management of the combined entity	The entity whose (former) management dominate the combined entity
Terms of the exchange of equity interests	The entity that pays a premium over pre-deal fair value of the other entity or entities

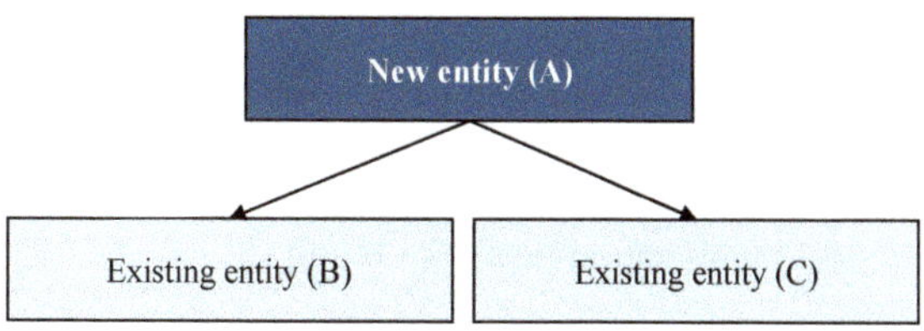

Fig. 2.1 Shareholders structure

The two following examples examine both the abovementioned scenarios.

Example starts

Entity B and C are existing entities, and combine through a new Entity (A), which issues new equity shares in itself in the following proportions: 80% to B's shareholders and 20% to C's shareholders. This kind of combination is commonly referred to as "consolidation." Entity B and C typically disappear and the new Entity A is the surviving entity after the transaction. Based on the relative voting rights, and in the absence of other factors suggesting otherwise, B is identified as the acquirer, because it is in control of the resulting Entity A.

The consolidated financial statements of A are presented as if B had legally acquired C. Note that Entity A lacks commercial substance because it is effectively a legal mechanism to achieve this outcome. Accordingly, the combination of A and B will be accounted for as a capital restructuring, whereby:

- the net assets of B remain at their previous carrying amounts;
- the consolidated statement of comprehensive income of A, including comparatives, will be based on the reporting period of B and will include the pre-combination results of B (although pro-forma statements of B and C would be helpful for investors);
- the group's equity will be that of B plus the fair value of C;
- the group's share capital, if any, will be that of A, the legal parent.

The combination of A and C will be a "normal" acquisition whereby:

- the identifiable net assets of C are fair valued on acquisition according to IFRS 3;
- the consolidated statement of comprehensive income of A will only include C's post-acquisition results.

Example ends

Example starts

Entity B and C are existing entities, and combine through a new Entity (A). The equity investors in A are a private equity business that owns 60% of A and the former equity investors in C who own 40%. Entity A pays cash to acquire the equity interests of B, and issues equity interests in A to acquire C. Therefore, following the transaction, all three legal entities survive.

Entity C is not identified as the acquirer since the equity investors in C do not hold a majority of the equity shares in A. In this case, Entity A is identified as the acquirer. The combination of A and B, and A and C, are "normal" acquisitions whereby:

- the identifiable net assets of both B and C are fair valued on acquisition according to IFRS 3;
- the consolidated statement of comprehensive income of A will include only the post-combination results of B and C.

Example ends

Relatedly, a combination in which the accounting acquirer is the legal acquiree is referred to as "reverse acquisition." This type of deals, which give rise to specific accounting issues and pose particular "problems" in the identification of the acquirer, will be discussed later in this chapter (Sect. 2.6).

2.3 Determining the Acquisition Date

The second step of the acquisition method is the identification of the acquisition date. IFRS 3 is rather "light" on this topic, but it does clarify that the acquisition date is the date on which the acquirer obtains control (as defined above) over the acquiree.

Generally, the acquisition date coincides with the date on which the acquirer legally transfers the consideration for the deal and, as a result, acquires the assets and assumes the liabilities of the acquiree. This date is usually referred to as the "closing date" of the deal.

Notwithstanding, the acquirer should consider all facts and circumstances in identifying the acquisition date, since it might obtain control on a date that is either earlier or later than the closing date. For instance, the acquisition date, according to IFRS 3, precedes the closing date if a written agreement (i.e., the purchase agreement) provides that the acquirer obtains control of the acquiree on a date before the closing date. Similarly, note that the consideration transferred may be paid over time (settled in installments) and/or be subject to forward adjustments depending on specific conditions defined between the acquirer and the acquiree.

2.4 Recognizing and Measuring Net Assets Acquired and Non-controlling Interests

The third step in applying the acquisition method is the recognition and measurement of the (net) assets acquired and non-controlling interests, if any. According to IFRS 3, at the acquisition date, the acquirer must recognize, separately from goodwill:

- the identifiable assets acquired;
- the liabilities assumed;
- non-controlling interests in the acquiree, if any.

To qualify for recognition, the identifiable net assets must meet the definition, at the acquisition date, of assets and liabilities contained in the IFRS Framework. For example, costs the acquirer expects but is not obliged to incur in the future (to effect its plan to exit an activity of an acquiree or to terminate the employment of or relocate an acquiree's employee) are not liabilities at the acquisition date. Therefore, the acquirer does not recognize those costs as part of applying the acquisition method. Instead, the acquirer recognizes such costs in its post-combination financial statements in accordance with other IFRS.

Moreover, the acquirer's application of the recognition principles and conditions may result in recognizing some assets and liabilities that the acquiree had not previously recognized in its financial statements. For example, the acquirer recognizes the acquired identifiable intangible assets, such as a brand name that the acquiree did not recognize as an asset in its financial statements, because the acquiree developed it internally and charged the related costs to period expenses. On the other hand, the acquirer, having paid for that (intangible) asset, should recognize it on its balance sheet.

The fundamental aspect of this step is that the acquirer has to measure and, then, recognize the identifiable (net) assets acquired in the acquiree in its consolidated financial statements at their acquisition-date fair value, irrespective of their carrying amount as shown into the acquiree's financial statements.

2.5 Recognizing and Measuring Goodwill

The final step required by the acquisition method is the recognition and measurement of goodwill (or gain from a bargain purchase). To this end, it is necessary to focus on two main aspects: the consideration transferred and the measurement of goodwill (and non-controlling interests).

2.5.1 Consideration Transferred

Consideration transferred in a business combination should be measured at fair value, which is calculated as the sum of the acquisition-date fair value of: the assets transferred by the acquirer, the liabilities incurred by the acquirer to the former owners of the acquiree, and the equity interests issued by the acquirer.

Any portion of the acquirer's share-based payment awards exchanged for awards held by the acquiree's employees, that is included in the consideration transferred in the business combination, should be measured in accordance with IFRS 2 (rather than at fair value) at the acquisition date.

Under IFRS 3, the consideration transferred includes only what is actually transferred in exchange for the acquiree. Therefore, all acquisition-related costs are excluded from this computation; these costs, instead, are reported directly in profit or loss as period expenses (see further).

Moreover, the consideration transferred may include more than one type of consideration. Potential forms of consideration include cash, other assets, a business or a subsidiary of the acquirer, contingent consideration (see further), ordinary or preferred equity instruments, options, warrants, and member interests of mutual entities.[2]

[2]Guidance on how to determine the fair value of the acquirer's equity interests issued is provided in IFRS 9.

In case of an equity consideration, the measurement date to ascertain its fair value is the acquisition date. No relevance is given to movements in share prices before or after this date, even though they happened after the announcement of the deal.

As already noticed, among other things, the consideration transferred may include assets or liabilities of the acquirer. These assets and liabilities (for example, inventory) may or may not have a carrying amount that differ from their fair value at the acquisition date. If their carrying amount indeed differs from the corresponding fair value, the acquirer should remeasure the transferred assets or liabilities to fair value as of the acquisition date and recognize any resulting gains or losses in the income statement.

The recognition of a gain or loss on assets or liabilities transferred is a direct application of the principle that crossing an accounting boundary (i.e., changing the nature of an investee from, say, associate to subsidiary or passive investment) involves a disposal.[3] Notwithstanding, sometimes the transferred assets or liabilities remain within the combined entity after the business combination (e.g., because the assets and liabilities were transferred to the acquiree rather than to its former owners), and the acquirer therefore retains control of them. In this situation, the acquirer should measure those assets and liabilities at their carrying amount immediately before the acquisition date. No gain or loss should be recognized in the income statement in respect of assets or liabilities controlled by the acquirer both before and after the business combination. The implication of not remeasuring assets and liabilities that remain within the group to fair value is that goodwill will be correspondingly lower compared to the situation where assets and liabilities are transferred outside the group and thus remeasured to fair value.

2.5.2 Acquisition-Related Costs

Acquisition-related costs are costs the acquirer incurs to effect a business combination. Those costs include finder's fees, advisory, legal, accounting, valuation, and other professional or consulting fees, general administrative costs (including the costs of maintaining an internal acquisitions department), and costs of registering and issuing debt and equity securities. The acquirer is required to account for acquisition-related costs as expenses in the periods in which those costs are incurred and the services are received, with only one exception for costs incurred

[3]This is exactly the same accounting treatment required for previously held equity interests in a target company in case of step acquisitions and/or step disposals (i.e., acquisitions and/or disposals achieved in stages rather than in a single deal). Therein, any previously held equity interest in the target company is remeasured at fair value only when control is obtained (step acquisitions) or when it is lost (step disposals). The difference between the carrying amount and the fair value of the previously held equity interest is reported directly in the income statement.

while issuing debt or equity securities. According to IAS 32, these transaction costs are accounted for as a reduction of proceeds of the related debt or equity instruments.[4]

Acquisition-related costs do not form part of the consideration transferred because these costs, whether for services performed by external parties or internal staff of the acquirer, do not generally represent assets of the acquirer at the acquisition date, since the benefits obtained are consumed as the services are received. Moreover, the amount that a seller is willing to accept as consideration for its business does not vary with the costs incurred by different potential buyers. Thus, acquisition-related costs are accounted for as separate transactions in which the acquirer simply pays for the services received. This accounting treatment stays the same also when acquisition-related costs are paid for by the acquiree or its former owners and then reimbursed by the acquirer.

2.5.3 Contingent Consideration

The consideration the acquirer transfers in exchange for the acquiree includes any asset or liability resulting from a contingent consideration agreement. Contingent consideration is usually defined as (IFRS 3):

> *an obligation of the acquirer to transfer additional assets or equity interests to the former owners of an acquiree as part of the exchange for control of the acquiree if specified future events occur or conditions are met. However, contingent consideration may also give the acquirer the right to the return of previously transferred consideration if specified conditions are met.*

Contingent considerations represent, therefore, a useful tool that can be used by both the acquirer and the acquiree to tackle some of the uncertainties surrounding the future performances of the post-deal entity, which, of course, are reflected in the consideration transferred within the business combination itself. That is why contingent consideration is recognized as part of the consideration transferred in exchange for the acquiree, measured at its acquisition-date fair value.

An obligation to pay contingent consideration is classified as a liability or as equity on the basis of the definitions of an equity instrument and a financial liability under IAS 32.

By the same token, where the purchase agreement includes a right to the return of previously transferred consideration if specified conditions for a repayment are met, that right to return is classified as an asset by the acquirer.

[4]Transaction costs that relate to the issue of a compound financial instrument are allocated to the liability and equity components of that instrument in proportion to the allocation of proceeds. Transaction costs that relate jointly to more than one transaction (e.g., costs of a concurrent offering of some shares and a stock exchange listing of other shares) are allocated to those transactions using a basis of allocation that is rational and consistent with similar transactions.

Example starts
Entity A acquires Entity B. The consideration is payable in three tranches:

- an immediate payment of £1,000,000;
- a further payment of £500,000 after one year, if profit before interest and tax (EBIT) for the first year following acquisition exceeds £200,000; and
- a further payment of £500,000 after two years if EBIT for the second year following acquisition exceeds £220,000.

The two payments that are conditional upon reaching earnings targets are contingent considerations. At the date of acquisition, the fair value of these two payments is assessed as £250,000. Consequently, on the date of acquisition, consideration of £1,250,000 is recognized.
Example ends

Contingent consideration classified as equity meets the definition of contingently issuable shares. As such, the contingent consideration may need to be included in the computation of basic and diluted earnings per share.

Contingent consideration is measured at its acquisition-date fair value. Therefore, it directly impacts the amount recognized as goodwill at that date. IFRS 3 has introduced a new approach to the accounting for changes in the value of contingent consideration subsequent to the acquisition date: changes that are the result of the acquirer obtaining additional information about facts and circumstances that existed at the acquisition date, and that occur within the measurement period (which may be a maximum of one year from the acquisition date), are recognized as adjustments against the original accounting for the acquisition (and so may impact goodwill).

Changes resulting from events after the acquisition date (e.g., meeting an earnings target, reaching a specified share price, or reaching a milestone on a research and development project) are not measurement period adjustments. Such changes are recorded at fair value separately from the business combination. If the amount of contingent consideration changes because of a post-acquisition event (such as meeting an earnings target), accounting for the change in consideration depends on whether the additional consideration is originally classified as an equity instrument or an asset or liability:

- if the contingent consideration is classified as an equity instrument, the original amount is not remeasured;
- if the additional consideration is classified as a financial asset or a financial liability, the contingent consideration is measured at fair value and gains and losses are recognized in either the income statement or other comprehensive income in accordance with IFRS 9.

If the additional consideration is not within the scope of IFRS 9, it is accounted for in accordance with IAS 37, or ASC 450, or other standards as appropriate.

2.5.4 Business Combinations with No Transfer of Consideration

An acquirer may obtain control of an acquiree without transferring any consideration. Examples include: (i) a case where an acquiree repurchases a sufficient number of its own shares for an existing investor to obtain control; (ii) minority veto rights lapse that previously kept the acquirer from controlling an acquiree in which the acquirer held the majority voting rights; (iii) a combination by contract alone. In such cases, an acquirer must be identified, and the acquisition method is applied as usual.

In a business combination achieved by contract alone, the acquirer transfers no consideration for the acquiree and holds no equity interests in it, either on the acquisition date or previously. In such situation, two entities simply enter into a contractual arrangement, which covers, for example, operation under a single management and equalization of voting power and earnings attributable to both entities' equity investors. Such structures may involve the formation of a dual-listed corporation.

<u>Example starts</u>
On June 29, 2001, BHP Billiton Plc (previously known as Billiton Plc), a UK listed company, and BHP Billiton Limited (previously known as BHP Limited), an Australian listed company, entered into a Dual Listed Companies (DLC) merger. The merger was effected by contractual arrangements between the companies, in addition to amendments to their constitutional documents. The effect of the DLC merger is that BHP Billiton Plc and its subsidiaries (the BHP Billiton Plc Group) and BHP Billiton Limited and its subsidiaries (the BHP Billiton Limited Group) operate together as a single economic entity (the BHP Billiton Group). Under the arrangements:

- the shareholders of BHP Billiton Plc and BHP Billiton Limited have a common economic interest in both Groups;
- the shareholders of BHP Billiton Plc and BHP Billiton Limited take key decisions, including the election of Directors, through a joint electoral procedure under which the shareholders of the two companies effectively vote on a joint basis;
- BHP Billiton Plc and BHP Billiton Limited have a common Board of Directors, a unified management structure and joint objectives;
- dividends and capital distributions made by the two companies are equalized;
- BHP Billiton Plc and BHP Billiton Limited each executed a deed poll guarantee, guaranteeing (subject to certain exceptions) the contractual obligations (whether actual or contingent, primary or secondary) of the other incurred after June 29, 2001 together with specified obligations existing at that date.

If either BHP Billiton Plc or BHP Billiton Limited proposes to pay a dividend to its shareholders, then the other company must pay a matching cash dividend of an equivalent amount per share to its shareholders. If either company is prohibited or unable to distribute matching dividend, then BHP Billiton Plc or BHP Billiton Limited will enter into such transactions with each other to enable both companies to pay dividends as nearly as practicable at the same time.

The DLC merger did not involve the change of legal ownership of any assets, any change of ownership of any existing shares or securities, the issue of any shares or securities or any consideration. However, each company issued one special voting share to a trustee company by means of which the joint electoral procedure is operated. In addition, to achieve a position where the economic and voting interests of one share in BHP Billiton Plc and one share in BHP Billiton Limited were identical, BHP Billiton Limited made a bonus issue of ordinary shares to the holders of its ordinary shares.

Example ends

How is the acquisition method applied in a combination without consideration? The answer is Deemed Consideration. In a business combination achieved without the transfer of any consideration, the acquirer substitutes the acquisition-date fair value of its interest in the acquiree (i.e., the deemd consideration) for the acquisition-date fair value of the consideration transferred to measure goodwill or a gain on a bargain purchase. The acquirer's interest in the acquiree may be limited to its right to equalization payments. In practice, the fair value may be negligible. The equity interests in the acquiree held by parties other than the acquirer are a non-controlling interest in the acquirer's post-combination financial statements even if the result is that all of the equity interests in the acquiree are attributed to the non-controlling interest.

2.5.5 Determining What Is Part of the Business Combination Transaction

The acquirer and the acquiree may have a pre-existing relationship or other arrangement before negotiations for the business combination begin, or they may enter into an arrangement during the negotiations that is separate from the business combination. In these situations, the acquirer is required to identify any amounts that are not part of what the acquirer and the acquiree exchanged in the business combination (i.e., amounts that are not part of the exchange for the acquiree).

The acquirer is required to recognize as part of applying the acquisition method only the consideration transferred to the acquiree, and the assets acquired and liabilities assumed in exchange for the acquiree. To determine whether a given transaction is part of the exchange for the acquiree or whether the transaction is separate from the business combination, the following factors are relevant:

(a) **The reasons for the transaction**—Understanding the reasons why the parties to a combination entered into a particular transaction or arrangement may provide insights into whether it is part of the consideration transferred and the assets acquired or liabilities assumed. For example, payments made by the acquirer to vendor(s) of the acquiree may be part of a business combination. However, this principle would not apply to any costs incurred by the acquirer on its own behalf in making the acquisition, because these costs must be accounted for outside the business combination and reported in profit or loss as period expenses.

(b) **Who initiated the transaction**—Understanding who initiated the transaction may also provide insights into whether it is part of the exchange for the acquiree. For example, a transaction or other event initiated by the acquirer may be entered into for providing future economic benefits to the acquirer with little or no benefit received by the acquiree. On the other hand, a transaction or arrangement initiated by the acquiree or its former owners is less likely to be for the benefit of the acquirer or the combined entity and more likely to be part of the business combination transaction.

Example starts

An acquirer may acquire a business from the government in a privatization transaction. These legal arrangements sometimes have obligations that are effectively imposed upon the acquirer by the government (e.g., a requirement to retain a certain level of staff, to maintain a presence in a certain geographical location, or to meet other government policy objectives). In some cases, these arrangements may impact the consideration that the acquirer is prepared to pay, which might generally be higher if the obligations did not exist. These transactions are generally initiated by the relevant government as the vendor for its own benefit (i.e., meeting the policy objectives). Therefore, no adjustment would be made to the consideration as a result of the obligations. However, in some cases, a liability may be recognized as part of the purchase price allocation if the relevant recognition criteria are met.

Example ends

(c) **The timing of the transaction**—The timing of the transaction may also provide insights into whether it is part of the exchange for the acquiree. For example, a transaction between the acquirer and the acquiree that takes place during the negotiation of the terms of a business combination may have been entered into in contemplation of the business combination to provide future economic benefit to the acquirer or the combined entity. If so, the acquiree or its former owners are likely to receive little or no benefit from the transaction except for the benefits they receive as part of the combined entity.

The following are examples of separate transactions that are not to be included in applying the acquisition method:

- a transaction that settles pre-existing relationships between the acquirer and the acquiree;
- a transaction that remunerates employees or former owners of the acquiree for future services;

- a transaction that reimburses the acquiree or its former owners for paying the acquirer's acquisition-related costs.

Example starts
TC appointed a candidate as its new CEO under a ten-year contract. The contract required TC to pay the candidate £5 million if TC is acquired before the contract expires. AC acquires TC eight years later. The CEO was still employed at the acquisition date and will receive the additional payment under the existing contract. In this example, TC entered into the employment agreement before the negotiations of the combination began, and the purpose of the agreement was to obtain the services of the CEO. Thus, there is no evidence that the agreement was arranged primarily to provide benefits to AC or the combined entity. Therefore, the liability to pay £5 million is included in the application of the acquisition method, as AC should have considered it when negotiating the acquisition price.
Example ends

Example starts
Facts are as in the previous example, except that TC entered into the agreement with the CEO at the suggestion of AC during the negotiations for the business combination, and the payment is contingent on the CEO remaining in employment for 3 years following a successful acquisition. The primary purpose of the agreement is to retain the services of the CEO, following the acquisition. Since the CEO is not a shareholder, and the payment is contingent on continuing employment, the payment is accounted for as post-acquisition remuneration separately from the application of the acquisition method.
Example ends

2.5.6 Goodwill

Goodwill arising from a business combination is determined as follows:

Goodwill =	Consideration transferred to obtain control
+	Amount of non-controlling interests (either full or partial method), if any
+	Fair value of previously held equity interests
–	Fair value of the identifiable net assets of the Acquiree

The main issues to consider in determining goodwill are the following:

- a business combination occurs only when an acquirer obtains control of an acquiree. Therefore, to measure goodwill at the time of acquisition, accounting for a business combination reflects the fair value of any previously held equity interests in the acquiree;
- non-controlling interests can be measured in one of two ways: as the share of the identifiable net assets of the acquiree (partial method) or the fair value of

the non-controlling interests (full method). The latter recognizes the non-controlling interest's share of goodwill. Under IFRS, reporting entities can opt for the partial or full goodwill method on a transaction basis. Under US GAAP, the full goodwill method is mandatory.

The process of recognizing and measuring goodwill must be completed within one year from the acquisition date.

Example starts

Entity P acquired Entity Q in two stages:

- in 2011, P acquired a 30% equity interest for cash consideration of £32,000 when the fair value of Q's identifiable net assets was £100,000. This first investment in Q would likely be reported into P's financial statements as an associate under the equity method;
- in 2015, P acquired a further 50% equity interest for cash consideration of £75,000. On the acquisition date, the fair value of Q's identifiable net assets was £120,000. The fair value of P's original 30% holding was £40,000 and the fair value of the 20% non-controlling interests was assessed at £28,000.

Here is goodwill under both methods for computing non-controlling interests:

£	Partial	Full
Fair value of consideration	75,000	75,000
Non-controlling interests	24,000	28,000
Previously held interest	40,000	40,000
Total	**139,000**	**143,000**
Fair value of identifiable net assets	(120,000)	(120,000)
Goodwill	**19,000**	**23,000**

Following the transaction, P would recognize a gain of (£40,000 – £32,000=) £8,000 on previously held 30% stake in Q (assuming that, on the acquisition date, the book value of its stake in Q was still £32,000). Under the full goodwill method, then, the post-deal consolidated financial statements will show, among non-current assets, the amount of goodwill pertaining to both controlling, and non-controlling interests (£23,000).

Example ends

In business combinations where the acquirer and the acquiree (or its former owners) exchange only equity interests, the fair value of the acquiree's equity interests may be a more reliable measure of fair value than the fair value of the acquirer's equity interests (for instance, when the acquirer is private, while the acquiree is public). In this case, the acquirer should determine the amount of goodwill by using the fair value of the acquiree's own equity interests rather than the fair value of the equity interests transferred.

Example starts
An unlisted private equity entity acquires a publicly listed entity through an exchange of equity instruments. The public price of the listed equity instruments of the acquiree at the date of exchange is probably a more reliable indicator of fair value than the valuation methods used to measure the fair value of the private acquirer's equity instruments. If acquisition is performed without consideration, goodwill is determined by using the fair value of the acquirer's interest in the acquiree at the date of acquisition, instead of the fair value of the consideration transferred.
Example ends

2.5.7 Bargain Purchase Price (or Negative Goodwill)

A bargain purchase is a business combination in which the resulting goodwill is negative. That is, the net fair value of the identifiable assets acquired and liabilities assumed exceeds the aggregate of the consideration transferred, the non-controlling interests and the fair value of any previously held equity interest in the acquiree. For example, negative goodwill may arise in a business combination that is a forced sale.

In a business combination with a bargain purchase, the acquirer recognizes the negative goodwill as a gain in the income statement at the acquisition date. However, before recognizing any gain, the acquirer should reassess whether it has correctly identified and measured at fair value all the assets acquired and liabilities assumed. The acquirer should recognize any additional assets or liabilities that are identified in that review. The acquirer is then required to review the procedures used to measure the following amounts:

- the identifiable assets acquired and liabilities assumed;
- the non-controlling interests in the acquiree, if any;
- the acquirer's previously held equity interest in the acquiree (for an acquisition in stages); and
- the consideration transferred.

Example starts
On January 1, 2015, Tal acquires 80% of the equity interests of Gal, a private entity, for £150 in cash. At that date, Gal reported net identifiable assets equal to £200 (see further). The management of GAL had to dispose of their investments by a specified date, hence the low consideration paid. The management of Tal initially measures the identifiable assets at £250 and the liabilities assumed at £50. Tal engages an independent consultant, who determines that the fair value of the 20% non-controlling interests in Gal is £42.

The amount of Gal's identifiable net assets (£200) exceeds the fair value of the consideration transferred plus the fair value of the non-controlling interests in Gal ($150+42<200$). Therefore, Tal reviews the procedures it used to identify and measure the assets acquired and liabilities assumed and to measure the fair value of both the non-controlling interests in Gal and the consideration transferred. Following the review, Tal decides that the procedures and resulting measures were appropriate. Tal measures the gain on its purchase of the 80% interest as follows:

	£
Amount of the identifiable net assets acquired (£250–£50)	£200
Fair value of the consideration transferred for Tal's 80% interest in Gal	(150)
Fair value of non-controlling interests in Gal	(42)
Subtotal	**(192)**
Gain on bargain purchase of 80% interest	8

Tal would record its acquisition of Gal in its consolidated financial statements as follows:

£	Dr.	Cr.
Identifiable assets acquired	250	
Cash		150
Liabilities assumed		50
Gain on the bargain purchase		8
Non-controlling interest in Gal		42

If the acquirer chooses to measure the non-controlling interests in Gal on the basis of its proportionate interest in the identifiable net assets of the acquiree (partial method), the recognized amount of the non-controlling interests would be £40 (£200 × 20%). The gain on the bargain purchase then would be (£200 – £150 + £40 =) £10.

Example ends

2.6 Reverse Acquisitions

A reverse acquisition occurs when the legal acquirer (the entity that issues securities or pays the consideration in cash) is identified as the acquiree for accounting purposes. The entity whose equity interests are acquired (the legal acquiree) must be the acquirer for accounting purposes for the transaction to be considered a reverse acquisition.

Example starts

Reverse acquisitions sometimes occur when a private entity wants to become a public entity, but does not want to register its equity shares. To accomplish this, the private entity will arrange for a public entity to acquire its equity interests in exchange for the equity interests of the public entity. Here, the public entity is the legal acquirer because it issued its equity interests to the owners of the private entity, and the private entity is the legal acquiree because its equity interests were acquired. However, based on the guidance in IFRS 3:

- the public entity is the acquiree for accounting purposes (the accounting acquiree);
- the private entity is the acquirer for accounting purposes (the accounting acquirer).

Example ends

Business combinations are limited to circumstances where the acquiree is a business.[5] It follows, for reverse acquisitions, that the accounting acquiree must meet the definition of a business for the transaction to be accounted for as a reverse acquisition. This restriction appears to exclude from the scope of reverse acquisitions cases where a private entity reversing into a publicly listed "cash shell" (i.e., an entity with a public listing but with no ongoing activities) and a new entity becoming the new parent of an existing group through an exchange of equity instruments. Under IFRS 3, such transactions should not be described as reverse acquisitions. An appropriate accounting policy may describe them as "capital restructurings" or "reverse asset acquisitions." Such an accounting policy may result in consolidated financial statements that are similar to those produced under reverse acquisition accounting.

2.6.1 Accounting for a Reverse Acquisition

The aim is to achieve an accounting outcome that reflects the consolidated financial statements as if the accounting acquirer had legally acquired the accounting acquiree. In other words, the legal form of the business combination should not impact the accounting for the substance of the business combination.

Consolidated financial statements following a reverse acquisition are issued under the name of the legal parent (accounting acquiree) but described in the notes as a continuation of the financial statements of the legal subsidiary (accounting acquirer), with one adjustment, which is to adjust retroactively the accounting acquirer's legal capital to reflect the legal capital of the accounting acquiree. That adjustment is required to reflect the capital of the legal parent (the accounting acquiree).

In other words, the assets and liabilities reported in the post-deal consolidated financial statements will be based on the pre-deal book values of the legal subsidiary (the accounting acquirer). IFRS 3's recognition and measurement rules (fair valuation of assets/liabilities and the determination of goodwill) will be

[5] IFRS 3 defines a business as: "*an integrated set of activities and assets that is capable of being conducted and managed for the purpose of providing a return in the form of dividends, lower costs or other economic benefits directly to investors or other owners, members or participants*".

applied only to the identifiable net assets of the legal parent (the accounting acquiree). Comparative financial information is retroactively adjusted to reflect the legal capital of the legal parent (accounting acquiree). Separate entity financial statements for the legal parent, if required, would be prepared on a standalone basis. Where the entity was formed shortly before the combination, its entity financial statements would cover only its actual accounting period.

2.6.2 Detailed Accounting Entries

IFRS 3 contains detailed guidance on the preparation of consolidated financial statements for a reverse acquisition. This guidance is presented below as a comparison between the "conventional" (an acquisition where the accounting acquirer and the legal acquirer are the same entity) and the "reverse acquisition" cases. Note that the terminology used for a reverse acquisition is that the accounting acquirer is the legal subsidiary, and the accounting acquiree is the legal parent (Table 2.3).

Pre-combination net income and net assets are those of the legal subsidiary (accounting acquirer), and present no particular problems. Pre-combination equity is, in theory, the pre-combination equity of the legal subsidiary but adjusted retroactively to reflect the legal capital of the legal parent. IFRS 3 describes the position at the date of combination as follows:

- the consolidated financial statements reflect the retained earnings and other equity balances of the legal subsidiary (accounting acquirer) before the business combination;
- the amount recognized as issued equity interests in the consolidated financial statements is determined by adding the issued equity interest of the legal subsidiary (the accounting acquirer) outstanding immediately before the business combination to the fair value of the legal parent (accounting acquiree) determined in accordance with the requirements of IFRS 3.[6]

Applying this guidance to periods before the combination:

- the total amount shown as equity is the total shown as equity in the legal subsidiary; and
- the amount shown as equity instruments (e.g., share capital) is the amount shown in the legal subsidiary adjusted by the exchange ratio. In the case of

[6]The equity structure (i.e., the number and type of equity interests issued) reflects the equity structure of the legal parent (the accounting acquiree), including the equity interests the legal parent issued to effect the combination. Accordingly, the equity structure of the legal subsidiary (the accounting acquirer) is restated using the exchange ratio established in the acquisition agreement to reflect the number of shares of the legal parent (the accounting acquiree) issued in the reverse acquisition.

Table 2.3 Reverse acquisitions guidance

	Conventional acquisition	Reverse acquisition
Consolidated financial statements	In the name of the legal parent	In the name of the legal parent[a]
Consideration transferred	Fair value of consideration given by legal parent	Fair value of the notional number of equity instruments that the legal subsidiary would have had to issue to the legal parent to give the owners of the legal parent the same % ownership in the combined entity
Net assets of legal subsidiary (accounting acquirer)	Recognized and measured in accordance with IFRS 3 (generally restated to fair value)	Not restated from pre-combination carrying amounts
Net assets of legal parent (accounting acquiree)	Not restated from pre-combination carrying amounts	Recognized and measured in accordance with the requirements for acquirees under IFRS 3
Goodwill/gain on bargain purchase	Consideration transferred less identified net assets of legal subsidiary	Consideration transferred less identified net assets of legal parent
Consolidated retained earnings.	Legal parent only	Legal subsidiary only
Consolidated equity instruments	Equity instruments of legal parent	Issued equity instruments of legal subsidiary outstanding before the business combination plus the fair value of the legal parent
Non-controlling interests (NCIs) in legal subsidiary	NCIs' proportionate share of legal subsidiary net assets at fair value, or at fair value of NCIs	NCIs' proportionate share of legal subsidiary net assets at pre-combination carrying amounts. No fair value option
Comparative information	Legal parent only	Legal subsidiary only, but retroactively adjusted to reflect the legal capital of the legal parent
Earnings per share of current period	Earnings based on consolidated earnings. Weighted average no. of shares reflects actual shares issued for legal subsidiary from date of acquisition	Earnings based on consolidated earnings. Weighted average no. of shares reflects legal subsidiary's weighted average pre-deal shares times the established exchange ratio, and the weighted average actual shares of the legal parent in issue after the acquisition date

(continued)

Table 2.3 (continued)

	Conventional acquisition	Reverse acquisition
Earnings per share of comparative period	Acquirer only	Earnings of legal subsidiary. Legal subsidiary's weighted average ordinary shares times exchange ratio established at acquisition

[a]With disclosure in the notes that they are a continuation of the statements of the legal subsidiary

share capital with a fixed nominal value, the result may be higher or lower than the legal subsidiary's actual share capital pre-combination. The resulting adjustment is reflected as a reduction in, or addition to, equity reserves.

Example starts

Entity A's and B's balance sheets include the following amounts as of December 31, 2018:

£	Entity A	Entity B
Share capital – £1 nominal (par) shares	100	300
Retained earnings	200	500
Net assets at carrying amount	**300**	**800**
Net assets at fair value	500	2,000
Fair value of whole business	5,000	25,000

On that date, Entity A issued 500 new shares in exchange for the entire share capital of Entity B. Because the owners of Entity B obtain a 5/6 (83.3%) share of the equity of Entity A, Entity B is identified as the acquirer. Since Entity A issued 500 shares in itself in exchange for 300 shares in Entity B, the exchange ratio is 5/3 (1.66 shares of Entity A for each share of Entity B).

The consideration transferred would be £5,000. This equals the fair value of 60 new shares in Entity B, being the notional number that Entity B would issue to give the shareholders of Entity A 1/6 of the combined entity (5,000/25,000 × 300). It also represents the fair value of Entity A as an entity.

£	Combination	Pre-combination
Share capital - £1 nominal shares	600	500
Other reserves (additional paid-in capital)	4,700	(200)
Issued equity instruments	**5,300**	**300**
Retained earnings	500	500
Total equity	**5,800**	**800**

Share capital at the date of combination is 600, being the actual Entity A's shares in issue. Share capital pre-combination is £500, being the issued shares of Entity B (£300) adjusted for the exchange ratio. Issued equity instruments at the date of combination are the issued equity instruments of Entity B (£300) plus the consideration transferred (£5,000). Issued equity instruments pre-combination are those of Entity B (£300). Retained earnings at the date of combination, and pre-combination, are those of Entity B (£500). The balance of other reserves pre-combination (negative £200) represents the capitalization of reserves into share capital (500 shares in Entity A issued in exchange for 300 shares in Entity B).

Earnings per share would be based on the consolidated earnings (pre-combination earnings of Entity B, and post-combination earnings of Entity A + B). The weighted average number of shares would be based on 500 shares pre-combination (being the number of shares in Entity A issued to shareholders of Entity B) and 600 shares post-combination.

Example ends

Example starts

This example illustrates the accounting for a reverse acquisition in which Entity B (legal subsidiary) acquires Entity A (the legal parent issuing equity instruments), in a reverse acquisition on September 30, 2019. Ignore income tax effects. Here is additional information:

- on September 30, 2019, Entity A issues 2.5 shares in exchange for each ordinary share of Entity B. All of Entity B's shareholders exchange their shares in Entity B. Therefore, Entity A issues 150 ordinary shares in exchange for all 60 ordinary shares of Entity B;
- the fair value of each ordinary share of Entity B as of September 30, 2019 is €40. The quoted market price of Entity A's ordinary shares at that date is €16;
- the fair values of Entity A's identifiable assets and liabilities as of September 30, 2019 are the same as their carrying amounts, except that the fair value of Entity A's non-current assets as of September 30, 2019 is €1500.

Entity A's and B's balance sheets just before the transaction are:

€	Entity A	Entity B
Current assets	500	700
Non-current assets	1,300	3,000
Total assets	**1,800**	**3,700**
Current liabilities	300	600
Non-current liabilities	400	1,100
Total liabilities	**700**	**1,700**
Issues equity (100 for A, 60 for B)	300	600
Retained earnings	800	1,400
Total shareholders' equity	**1,100**	**2,000**
Total liabilities and shareholders' equity	**1,800**	**3,700**

As a result of Entity A (legal parent, accounting acquiree) issuing 150 ordinary shares, Entity B's shareholders own 60% of the issued shares of the combined entity (i.e., 150 of 250 issued shares). The remaining 40% are owned by Entity A's shareholders. If the business combination had taken the form of Entity B issuing additional ordinary shares to Entity A's shareholders in exchange for their ordinary shares in Entity A, Entity B would have had to issue 40 shares for the ratio of ownership interest in the combined entity to be the same. Entity B's shareholders would then own 60 of the 100 issued shares of Entity B (i.e., 60% of the combined entity). As a result, the fair value of the consideration effectively transferred by Entity B and the group's interest in Entity A is €1,600 (40 shares with a fair value per share of €40).

The fair value of the consideration effectively transferred should be based on the most reliable measure. In this example, the quoted market price of Entity A's shares provides a more reliable basis for measuring the consideration effectively transferred than the estimated fair value of the shares in Entity B, and the consideration is measured using the market price of Entity A's shares (i.e., 100 shares with a fair value per share of €16).

Goodwill is measured as the excess of the fair value of the consideration effectively transferred (the group's interest in Entity A) over the net amount of Entity A's recognized identifiable net assets:

	€
Consideration (100 shares x €16)	1,600
Entity A's net identifiable assets	1,300
Goodwill	**300**

The consolidated balance sheet as of September 30, 2019 would be as follows

	€
Current assets (700+500)	1,200
Non-current assets (1,500+3,000)	4,500
Goodwill	300
Total assets	**6,000**
Current liabilities (600+300)	900
Non-current liabilities (1,100+400)	1,500
Total Liabilities	**2,400**
Issued equity (250 Shares) (600+1,600)	2,200
Retained earnings	1,400
Total shareholders' equity	**3,600**
Total liabilities and shareholders' equity	**6,000**

The amount recognized as issued equity interests in the consolidated financial statements (€2,200) is determined by adding the issued equity of the legal subsidiary (accounting acquirer) immediately before the business combination (€600) and the fair value of the consideration effectively transferred (€1,600). However, the equity structure appearing in the consolidated financial statements (i.e., the number and type of equity interests issued) must reflect the equity structure of the legal parent, including the equity interests issued by the legal parent to effect the combination.

Assume that Entity B's earnings for the annual period ended on December 31, 2018 and 2019 were €600 and €800, respectively. Assume also that there was no change in the number of ordinary shares issued by Entity B during the annual period ended on December 31, 2018 and during the period from January 1, 2019 to the date of the reverse acquisition on September 30, 2019. Earnings per share for the annual period ended on December 31, 2019 is calculated as follows:

	€
Shares deemed to be outstanding from January 1, 2019 to the acquisition date[a]	150
Shares outstanding from the acquisition date to December 31, 2019	250
Weighted average number of shares outstanding [(150 × 9/12) + (250 × 3/12]	**175**
Earnings per share [800/175]	**4.57**

[a]The number of ordinary shares issued by Entity A (legal parent, accounting acquiree) in the reverse acquisition

Restated earnings per share for the annual period ended on December 31, 2018 is €4.00.[7]

Example ends

Example starts

The facts are the same as in the previous example, except that there are non-controlling interests because 10% of the shareholders in Entity B did not take part in the exchange transaction. Their interest is limited to Entity B with no interest in the combined entity.

As a result, there is a 10% non-controlling interest in Entity A's consolidated financial statements. The non-controlling interest should reflect the proportionate interest in the pre-combination carrying amounts of the legal subsidiary's net assets. Therefore, the non-controlling interest is 10% of the pre-combination carrying amount of Entity B's net assets, that is €200.

The existence of the non-controlling interests does not affect the fair value of the consideration that is effectively transferred as all of the shareholders of the legal parent participate in the exchange. Therefore, it does not form part of the goodwill calculation, because there is no non-controlling interest in the acquiree

[7]Entity B's earnings (€600) divided by Entity A's shares issued in the reverse acquisition (150).

(Entity A). Rather, part of the equity of the acquirer (Entity B) is reclassified as non-controlling interests. Accordingly, goodwill arising on the reverse acquisition is still calculated as the consideration transferred (€1,600) less the fair value of identifiable net assets (€1,300), that is €300.

The amounts recognized within equity will be as follows:

Issued equity—Previous balance	600
Reclassified to non-controlling interest (10% × 600)	(60)
Fair value of consideration	1,600
Issued equity—Balance after acquisition	**2,140**

Retained earnings—Previous balance	1400
Reclassified to non-controlling interests (10% × 1,400)	(140)
Retained earnings—Balance after acquisition	**1,260**

Non-controlling interests—Reclassified from parent equity 200	200
Total shareholders' equity	**3,600**

Example ends

2.7 Summary

In this chapter, we focus on the purchase (acquisition) method, which is applied by an investor to account for controlling interests in the investee. The first element in applying the purchase method is identifying the acquirer and the acquiree in a business combination. In each transaction where one company achieves control over the investee, we must identify the acquiring company and the acquired business, because only the acquired business' assets and liabilities are included in the consolidated financial statements at fair value, while the acquiring company's assets and liabilities retain their accounting basis. While in most transactions the identification of the acquiring and the acquired companies is straightforward, there are cases where this process requires judgment, such as in reverse acquisitions.

The second element we discuss is the determination of the acquisition date. Identifying the acquisition date is important because from that date onwards, the acquired business' income is included in the consolidated income statement. The third element is the determination of the acquisition consideration. While in many cases, it is easy to determine the consideration (cash or shares with readily available market price), this process becomes more challenging in transactions with non-monetary and contingent consideration.

Next, we discuss the measurement of goodwill and non-controlling interests (NCIs) under the full and partial methods. We also discuss the accounting treatment in a case of negative goodwill. We highlight the difference between IFRS and US GAAP in measuring goodwill. While IFRS allows both the partial and full fair value measures of goodwill and NCI, under US GAAP only the full fair value method is allowed for goodwill and NCI.

References

Financial Accounting Standards Board (FASB), *ASC 450 Contingencies*, as updated lastly in 2010.

Financial Accounting Standards Board (FASB), *ASC 805 Business Combinations*, as updated lastly in 2019.

Financial Accounting Standards Board (FASB), *ASC 810 Consolidation*, as updated lastly in 2018.

International Accounting Standards Board (IASB), *IAS 32 Financial Instruments: Presentation*, as amended lastly in 2012.

International Accounting Standards Board (IASB), *IAS 37 Provisions, Contingent Liabilities and Contingent Assets*, as amended lastly in 2020.

International Accounting Standards Board (IASB), *IFRS Framework*, as amended lastly in 2018.

International Accounting Standards Board (IASB), *IFRS 2 Share-Based Payments*, as amended lastly in 2016.

International Accounting Standards Board (IASB), *IFRS 3 Business Combinations*, as amended lastly in 2020.

International Accounting Standards Board (IASB), *IFRS 9 Financial Instruments*, as amended lastly in 2020.

International Accounting Standards Board (IASB), *IFRS 10 Consolidated Financial Statements*, as amended lastly in 2015.

3 More Issues in Purchase Accounting

3.1 Acquisition Provisions

To apply the acquisition method of accounting, the acquirer must determine the fair value of net identifiable assets acquired. In turn, measuring the fair value of net assets acquired has a direct effect on the measurement of both goodwill and non-controlling interests. In addition, fair value adjustments for assets, liabilities and goodwill may have a significant effect on the acquirer's subsequent reported income in the consolidated financial statements.

Consider the following simple example. An acquirer agrees to pay £100 in cash for all the voting shares of the acquiree. At the time of acquisition, the fair value of net assets acquired is £50. In this case, goodwill would be (£100 − £50=) £50 with no difference between the full or partial method of accounting, because there are no minorities. Now suppose that the acquirer decides to establish a "provision for reorganization costs" of £20 and include this provision on the acquiree's balance sheet at the date of acquisition as part of the purchase price allocation. In this case, the fair value of net assets acquired would be (£50 − £20=) £30 and goodwill would be (£100 − £30=) £70.

Why is that so important? Consider the subsequent year. The acquiree will incur a cost of £20 in reorganizing acquired business. Without the provision, the accounting entry would be:

£	Dr.	Cr.
Reorganization costs (income statement)	20	
Cash		20

Electronic supplementary material The online version of this chapter (https://doi.org/10.1007/978-3-030-61769-1_3) contains supplementary material, which is available to authorized users.

E. Amir and M. Ghitti, *Financial Analysis of Mergers and Acquisitions*,
https://doi.org/10.1007/978-3-030-61769-1_3

With the provision, the accounting entry would instead be:

£	Dr.	Cr.
Provision for reorganization	20	
Cash		20

That is, establishing a provision at acquisition enables post-acquisition costs to bypass the income statement and increase reported income in subsequent periods.[1]

An increase in provisions by £1 also increases goodwill by £1. Hence, goodwill is more likely to be impaired later on.[2] Alternatively, it is possible that other depreciable or amortizable assets increase because of establishing a provision, so depreciation/amortization expenses will be higher in subsequent periods. To conclude, the ability to establish such provisions represents potential opportunity to manage post-acquisition profits.

3.1.1 Onerous Contracts

One way to establish acquisition provisions is by using "onerous contracts". According to IAS 37, an onerous contract is "*a contract in which the unavoidable costs of meeting the obligations under the contract exceed the economic benefits expected to be received under it.*"[3] The required accounting treatment is to establish a provision equal to the discounted gross costs less the discounted expected benefits (this amount is referred to as a "present obligation"). In other words, whenever a contract becomes onerous (as defined above) the reporting entity must immediately recognize the expected loss in the income statement rather than expensing it throughout the residual life of the contract itself.

At acquisition, the acquirer should include onerous contracts in computing the fair value of net assets acquired only if the onerous contract to the acquiree indeed exists at the acquisition date. Including the onerous contract as a liability at acquisition requires support for key assumptions used in assessing the loss-making contract, such as market prices and the unavoidable costs to fulfill the contract. Everything else being the same, the higher the liability for an onerous contract, the higher the goodwill resulting from the acquisition method.

Example starts

Acquire Company acquires Target Company. Target Company is obligated by a non-cancelable contract to construct a building for a fixed price. An assessment

[1]Contingencies and provisions are recognized according to IAS 37 and ASC 410, 420, and 450.

[2]Goodwill is not subject to amortization since it has an indefinite useful life. So are indefinite-lived intangible assets. Instead, they are tested annually for impairment according to IAS 36 and ASC 350, at least once a year.

[3]Under US GAAP, onerous contracts are dealt with in ASC 450.

of the unavoidable costs to complete the project exceed the contract's fixed price. Acquire Company will include, in computing the fair value of net assets acquired, a liability equal to the difference between the present value of the unavoidable costs of completion and the present value of the revenues. The present obligation arising from the onerous contract should be recognized (as a provision) in Target's financial statements irrespective of the business combination with Acquire.

Similar effects exist when the acquirer reassesses the fair value of existing liabilities at acquisition. Overstating the acquiree's liabilities at acquisition is likely to result in overstating subsequent reported profits, assuming no impairment loss on goodwill arising from the deal.

Example ends

Example starts

Acquire Company acquires Target Company, who operates a nuclear power plant. The carrying amount of the plant in Target's financial statements is £400, but an appraiser values the fair value of the plant at £500. In addition, Target recognizes a liability for decommissioning the plant in 10 years at the amount of £50. The appraiser values the decommissioning liability at £150. In computing the fair value of net assets acquired, Acquire includes a power plant at fair value of £500 and a decommissioning liability at £150.

Example ends

3.1.2 Pension and Postretirement Benefits

Acquired companies often provide their employees with defined benefit pension and other postretirement benefits.[4] Employee benefit plans may be amended in the form of settlements and curtailments. A settlement is a transaction that eliminates all or part of the benefit obligation for all or part of the benefits provided under the plan. A curtailment is a transaction where the sponsoring entity reduces the number of employees covered by a plan, or amends the terms of the plan such that a material element of future service by current employees will no longer qualify for benefits or will qualify only for reduced benefits.

A business combination often involves acquiring companies who sponsor defined benefit pension and other postretirement benefit plans. In computing the fair value of net assets acquired, the acquirer should measure the present value of the defined benefit obligations less the fair value of plan assets to determine the net employee benefit assets or liabilities to be included in the fair value of net assets acquired. However, IFRS (IAS 19 and IFRIC 14) require that if there is a net employee benefit asset, it is recognized as part of the fair value of net assets acquired only to the extent that it will be available to the acquirer in the form of

[4] See IAS 19 and ASC 715.

refunds from the plan or a reduction in future contributions. Furthermore, settlements or curtailments are recognized in the measurement of the plan's benefit obligations only if the settlement or curtailment event has occurred by the acquisition date.

Example starts
Parent Company acquires all the assets and liabilities of Target Company. Target's financial statements include a net defined benefit pension liability of £250. Parent measures the net present value of expected pension payments at £600 and the fair value of pension assets at £300. Parent expects to amend the pension plan such that the present value of the pension liability will be reduced to £500. While it is probable that the amendments will be made, these amendments are not yet in place at acquisition date. Parent will recognize a net pension liability of (£600 – £300 =) £300 as part of the fair value of net assets acquired without the effect of the plan amendments.
Example ends

3.2 Step Acquisitions

Parent companies often achieve control over subsidiaries in steps. For example, a company may acquire 10% of the acquiree's voting shares, and then an additional 30%, and finally 20% more to achieve a total of 60% of the acquiree's voting rights (and thus control). The accounting method for the investment will change as the level of ownership does.

A business combination occurs only when a transaction gives one entity control of another. Whenever this happens:

- the acquiree's identifiable net assets are remeasured to fair value at the date of acquisition (i.e., the date that control changes);
- non-controlling interests are measured on the date of acquisition either using the full fair value method or the partial method (percentage of identifiable net assets acquired);
- any equity interest previously held as a financial asset (IFRS 9/ASC 320, 321) is treated as if it were disposed of (at its carrying amount) and reacquired at fair value on the acquisition date. Accordingly, any resulting gain/loss is recognized in the income statement. Any change in value of the equity interest that were previously recognized in other comprehensive income is reclassified from equity to the income statement.

An equity interest previously held under the equity method (IAS 28/ASC 323) is similarly treated as if it were disposed of and reacquired at fair value on the date of acquisition. Accordingly, any resulting gain/loss relative to its carrying amount is recognized in the income statement. Any amount that has previously been recognized in other comprehensive income, and that would be reclassified to the income statement following a disposal, is similarly reclassified from equity to the income statement.[5]

Example starts

Tal acquired a 75% controlling interest in GAL in two stages. In 2016, Tal acquired a 15% equity interest for a cash consideration of £10,000. Tal classified the interest at fair value through other comprehensive income (FVOCI) under IFRS 9, since it did not buy the 15% stake in Gal for short-term trading purposes (the investment is not held for trading). From 2016 to the end of 2018, Tal reported fair value increases of £2,000 in other comprehensive income. In 2019, Tal acquired a further 60% equity interest for a cash consideration of £60,000. Tal identified net assets of Gal with a fair value of £80,000. Tal elected to measure non-controlling interests at their share of net assets (partial method). On the date of acquisition, the previously held 15% interest had a fair value of £12,500.

In 2019, Tal includes £2,500 in the income statement, as follows:

	£
Gain on "disposal" of 15% investment (£12,500 – £12,000)	500
Gain previously reported in other comprehensive income (£12,000 – £10,000)	2,000
Total	**2,500**

In 2019, Tal measures goodwill as follows:

	£
Consideration transferred to obtain control	60,000
Non-controlling interests (25% × £80,000), based on share of net assets	20,000
Fair value of previously held interest	12,500
Sub-total	**92,500**
Fair value of Gal's net assets	(80,000)
Goodwill	**12,500**

The accounting entry to record the acquisition is:

£	Dr.	Cr.
Net assets	80,000	
Goodwill	12,500	
Equity (OCI recycled)	2,000	

[5]According to IAS 16, for example, the revaluation surplus included in other comprehensive income in respect of an item of property, plant and equipment (PPE) may be transferred directly to retained earnings when the asset is disposed.

£	Dr.	Cr.
Cash		60,000
Non-controlling interests		20,000
Investment (IFRS 9, eliminated)		12,000
Gain (income statement)		2,500

Example ends

Example starts

LBS Ltd. acquired a 75% controlling interest in City Ltd. in two steps. In 2014, LBS acquired a 40% equity interest for a cash consideration of £40,000. LBS classified the interest as an associate and applied the equity method of accounting. At the date that LBS acquired its interest, the fair value of City's identifiable net assets was £80,000. From 2014 to 2019, LBS recognized its share of undistributed profits totalling £5,000, and in addition included its share of an IAS 16 revaluation gain of £3,000 in other comprehensive income. Therefore, in 2019, the carrying amount of LBS's interest in City was £48,000. In 2019, LBS acquired a further 35% equity interest for a cash consideration of £55,000. LBS identified net assets of City with a fair value of £110,000. LBS elected to measure non-controlling interests at fair value of £30,000. On the date of acquisition, the previously held 40% interest had a fair value of £50,000.

In 2019 (ignoring any profits earned prior to the acquisition) LBS includes £2,000 in the income statement, as follows:

	£
Fair value of previously held interest	50,000
Carrying amount (equity method)	(48,000)
Total	**2,000**

The revaluation gain of £3,000 previously recognized in other comprehensive income is not reclassified to the income statement because it would not be reclassified if the interest in City were disposed of.

In 2019, LBS measures goodwill as follows:

	£
Consideration transferred to obtain control	55,000
Non-controlling interests (fair value)	30,000
Fair value of previously held interest	50,000
Sub-total	**135,000**
Fair value of City's net assets	(110,000)
Goodwill	**25,000**

The accounting entry to record the acquisition is:

£	Dr.	Cr.
Net assets	110,000	
Goodwill	25,000	
Cash		55,000
Non-controlling interests		30,000
Investment (IAS 28, eliminated)		48,000
Gain (income statement)		2,000

Example ends

When a company holds a controlling interest in another company, but less than 100% of the voting rights, this situation is referred to as partial control. What happens when a controlling company with less than 100% of the voting rights acquires the remaining interest to achieve 100% holding, or full control? In such case, the transaction is viewed as a transaction between two groups of shareholders. That is, transactions whereby the parent acquires further equity interests from non-controlling interests, or disposes of equity interests but without losing control, are accounted for as equity transactions (i.e. transactions with owners in their capacity as owners). As in other shareholders' equity transactions, no gain/loss is recognized in the income statement and no additional goodwill is recognized.

Example starts

Continue from the LBS-City example above. In 2020, LBS Ltd. acquired the remaining 25% equity interest in City for a cash consideration of £53,000. LBS identified net assets of City with a fair value of £145,000. Non-controlling interests are recorded at £35,000. On the date of acquisition, the previously held 75% interest had a fair value of £140,000.

This example contains some irrelevant information. Specifically, the fair value of City's net assets and the fair value of the previously held 75% are irrelevant for this transaction because LBS already has control over City. Hence, there is no gain recognition and no additional goodwill.

The journal entry is:

£	Dr.	Cr.
Non-controlling interests	35,000	
Equity (plug)	18,000	
Cash		53,000

The £18,000 reported as "negative" equity reflects the "premium" paid to non-controlling interests over their carrying amount in the consolidated financial statements of LBS.

Example ends

3.3 Disposal of Subsidiaries

When a parent company disposes of a subsidiary, the parent will recognize gains/losses from disposal in the income statement only when control is lost. When the parent loses control, it should:

- derecognize the carrying amount of assets (including goodwill), liabilities and non-controlling interests;
- recognize the fair value of the consideration received;
- recognize any distribution of shares to owners;
- recognize the fair value of any residual interest retained;
- reclassify to the income statement any amounts (i.e., the entire amount, not a proportion) relating to the subsidiary's assets and liabilities previously recognized in other comprehensive income as if the assets and liabilities had been disposed of directly;
- recognize any resulting difference as a gain or loss in the parent's income statement.

In contrast, when the stake held by the parent company changes but control is retained, the transaction is recorded as an exchange with the non-controlling shareholders, entirely within the consolidated equity. Such transaction is known as a "step-down."

<u>**Example starts**</u>

On January 1, 2004, Acquire purchases 80% of Target for £80,000 when the fair value of net assets acquired is £87,500. Acquire disposes of this holding on December 31, 2016 for £100,000 when the carrying amount of Target, as included in the consolidated accounts of Acquire (excluding goodwill) is £112,500.

Goodwill was recognized at acquisition at (£80,000 − [£87,500 × 80%]=) £10,000. The carrying amount of goodwill at disposal was £6,000. Non-controlling Interests and goodwill are measured using the partial method. On disposal, the gain is going to be:

$$(\pounds 100,000 - [80\% \times \pounds 112,500 + \pounds 6,000] =) \pounds 4,000.$$

The journal entry is:

£	Dr.	Cr.
Cash	100,000	
Non-controlling interests	22,500	
Net assets		112,500
Goodwill		6,000
Gain (income statement)		4,000

If goodwill was previously written-off to reserves (the old approach allowed under UK accounting rules prior to the adoption of IFRS), it would have been included in the computation of the gain on disposal. This will only apply if a first-time adopter of IFRS chooses not to "reinstate" goodwill under IFRS 1 ("business combinations exemption").

Example ends

When a parent company sells part of its holdings but retains a controlling interest, the transaction is viewed as a transaction between two groups of shareholders—an equity transaction. Hence, no gains/losses are recognized in the income statement.

Example starts

On January 1, 2009, Acquire purchases 100% of Target for £500,000 when the fair value of net assets acquired was £400,000. At the time of acquisition, goodwill was assessed at £100,000. On December 31, 2019, Acquire sells 40% of its holdings for £450,000 in cash, when the carrying amount of Target, as included in consolidated financial statements, excluding goodwill, was £800,000. At the time of disposal, goodwill was £50,000. Non-controlling interests, according to the partial method, were valued at [40% × (£800,000 + £50,000) =] £340,000.[6]

The journal entry is:

£	Dr.	Cr.
Cash	450,000	
Non-controlling interests		340,000
Equity		110,000

Example ends

Example starts

On January 1, 2009, Acquire purchases 100% of Target for £500,000 when the fair value of net assets acquired was £400,000. At the time of acquisition, Acquired recognized £100,000 of goodwill. On December 31, 2019, Acquire sells 60% of its holdings for £675,000 in cash, when the carrying amount of Target, as included in consolidated financial statements, excluding goodwill, was £800,000. At the time of disposal, goodwill was £50,000. The fair value of the remaining 40% holdings is £420,000 (including goodwill valued at £45,000).

The gain from disposal, recognized in the income statement, is equal to:

$$(£675,000 + £420,000 - £800,000 - £50,000 =) £245,000.$$

[6]There is no consensus on what happens to the non-controlling interests' share of goodwill when accounting for transactions with non-controlling interests like this one (i.e., step-down transaction). One view (proposed here) is that the parent should reallocate a proportion of goodwill between controlling and non-controlling interests whenever their relative ownership interests change. This is so irrespective of the way chosen to calculate goodwill (partial vs full method). Anyway, there is no adjustment to the overall carrying amount of goodwill since control is retained. This view is proposed, for instance, by both Deloitte and Ernst & Young in their international accounting manuals.

The remaining investment is then recorded at fair value and the equity method is used henceforth. The journal entry is:

£	Dr.	Cr.
Cash	675,000	
Investment in Associate (IAS 28)[a]	420,000	
Goodwill		50,000
Net assets		800,000
Gain (income statement)		245,000

[a]Including a goodwill component of £45,000

<u>**Example ends**</u>

<u>**Example starts**</u>

On January 1, 2010, Company A acquired all the voting shares of Company B for £1500 in cash, when Company B's fair value of net assets acquired was £900. Goodwill was recognized at £600. Since the acquisition, goodwill was neither amortized nor impaired. On January 1, 2018, Company A sells all the shares of Company B to Company C in exchange for 75% of the voting shares of Company C. Here are more details:

Net assets	Carrying amount	Fair value
Company A	10,000[a]	–
Company B	1,000	1,300
Company C	380	500

[a]Excluding the investment in Company B

Since Company A controls Company B before and after the transaction, there is no gain/loss recognized in the income statement on the partial disposal of Company B. In addition, Company C was not controlled before the transaction, but is controlled afterwards. Hence, Company C is fair valued at the acquisition date and goodwill is recognized. We will measure non-controlling interests in Company C as the percentage of net assets acquired (partial method), while we will keep full goodwill for Company B (Fig. 3.1).

Prior to the transaction, A's shareholders held (A + B) while C's shareholders held C. After the transaction, A's shareholders hold A + 0.75 × (C + B), while C's shareholders hold 0.25 × (C + B). The changes in value are:

- A's shareholders: 0.75C – 0.25B;
- C's shareholders: 0.25B – 0.75C.

Therefore, if the transaction is fair then: (0.75C – 0.25B) ought to be equal to (0.25B – 0.75C), or B = 3C (including goodwill). Assume the fair value of B is £3,000, and the fair value of C is £1,000. Then, it follows that A's shareholders

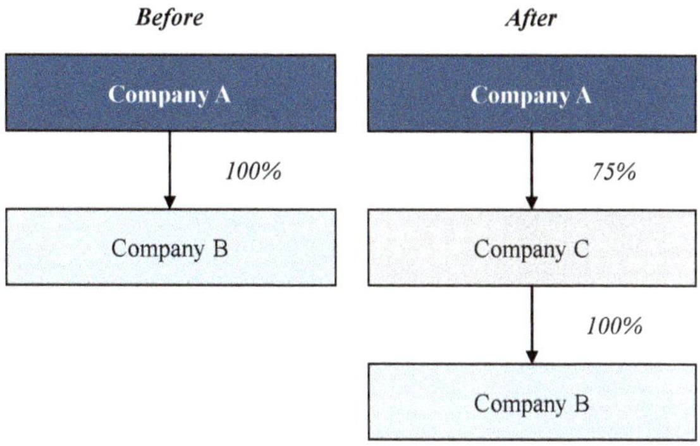

Fig. 3.1 Shareholders structure (pre and post transaction)

contribute 0.25 × B or £750, while C's shareholders contribute 0.75 × C or £750. Therefore, the acquisition consideration of Company C is £750, and the proceeds from the disposal of Company B are £750. Here are some details on the solution:

1. From a group viewpoint, A has disposed 25% of Company B. Hence, goodwill related to the original acquisition of Company B is not amended (assuming that Company A recognized goodwill for Company B using the full method of accounting); it stays at £600.
2. Unrecognized gain/loss on disposal of B is:

	£
Consideration received (fair value)	750
Non-controlling interests	(250)[a]
Increase in shareholders' equity	**500**

[a]£1,000 × 25%

3. Goodwill on acquisition of Company C is computed as:

	£
Consideration (fair value)	750
Net assets acquired (fair value)	(375)[a]
Goodwill	**375**

[a]£500 × 75%

4. Non-controlling interests on the acquisition of Company C are (£500 × 25% =) £125.

Putting it all together, company A's consolidated balance sheet after the transaction is as follows:

£	From A	From B	From C	Total
Goodwill	–	600	375	975
Other net assets	10,000	1,000	500	11,500
Total	**10,000**	**1,600**	**875**	**12,475**
Shareholders' equity	11,600	–	–	11,600
Additional paid-in capital	–	500	–	500
Non-controlling interests	–	250	125	375
Total	**11,600**	**750**	**125**	**12,475**

Example ends

Example starts

Company A has a wholly owned subsidiary, Company B. Company C has a wholly owned subsidiary, Company D. Here are details on the subsidiaries:

Company	Carrying amount ($)		Fair value ($)	
	Net assets	Goodwill	Net assets	Entire Company
B (owned by A)	400	100	600	800
D (owned by C)	300	–	400	800

Companies A and C form Company NewCo and contribute to it the businesses and net assets of Companies B and D, respectively. In return, A and C each receive 50% of the shares in NewCo. For Company A, the transaction is equivalent to an exchange of 50% of B in return for 50% of D. For Company C, the transaction is equivalent to an exchange of 50% of D in return for 50% of B. For both A and C, control is lost and a gain/loss is recognized in the income statement. Both A and C account for the investment in NewCo, whose fair value is equal to $1,600 (sum of fair value of B and D), under the equity method (IAS 28/ASC 323) (Fig. 3.2).

Company	Fair value ($)	Carrying amount ($)		Gain ($)
	Investment	Disposed	Goodwill	
A	800	400	100	300
C	800	300	–	500

The journal entry for Company A is:

£	Dr.	Cr.
Investment in NewCo (equity method)	800	
Net assets		400
Goodwill		100
Gain (income statement)		300

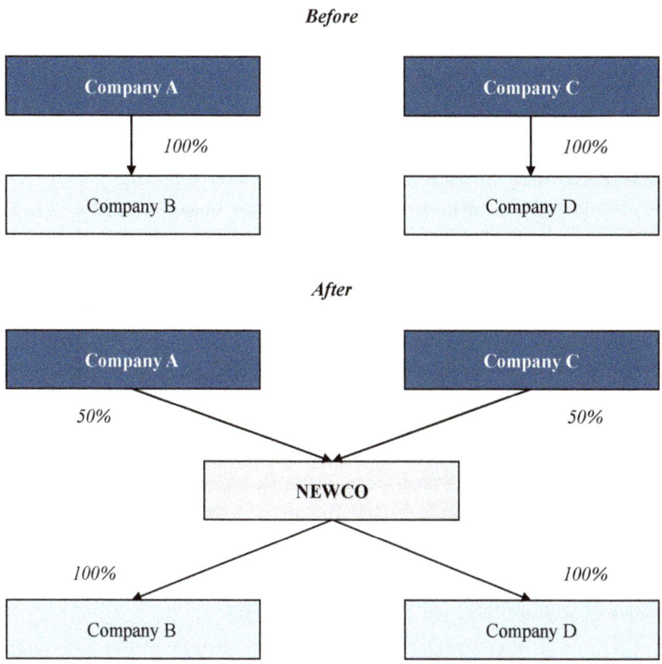

Fig. 3.2 Shareholders structure (pre and post transaction)

The journal entry for Company C is:

£	Dr.	Cr.
Investment in NewCo (equity method)	800	
Net assets		300
Gain (income statement)		500

Example ends

3.4 Consolidated Cash Flow Statement

A consolidated cash flow statement includes the cash flows of the entire consolidated entities in a group. Several accounting issues are relevant only in the presence of consolidated financial statements.[7] Specifically, acquisition of subsidiaries during the period gives rise to cash flow from investing activities. However, the cash flow statement will include in cash from investing activities only the cash

[7]See IAS 7 and ASC 230.

paid for the subsidiary net of the cash acquired (cash balance included on the subsidiary's balance sheet at acquisition). In addition, if the parent company sells a subsidiary, the consolidated cash flow statement will include in cash from investing activities only the cash received net of the cash balance included in the disposed subsidiary.

Dividends paid, that are included in cash flows from financing activities, will include dividends paid to non-controlling interests in subsidiaries.[8] However, dividends paid/received within the group will not appear as cash flows in the consolidated cash flow statement. Furthermore, changes in working capital accounts could be affected by acquisitions of subsidiaries during the period. Hence, the balance sheet change in working capital accounts does not necessarily represent an adjustment to income in the cash flows from operating activities section of the cash flow statement.

Example starts

Consider the consolidated income statement, balance sheet, and supporting information, for Acquire Company for fiscals 1 and 2. During the year, Acquire Company acquired all the voting shares of Target Company. The consideration paid and the purchase price allocation (PPA) are presented below. Present the consolidated cash flow statement for Acquire Company.

Statement of changes in retained profit	£
Net profit	1,957
Dividends declared	(503)
Retained profit for the year	**1,454**

Income statement	£
Revenues	12,685
Cost of sales	(7,542)
Gross profit	**5,143**
Operating expenses	(1,705)
Depreciation of tangible fixed assets	(705)
Amortization and impairment of intangible fixed assets:	(92)
Goodwill impairment	(198)
Operating profit	2,443
Profit on disposal of tangible fixed assets	254
Dividends received	126

[8]According to IAS 7, dividends paid may also be classified as a component of cash flows from operating activities in order to assist users of financial statements to determine the ability of an entity to pay dividends out of operating cash flows.

Income statement	£
Profit before interest and tax	2,823
Interest income	45
Interest charges	(169)
Profit before tax	2,699
Income tax expenses	(814)
Profit after tax	1,885
Share in the net income of equity method investments	475
Profits attributable to non-controlling interest	(403)
Profit attributable to ordinary shareholders	1,957

Balance sheet (£)	Year 2	Year 1
Inventory	785	412
Trade receivables	650	385
Other receivables	125	86
Prepaid expenses	201	165
Short-term investments	651	513
Cash	1,734	1,010
Total current assets	**4,146**	**2,571**
Goodwill	3,587	1,047
Other intangibles	1,654	105
Tangible fixed assets	9,514	7,843
Investments under the equity method	2,015	1,834
Investments, at cost	783	201
Total assets	**21,699**	**13,601**
Trade payables	456	306
Other payables	320	115
Accrued expenses	218	106
Corporate taxes payable	521	201
Dividends payable	416	400
Current maturities of long-term debt	105	78
Total current liabilities	**2,036**	**1,206**
Long-term debt	2,046	1,543
Deferred taxes	35	1,315
Total liabilities	**4,117**	**4,064**
Share capital	3,750	1,000
Share premium	6,541	3,012

Balance sheet (£)	Year 2	Year 1
Retained profits	5,826	4,372
Shareholders' equity	**16,117**	**8,384**
Non-controlling interests	1,465	1,153
Total equity	**17,582**	**9,537**
Total liabilities and shareholders' equity	**21,699**	**13,601**

Other information

1. Acquisition during the year

	£
Cash	984
Ordinary shares	2,681
Total consideration	**3,665**
	£
Intangible fixed assets	725
Tangible fixed assets	513
Inventory	207
Trade receivables	135
Prepaid expenses	48
Cash	219
Trade payables	(178)
Accrued expenses	(84)
Corporate tax payables	(173)
Deferred taxes	(485)
Fair value of net assets acquired	**927**
Goodwill	**2,738**

2. Disposal of tangible fixed assets

	£
Original cost	784
Accumulated depreciation at disposal	(675)
Net book value at disposal	**109**

3. Receipts/payments for tangible fixed assets

Within other receivables and other payables there are the following amounts in respect of receipts (payments for tangible fixed assets):

£	Year 2	Year 1
Other receivables	47	31
Other payables	169	70

4. Share in the net profit of investments under the equity method

	£
Share in operating profit	684
Share in operating expenses	(83)
Share in income tax expenses	(126)
Share in the net profit	**475**

Solution

We will analyze each balance sheet account, starting with goodwill. Note that each account may be affected by the acquisition's purchase price allocation.

Goodwill	£
Beginning balance	1,047
Acquired goodwill	2,738
Impairment (income statement)	(198)
Total	**3,587**
Closing balance	3,587
Difference	–

Other intangibles	£
Beginning balance	105
Acquired intangibles	725
Amortization (income statement)	(92)
Total	**738**
Closing balance	1,654
Difference	**916**

The difference represents cash payments to acquire intangible fixed assets, which are not part of the acquisition.

Tangible fixed assets	£
Beginning balance	7,843
Acquired tangible fixed assets	513
Net book value of disposals (Note 2)	(109)
Depreciation (income statement)	(705)
Total	**7,542**
Closing balance	9,514
Difference	**1,972**

The difference represents additions (not necessarily cash) to tangible fixed assets, which are not part of the acquisition. To get the amount of cash actually paid, we need to look at other payables:

Other payables	£
Beginning balance (Note 3)	70
Additions	1,972
Total	**2,042**
Closing balance (Note 3)	169
Cash paid for tangible fixed assets	**1,873**

Next, we will compute the cash received from disposal of tangible fixed assets.

Tangible fixed assets (disposals)	£
Net book value of disposals (Note 2)	109
Profit from disposals (income statement)	254
Proceeds from disposals	**363**
Beginning balance of other receivables (Note 3)	31
Proceeds from disposal	363
Closing balance of other receivables (Note 3)	(47)
Cash received from fixed assets disposals	**347**

We now move to changes in operating working capital. These changes will appear as adjustments to operating income in computing the cash flows from operating activities.

£	BOP[a]	EOP[b]	Difference	Acquisition	Change
Inventory	412	785	373	207	166
Trade receivables	385	650	265	135	130
Other receivables[c]	55	78	23	–	23
Prepaid expenses	165	201	36	48	(12)
Trade payables	(306)	(456)	(150)	(178)	28

£	BOP[a]	EOP[b]	Difference	Acquisition	Change
Other payables[d]	(45)	(151)	(106)	–	(106)
Accrued expenses	(106)	(218)	(112)	(84)	(28)

[a]Beginning of period
[b]End of period
[c]Excluding other receivables and payables related to tangible fixed assets
[d]Idem

The changes in investments are computed as follows.

Equity method investment	£
Beginning balance	1,834
Share in net income of associates	475
Total	**2,309**
Closing balance	2,015
Difference	**294**

The difference represents the dividends received from investments under the equity method.

Investments at cost (£)	BOP	EOP	Difference
Short-term investment	651	513	138
Long-term investment	783	201	582
Total	**1,434**	**714**	**720**

These differences arise from payments made to acquire new investments. Deferred taxes and corporate tax payables changes are the following.

Deferred taxes	£
Beginning balance	1,315
Deferred taxes in acquisition	485
Total	**1,800**
Closing balance	35
Difference	**1,765**

The income tax expense on the income statement is £814. Together with a reduction in deferred taxes of £1,765, a credit to corporation tax payable of £2,579 arises.

Corporate tax payables	£
Beginning balance	201
Payables this year	2,579

Corporate tax payables	£
Corporate tax payables in acquisition	173
Closing balance	**2,953**
Difference (corporate tax paid in cash)	521
Difference	**2,432**

Dividends declared and paid are computed next.

Dividends	£
Beginning balance (dividends payable)	400
Dividends declared	503
Closing balance	**903**
Closing balance	416
Difference (dividends paid in cash)	**487**

The difference between short- and long-term debt from year 1 (beginning balance) to year 2 (closing balance) represents the new debt issued.

£	Short-term debt	Long-term debt	Total debt
Beginning balance	78	1,543	1,621
Closing balance	105	2,046	2,151
Debt issued	**27**	**503**	**530**

We now have to compute the cash movements within shareholders' equity (including non-controlling interests).

£	Share capital	Premium	Change
Beginning balance	1,000	3,750	2,750
Closing balance	3,012	6,541	3,529
Total			**6,279**
Acquisition consideration			(2,681)
Difference (shares issued)			**3,598**

Non-controlling interests (NCI)	£
Beginning balance	1,153
Net profit pertaining to NCI	403
Total	**1,556**
Closing balance	1,465
Difference (dividends to NCI)	**91**

Consolidated cash flow statement	£
Operating profit	2,443
Depreciation of tangible fixed assets	705
Amortization/impairment of intangible fixed assets	290
(Increase)/decrease in working capital:	
Inventory	(166)
Trade receivables	(130)
Other receivables	(23)
Prepaid expenses	12
Trade payables	(28)
Other payables	106
Accrued expenses	28
Cash flows from operating activities	**3,237**
Dividends received from equity investments	294
Interest received	45
Interest paid	(169)
Dividends received	126
Corporation tax paid	(2,432)
Net cash flows from operating activities	**(2,136)**
Payments to acquire intangible fixed assets	(916)
Payments to acquire tangible fixed assets	(1,873)
Proceeds from disposal of tangible fixed assets	347
Payments to acquire investments (cost)	(720)
Acquisitions (net of 219 cash acquired)	(765)
Cash flows from investing activities	**(3,927)**
Issuance of long-term debt	530
Issuance of ordinary shares	3,598
Dividends paid to minority interests	(91)
Equity dividends paid	(487)
Cash flows from financing activities	**3,550**
Increase in cash	724
Opening balance of cash	1,010
Closing balance of cash	**1,734**

Example ends

3.5 Summary

In this chapter we discuss additional issues related to the application of the purchase (acquisition) method of accounting. To apply the purchase method, we need to assess the fair value of all identifiable assets and liabilities of the acquiree at the time of acquisition and determine goodwill and non-controlling interests. To determine the fair value of net assets acquired, the acquirer must identify, measure, and recognize provisions that exist at the time of acquisition. We discuss the effect of these provisions on the measurement of goodwill and in particular on income subsequent to the acquisition date. We demonstrate how increasing provisions could result in higher goodwill and higher subsequent income.

We also discusses acquisitions in which the acquirer achieves control in multiple steps. For example, an acquirer may acquire 25% of the voting shares in the first step, and only later achieve control by acquiring an additional 40% of the voting shares. We emphasize that goodwill is measured and recognized only when control is achieved. Furthermore, in each step, the previously held holdings are deemed to be sold and reacquired at fair value with gains/losses recognized.

We continue with the accounting treatment of complete and partial disposal of subsidiaries. In particular, we focus on when disposal of subsidiaries results in the recognition of gains/losses in the income statement and when disposals are recorded as transactions between equity holders. Finally, we explain and demonstrate the preparation of the consolidated cash flow statement in the presence of acquisitions.

References

Financial Accounting Standards Board (FASB), *ASC 230 Statement of Cash Flows*, as updated lastly in 2016.

Financial Accounting Standards Board (FASB), *ASC 320 Investments—Debt and Equity Securities*, as updated lastly in 2018.

Financial Accounting Standards Board (FASB), *ASC 321 Investments—Equity Securities*, as updated lastly in 2020.

Financial Accounting Standards Board (FASB), *ASC 323 Investments—Equity Method and Joint Ventures*, as updated lastly in 2020.

Financial Accounting Standards Board (FASB), *ASC 350 Intangibles—Goodwill and Other*, as updated lastly in 2019.

Financial Accounting Standards Board (FASB), *ASC 410 Asset Retirement and Environmental Obligations*, as updated lastly in 2002.

Financial Accounting Standards Board (FASB), *ASC 420 Exit or Disposal Cost Obligations*.

Financial Accounting Standards Board (FASB), *ASC 450 Contingencies*, as updated lastly in 2010.

Financial Accounting Standards Board (FASB), *ASC 715 Compensation—Retirement Benefits* as updated lastly in 2018.

International Accounting Standards Board (IASB), *IAS 7 Statement of Cash flows*, as amended lastly in 2016.

International Accounting Standards Board (IASB), *IAS 16 Property, Plant and Equipment*, as amended lastly in 2020.

International Accounting Standards Board (IASB), *IAS 19 Employee Benefits*, as amended lastly in 2018.
International Accounting Standards Board (IASB), *IAS 28 Investments in Associates and Joint Ventures*, as amended lastly in 2017.
International Accounting Standards Board (IASB), *IAS 36 Impairment of Assets*, as amended lastly in 2013.
International Accounting Standards Board (IASB), *IAS 37 Provisions, Contingent Liabilities and Contingent Assets*, as amended lastly in 2020.
International Financial Reporting Interpretations Committee (IFRIC), *IFRIC 14 Availability of Refunds from a Defined Benefit Plan Managed by an Independent Trustee*, as amended lastly in 2009.
International Accounting Standards Board (IASB), *IFRS 1 First-time Adoption*, as amended lastly in 2020.
International Accounting Standards Board (IASB), *IFRS 9 Financial Instruments*, as amended lastly in 2020.

Spin-Offs and Equity Carve-Outs 4

4.1 Introduction

Spin-offs, split-offs, and carve-outs are transactions that companies can use to divest assets, divisions, or subsidiaries. The choice of a specific method by the parent company depends on several factors discussed below. However, the ultimate goal is to recognize a situation where the market undervalues the parent company and hence attempt to correct this undervaluation and increase shareholders' value. An important issue in any divestiture is the preparation of separate financial statements for the divested elements. In this chapter, we will discuss the reasons for divestitures and examine the related accounting and reporting issues.

4.2 Spin-Offs

Spin-offs involve the creation of a new entity ("Spin-Co") to which certain assets of a parent company are transferred. In return for the spun-off assets, the parent receives shares in Spin-Co, which it automatically distributes to its existing shareholders.

In some spin-off transactions, the parent, rather than creating a subsidiary and transfer assets to it, might decide to distribute to its existing shareholders all or most of the shares already held in an existing subsidiary, thus creating an independent entity, which is not under the parent's control (according to IFRS 10/ASC 810). The distribution of shares is a pro-rata one, where each existing parent's shareholder receives shares of the spun-off subsidiary in proportion to the number of shares held in the parent company, without a cash exchange. Parent's shareholders thus become the shareholders of the newly spun-off entity. The most important issues about spin-offs are:

Electronic supplementary material The online version of this chapter (https://doi.org/10.1007/978-3-030-61769-1_4) contains supplementary material, which is available to authorized users.

E. Amir and M. Ghitti, *Financial Analysis of Mergers and Acquisitions*,
https://doi.org/10.1007/978-3-030-61769-1_4

- spin-offs are cash-free transactions. Technically, they represent distributions of non-cash assets (so called "dividends in kind")[1];
- spin-offs are non-reciprocal transactions. The parent's existing shareholders do not provide the parent company with anything in return for the distribution they received;
- spun-off assets are transferred to the parent's existing shareholders, typically through a separate legal entity;
- spun-off assets might comprise businesses, divisions or subsidiaries, not just individual assets and liabilities.

There are four main types of spin-offs:

a. *regular spin-off*, where the parent distributes 100% of a subsidiary's shares existing shareholders;
b. *majority spin-off*, where the parent distributes a majority (of at least 80%) of a subsidiary's shares, retaining a minority holding of less than 20% in it, often due to tax reasons (Fig. 4.1)[2];
c. *equity carve-out spin-off*, where an earlier equity carve-out (see further) of often less than 20% of a subsidiary's voting shares is followed by a spin-off;
d. *reverse Morris Trust spin-off*, where a spin-off aims at selling a group of assets owned by a parent company to a third party. To achieve this goal, the parent creates a subsidiary and transfers a group of assets to it. Then, the subsidiary is spun-off and merges with a third party company (the buyer). Depending on the exact structure of the transaction, this type of spin-off could result in much lower capital gain taxes.

Following the spin-off, the parent company would most likely recognize its residual investment in the spun-off subsidiary at fair value in accordance with IFRS 9/ASC 321 (or as an investment under the equity method, IAS 28/ASC 323, depending on the case).

The main reasons for a spin-off are:

[1]IFRS does not provide guidance on how an entity should measure distributions to its owners (whether cash or non-cash). IAS 1 simply requires an entity to present details of dividends recognized as distribution to owners either in the statement of changes in equity or in the notes to the financial statements. Some guidance on distribution of non-cash assets is provided by IFRIC 17.

[2]When a parent makes a distribution to its shareholders but retains control over the spun-off subsidiary, the former recognizes non-controlling interests in its interest held in the latter.

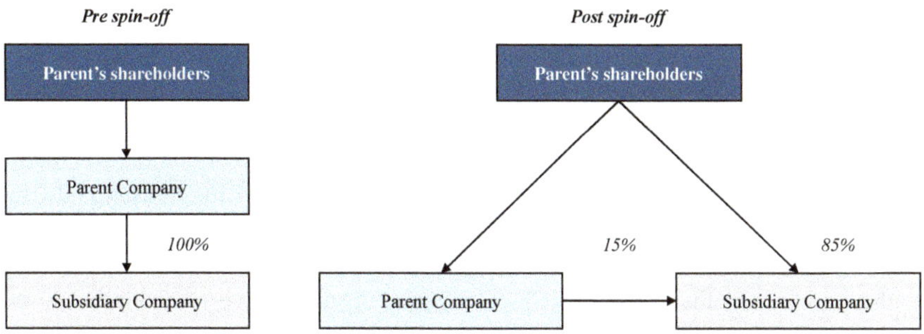

Fig. 4.1 Majority spin-off transaction

- a spin-off is an opportunity for a parent company to divest non-core businesses/assets and focus more on its core activities;
- a spin-off unlocks hidden value by creating a public market for the spun-off subsidiary's shares, in case of a subsequent listing on a stock exchange. This in turn makes the subsidiary more transparent to investors and analysts, and easier to value. Moreover, a public listing of the subsidiary's shares: (a) provides access to capital markets for the spun-off company; (b) promotes information production by analysts and sophisticated investors, reducing information asymmetry[3];
- a spin-off may help reducing the so called "conglomerate discount," which many large companies with a variety of activities suffer from;
- a spin-off grants shareholders more flexibility as to which part of the business to invest and how much risk to take (risk segmentation);
- a spin-off improves the overall management performance by better aligning management incentives with that of the spun-off subsidiary. The market value of the subsidiary's shares better represents the performance of the company, creating direct accountability to public shareholders, and increasing transparency into the management performance;
- a spin-off gives the spun-off subsidiary's management complete autonomy and improves the ability of management to control the company;
- a spin-off could be a response to regulatory restrictions (for example, anti-trust concerns);
- a spin-off is a corporate defense mechanism against takeovers. A spin-off could make an existing parent company of a spun-off subsidiary less attractive to hostile takeovers. The subsidiary, however, may become more attractive, if listed.

[3]In 2011, Marathon Oil Corp spun off Marathon Petroleum and the spun off company increased its dividends by 25% one quarter subsequently. In addition, the spun-off company's revenues increased 6.5% in 2012. During 2013, Kraft Foods spun off its snack foods division into a company called Mondelez keeping the grocery business. Initially, both companies reported a decline in sales but later on, share prices for both companies increased substantially. Clearly, spin-offs serve as a popular mechanism to increase shareholders' value by creating more focused businesses.

4.2.1 Tax Treatment

In Western countries, including the US, a spin-off is usually a tax-free distribution. That means both the parent company and its existing shareholders have no taxable capital gain on the spin-off distribution. To qualify for favorable tax treatment, the spin-off must generally meet certain requirements. Under the US tax code, for instance, these requirements are the following:

- the parent and the subsidiary have engaged in an "active trade or business" during the five years prior to the spin-off, and neither entity may have been acquired during that period in a taxable transaction. In addition, both companies must continue in an active trade or business following the separation;
- the parent must have tax control before the spin-off (more than 80% of the voting shares and value of all classes of the subsidiary's shares) and it must relinquish it following the spin-off (owning less than 80% vote and value);
- the spin-off must have a valid business purpose and cannot be used as a "device" to distribute earnings (dividends);
- the parent company's shareholders, collectively, must retain continuity of interest in both the parent and its spun-off subsidiary for a four-year period beginning two years before the spin-off by maintaining 50% equity ownership interest in both companies. A change in control of either company during this period could result in a capital gain for the parent company (the *anti-Morris Trust rule*).

If the spin-off does not qualify for tax-free treatment, shareholders who receive the distribution will have to pay taxes on the "ordinary income" equal to the fair market value of the subsidiary's shares they receive (as if it was "ordinary" dividends). In addition, the parent will pay capital gain tax on the difference between the fair market value of the subsidiary's shares distributed and the tax basis of the shares.

4.2.2 Accounting Treatment

The accounting for a spin-off is a disposal of a subsidiary representing the parent's decision to distribute non-cash assets (typically, but not necessarily, in the form of the subsidiary's shares) to its existing shareholders. From an accounting viewpoint, spin-offs pose two main challenges: when to recognize them and how to measure them. US GAAP and IFRS have similar rules about the timing of the recognition, but they differ as for its measurement.

4.2.2.1 Timing of the Recognition

Spin-offs are recognized when the distribution is appropriately authorized and is no longer at the discretion of the parent company. In substance, this is the date when the declaration of the distribution (e.g., by management or the board of directors) is approved by the relevant authority (e.g., shareholders) or the distribution is declared (e.g., by management or the board of directors), if no further approval (e.g., by shareholders) is required.

Similar to the payment of a cash dividend, the parent company will recognize a liability in relation to the spun-off assets. The journal entry will be:

	Dr.	Cr.
Retained earnings	–	
Dividend payable		–

When the spin-off is announced and until the transaction is completed, the parent company will deconsolidate the spun-off subsidiary and present, according to IFRS 5/ASC 205 (if applicable), the net assets of the spun-off entity in a single line item on the balance sheet (titled "assets of discontinued operations" or "assets held for distribution"). These net assets will be measured at the lower of their: (i) carrying amount; (ii) fair value less costs to sell. In addition, the parent company will identify the net income/loss attributed to the spun-off subsidiary and present it in one line in the income statement (titled "income/loss from discontinued operations," or similar).

When control of the spun-off assets is effectively transferred from the parent company to its shareholders, the parent company will recognize the spin-off by the following journal entry:

	Dr.	Cr.
Dividend payable	–	
Net assets of discontinued operations		–

If at the same time of the spin-off the assets belonging to the parent company are: (i) first transferred to the subsidiary (typically, with the incorporation of a new company) and (ii) then the subsidiary's shares are distributed to the parent company's shareholders, the subsidiary will record the following journal entry:

	Dr.	Cr.
Assets	–	
Liabilities		–
Equity[a]		–

[a]Allocated to common shares at par value and additional paid in capital (premium)

As pointed out earlier, US GAAP and IFRS differ here, so we will treat them separately.

4.2.2.2 Measurement—US GAAP

Under US GAAP, pro-rata spin-offs of consolidated subsidiaries or equity method investees are recognized at their carrying amount (book value basis) on the transaction date within equity (after impairment, if necessary). No gains or losses are recognized in the income statement.

In some situations, the parent company may retain an interest in the spinnee. In such cases, it should evaluate whether it has retained a controlling interest. If it has, the parent would account for the decrease in its ownership level as an equity transaction. If it has not, the parent would record its retained interest at an amount equal to its share of the carrying amount of the spinnee's net assets. Thereafter, the parent would account for its retained interest under applicable US GAAP.

Example starts

Juventus owns and operates a mall and a retail store, organized and managed in two separate divisions. The shareholders of Juventus would like to split the company into two entities. To achieve this, Juventus transfers the mall's assets and operations into a newly created subsidiary, Padua, and distributes Padua's shares to its shareholders on a pro basis, retaining a 20% non-controlling interest in Padua after the spin-off. The spin-off is announced and executed at the same time so there is no need to record the dividend payable. Assuming that the carrying amount of Padua's net assets is $100 on the date of the spin-off, the journal entry for the transaction is the following.

	Dr.	Cr.
Retained earnings ($100 × 80%)	80	
Equity method investment ($100 × 20%)	20	
Net assets of discontinued operations		100

Example ends

4.2.2.3 Measurement—IFRS

Under IFRS, spin-offs are recognized at fair value of the net assets to be distributed. Any difference between the net assets spun-off and the liability for the distribution is recognized in the parent company's income statement and presented separately from other items of the income statement. Since the fair value of net assets is usually higher than their carrying amount, a gain can be expected.

Example starts

The situation is the same as in the previous example though at the transaction date, the fair value of the spun-off assets is $150. The journal entry for Juventus consolidated financial statements is:

	Dr.	Cr.
Retained earnings ($150 × 80%)	120	
Equity investment ($150 × 20%)	30	

	Dr.	Cr.
Net assets		100
Gain (Income statement)		50

<u>**Example ends**</u>

4.3 Equity Carve-Outs

In an equity carve-out, a parent company sells a portion of the shares it owns in one subsidiary (often less than 20% of the voting share) to the public via an initial public offering (IPO). The carve-out thus creates a new publicly listed company with an independent management and board of directors. In addition, it may provide the parent with a cash infusion following the listing of its subsidiary.

The main purpose of an equity carve-out is to establish a public market valuation for the subsidiary in preparation for a subsequent spin-off of the parent's remaining interest in the subsidiary. Another purpose is to raise cash from selling a portion of the subsidiary to the public. Additionally, all the strategic rationales highlighted while discussing spin-offs apply to equity carve-outs as well. It is possible to arrange an equity carve-out in two different ways:

- the subsidiary issues shares to the public (primary shares) for cash. Then, it transfers the cash to its parent by way of dividends or loan repayment;
- the parent sells the subsidiary's shares directly to the public (secondary shares).

The main difference between these two approaches is that in one case shares are issued anew by the subsidiary, whereas in the other case the parent company sells (already existing) shares. In the former approach, the cash raised from the market goes to the subsidiary, while in the latter it goes to the parent. It is also possible to combine both primary shares and secondary shares in one transaction (Fig. 4.2).

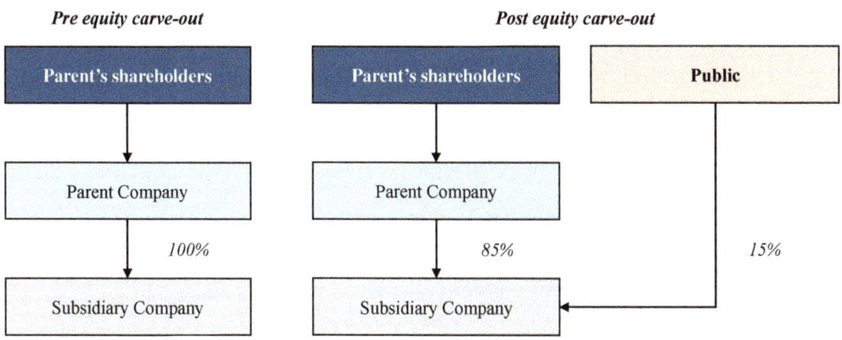

Fig. 4.2 Equity carve-out transaction

4.3.1 Tax Treatment

The structure of an equity carve-out may have serious tax implications for the parent company. If it sells secondary shares to the public for cash, the parent will have to pay a capital gain tax on the difference between the cash proceeds and the tax basis of the shares. However, if the subsidiary issues primary shares to the public, there is no tax event and neither the parent nor the subsidiary will pay taxes at the time of the carve-out. Therefore, issuing primary shares is tax-preferred, unless the tax basis of the parent's shares is higher than the expected cash proceeds.

Equity carve-outs typically do not exceed 20% of the parent's shares in the subsidiary for several reasons. First, if the parent reduces its control on the subsidiary to less than 80%, it will lose *tax control* of it (at least in the US) and any subsequent spin-off would not qualify as a tax-free transaction. Second, as long as the parent retains at least 80% of the voting shares in the subsidiary, dividends from the subsidiary to the parent will be generally tax-free (under the Dividends Received Deduction (DRD) in the US). Finally, if tax control is lost (that is, the parent holds less than 80% of the subsidiary according to the US tax code), the parent may no longer be able to consolidate the subsidiary for tax purposes. For example, if the parent has taxable profits and the subsidiary has taxable losses, tax deconsolidation may result in a tax liability to the parent since taxable losses may not be utilized.

4.3.2 Accounting Treatment

The accounting treatment of a carve-out depends on whether or not the parent company *controls* the subsidiary following the carve-out (i.e. whether the parent still owns more than 50% of the subsidiary's voting shares after the deal). If it does, as is often the case, gains/losses from the carve-out are recognized directly within the shareholders' equity section on the balance sheet (this, in fact, would qualify as a transaction with owners in their capacity as owners).

Example starts

Parent owns all 100 shares in Sub, which has net assets with a book value of £400. Sub issues 25 shares for £150 in cash. After the issue, Sub has 125 shares in total, and Parent holds 100 out of 125 shares (80%). Issuing 20% of the voting shares for £150 implies that the value of Sub's equity after the issues (so called "post-money" value) is (125/25 × £150=) £750, and the value of Sub before the issues (so called "pre-money" value) is (£750 – £150=) £600. The new Sub's shareholders hold 20% of the voting shares.

From an accounting viewpoint, Sub will record the following:

	Dr.	Cr.
Cash	150	
Shareholders' equity		150

In its consolidated financial statements, Parent will record the following:

	Dr.	Cr.
Cash	150	
Non-controlling interests (£550 × 20%)		110
Shareholders' equity		40

The amount of £40 represents the gain arising from the transaction with the shareholders. Indeed, Parent sold 20% stake whose carrying amount was £80 (20% × £400) for a cash consideration of £120 (80% × £150 = 20% × £600).
Example ends

Example starts
The situation is the same as in the previous example, except Parent sells 20% of its existing holding for (20% × £600 =) £120.

Sub does not record any entry, whereas Parent, in its consolidated financial statements, records the following:

	Dr.	Cr.
Cash	120	
Non-controlling interests (£400 × 20%)		80
Shareholders' equity		40

If Parent loses control of Sub, it will recognize a gain/loss on its consolidated income statement regardless of whether Parent issues primary or secondary shares. Also, Parent will be required to account for its investment in Sub using the equity method of accounting (IAS 28/ASC 323) rather than the consolidation method, if it keeps an investment in an associate, or under IFRS 9/ASC 321 if it keeps just a financial investment in Sub.
Example ends

4.4 Related Issues

We now briefly discuss some of the most interesting and frequent transaction-related issues pertaining to spin-offs and carve-outs:

- debt-for-debt swaps;
- debt-for-equity swaps;
- sponsored spin-offs;
- split-offs.

4.4.1 Debt-for-Debt Swaps

In a debt-for-debt swap, the parent company retires debt using a spin-off transaction. The general structure of the transaction is as follows:

- the parent transfers assets to the subsidiary in exchange for all its equity and debt (notes);
- a financial intermediary (e.g., an investment bank) purchases the parent's debt securities in the open market;
- the parent swaps with the investment bank its subsidiary's notes for its own debt securities with an equivalent value. The parent then retires its own debt securities;
- the investment bank sells the subsidiary's notes.

The result is that debt is now legally transferred to the subsidiary that can be then spun-off decreasing parent's leverage.

4.4.2 Debt-for-Equity Swaps

A debt-for-equity swap is similar to a debt-for-debt one, except that the parent swaps the subsidiary's notes for its own shares. Hence, a debt-for-equity swap is similar to a share repurchase financed by debt. The transaction is as follows:

- the parent transfers assets to the subsidiary in exchange for all its equity and debt (notes);
- financial intermediary (e.g., an investment bank) purchases the parent's shares in the open market;
- the parent swaps with the investment bank its subsidiary's notes for its own shares. The parent then retires its own shares;
- the investment bank sells the subsidiary's notes.

The result is that the debt arising from the transaction is issued by the subsidiary, which could be eventually spun-off.

4.4.3 Sponsored Spin-Offs

A sponsored spin-off is a transaction that involves a financial sponsor (e.g., a private equity fund) who makes a significant investment in a newly spun-off subsidiary. The involvement of a sophisticated investor provides the market assurance that the subsidiary is a viable business and endorses its management team. The mechanics of a sponsored spin-off are similar to those in Morris Trust transactions. In particular, to qualify for a tax-free treatment in US, the transaction must meet the conditions of US tax code, also known as the anti-Morris Trust rule (section 355 of the US tax code). This section limits the sponsor's investment to less than 50% of the vote and value of the subsidiary's outstanding shares at the time the investment is made. Holding a majority stake in the subsidiary soon after the spin-off could compromise the tax-free status of the spin-off. Hence, the sponsor does not control the subsidiary after the spin-off. In addition, the subsidiary will be a publicly listed company subject to regulatory restrictions, which is quite unusual for private equity funds. To exit the investment, the private equity investor could sell shares in the open market if their value appreciates. Alternatively, if their value declines, the private equity investor could obtain control of the subsidiary after a two-year waiting period, and exit later. A sponsored spin-off could also serve as mechanism to take over the parent. In this case, the parent spins off assets not wanted by the sponsor prior to the sponsor's investment in the parent.

4.4.4 Split-Offs

A split-off is a transaction in which the parent offers its shareholders to exchange its shares for shares of a newly formed subsidiary. To encourage the exchange, the offer includes a premium over the fair market value of the parent's shares. In case of oversubscription, shareholders receive shares on a pro-rata basis. In case of undersubscription, the parent could distribute the remaining subsidiary's shares in a pro-rata distribution to its investors in a regular spin-off. In essence, a split-off is a tax-efficient mechanism for the parent to redeem its own shares. However, this transaction suffers from certain drawbacks. First, there is uncertainty in executing the transaction (over versus under subscription). Second, there is potential of shareholder lawsuits if certain shareholders consider the premium offered by the parent unfair. To reduce the likelihood of a lawsuit, a split-off is often preceded by an equity carve-out to establish a fair market value of the subsidiary. On the other hand, a split-off involves fewer shareholders than a spin-off, because a split-off better aligns shareholders' preferences with their equity holdings compared to regular spin-off.

4.5 Summary

Spin-offs, carve outs, and split-offs are popular ways for parent companies to divest assets, divisions or subsidiaries. All three transactions often result in separate public equity of the divested assets. In an equity carve-out, the parent company sells a portion (usually less than 20% of the voting shares) of the shares it owns in a subsidiary to the public via an initial public offering (IPO). The carve-out thus creates a new publicly listed company with an independent management and board of directors. In addition, it may provide the parent with a cash infusion following the listing of its subsidiary.

A spin-off transaction involves the creation of a new entity to which certain assets of the parent company are transferred. In return for the spun-off assets, the parent receives shares in the newly created company, which are automatically distributed to its existing shareholders. Often, a spin-off is preceded by an equity carve-out. A split-off, instead, is a transaction in which the parent offers its shareholders to exchange its shares for shares of a newly formed subsidiary.

The main reason for creating a separate public entity is to increase the value of the parent's shares by focusing on core business. Another motivation is to make the divested assets more visible to market participants, induce information gathering, and by that increase its value.

In this chapter, we will discuss the motivation for these transactions. We will also explain their accounting treatment highlighting differences between IFRS and US GAAP. We will also briefly discuss the tax consequences of these transactions.

References

Financial Accounting Standards Board (FASB), *ASC 205 Presentation of Financial Statements*, as updated lastly in 2012.

Financial Accounting Standards Board (FASB), *ASC 321 Investments—Equity Securities*, as updated lastly in 2020.

Financial Accounting Standards Board (FASB), *ASC 323 Investments—Equity Method and Joint Ventures*, as updated lastly in 2020.

Financial Accounting Standards Board (FASB), *ASC 810 Consolidation*, as updated lastly in 2018.

International Accounting Standards Board (IASB), *IAS 1 Presentation of Financial Statements*, as amended lastly in 2020.

International Accounting Standards Board (IASB), *IAS 28 Investment in Associates and Joint Ventures*, as amended lastly in 2017.

International Financial Reporting Interpretations Committee (IFRIC), *IFRIC 17 Distribution of Non-cash Assets to Owners*, 2008.

International Financial Reporting Interpretations Committee (IFRIC), *IFRS 5 Non-current Assets Held for Sale and Discontinued Operations*, as amended lastly in 2014.

International Accounting Standards Board (IASB), *IFRS 9 Financial Instruments*, as amended lastly in 2020.

International Accounting Standards Board (IASB), *IFRS 10 Consolidated Financial Statements*, as amended lastly in 2015.

Special Purpose Entities

5

5.1 Introduction

A special purpose entity (SPE) is an entity created to accomplish a narrow and well-defined (often temporary) objective of the sponsoring/originator entity. The sponsoring/originator entity is the entity on whose behalf the SPE is created and operates.[1] In addition to the sponsor entity, though, a variety of other parties can be involved in a SPE (depending on the sponsor's purpose in establishing the SPE).[2]

SPEs are widely used in practice and have certain common characteristics. Irrespective of their ultimate goal, though, SPEs are typically designed so that voting rights do not represent the primary factor in deciding who controls them. The activities of SPEs, in fact, are (generally) laid out by contractual arrangements signed among the sponsoring/originating entity and other investors. Therefore, deciding: (i) whether a particular entity is a SPE and (ii) who (if any) needs to consolidate it requires significant judgment. Moreover, SPEs are generally structured to be bankruptcy remote from the sponsoring entity.[3]

[1]Under US GAAP, SPEs fall into the broader category of the so-called "variable interest entity" (VIE), whereas under IFRS, SPEs are referred to as "structured entities" (IFRS 12).

[2]For instance, if a sponsoring entity transfers assets to a SPE, the assets held by the SPE are typically serviced by a servicing provider on behalf of the SPE through a servicing agreement. The same is true for the administrative functions of the SPE (typically performed by a trustee or an administrative agent).

[3]If the sponsoring entity were to enter a bankruptcy procedure, its creditors would not be allowed to seize any of the SPE's assets.

Electronic supplementary material The online version of this chapter (https://doi.org/10.1007/978-3-030-61769-1_5) contains supplementary material, which is available to authorized users.

E. Amir and M. Ghitti, *Financial Analysis of Mergers and Acquisitions*,
https://doi.org/10.1007/978-3-030-61769-1_5

SPEs were typically structured so that sponsoring entities had, *de facto*, financial control over them while other parties retained the majority of the voting interests (even though activities were carried out according to pre-agreed upon contractual arrangements). In addition, the investors who held the majority voting stakes in a SPE often funded their investment by issuing debt securities guaranteed by the sponsoring entity, and received a fix return from their involvement with the SPE (see the second example below). In the past, such agreements allowed sponsoring entities to avoid consolidating the SPE, and hence avoid disclosing the assets and liabilities of the SPE. Avoiding consolidation of the SPE often resulted in large amounts of off-balance sheet financing, that is, the sponsoring entity did not recognize a significant amount of debt in its balance sheet. Lower amounts of recognized debt, allowed sponsoring entities to show better financial ratios and overall performances, such as higher returns on assets and lower indebtedness relative to equity capital.

From an accounting perspective, the issues of whether a SPE should be consolidated and who should consolidate it have been subjects of much debate among standard setters, regulators and other interest groups. The consolidation issue has been exacerbated since the scandals (and, to some extent, accounting frauds) perpetrated by companies such as Enron, which heavily relied on SPEs to "hide" part of its debt and, therefore, risk in off-balance sheet vehicles.

SPEs may be used in different ways, but the most widespread use of SPEs is in the financial services industry, where the sponsor is typically a major bank, finance or insurance company. In particular, SPEs play a crucial role in securitizations and other asset-backed financing arrangements.[4] Asset securitization is a process by which an entity pools together and repackages cash flow producing financial assets into securities (asset-backed) that are then typically sold to investors, in different tranches according to their riskiness. The process often uses the SPE to isolate the underlying assets from the selling institution in a bankruptcy remote vehicle.

SPEs may also be used to segregate and finance certain projects (property and/or research and development activities) in a tax-efficient manner, to issue and invest in complicated debt securities, and for the purpose of regulatory compliance.

SPEs share some of the governance characteristics designed to ensure that they engage in the narrow range of activities for which they were established. SPEs are usually not structured as a simple limited liability corporation, though they might assume a wide variety of legal forms (limited liability companies, trusts, partnerships, unincorporated entities, and so forth). SPEs usually have professional directors appointed by an administration company and they are often located in tax havens and/or financial centers. They also have a mechanism in place to ensure

[4]SPE may allow businesses to remove assets from their balance sheets for both financial and accounting purposes, therefore, freeing up capital that would otherwise be required to cover for the underlying riskiness of the assets themselves.

that ordinary shares (if issued) do not confer ownership benefits. For example, most of the SPE's profit is paid out as interest or fees, the SPE is very thinly capitalized, and its shares are often held by a charitable trust.

5.2 Accounting for SPEs Under IFRS and US GAAP

5.2.1 Accounting Under IFRS

The main question regarding SPEs is who controls them and, therefore, who should consolidate them in its financial statements. Ascertaining the answer to this question may be problematic since, as anticipated, SPEs are usually structured so that control is not based on voting or other similar rights but, rather, on contractual agreements. Under such circumstances, therefore, it is necessary to consider the purpose and design of the SPE. Specifically, it is necessary to consider the risks and who is exposed to these risks. In addition, it is necessary to consider the potential benefits and returns and who is expected to enjoy these benefits/returns.

Under IFRS, the relevant accounting standards that deal with control and consolidations are IFRS 3 and IFRS 10. Another relevant standard is IFRS 12, which provides detailed guidance on disclosure requirements about interests in subsidiaries, joint arrangements, associates and unconsolidated/structured entities.

Both IFRS 3 and IFRS 10 do not include a specific definition of a SPE. These standards do not include specific guidance on SPEs either, although the accounting treatment of SPEs is within the scope of IFRS 10, which provides consolidation guidance for all types of entities. Moreover, because SPEs are often used in securitizations and transactions involving a transfer of financial assets, the financial reporting impact of these transactions depends on the derecognition requirements of these assets as described in IFRS 9. If the asset transfer "fails" derecognition because the transferor retains substantially all the risks and rewards of the transferred assets, the accounting effect is very similar to consolidation of the SPE.

While IFRS 10 has no separate guidance on SPEs, it does have guidance on assessing control (and hence, on the need for consolidation) over entities for which voting rights do not have a significant effect on returns, and, in broader terms, do not represent the primary factor in deciding who controls them, as is the case for SPEs. Furthermore, to improve the disclosure about SPEs, IFRS 12 specifically addresses "structured entities," which encompass the definition of most SPEs, for which, specific disclosure must be provided. A structured entity is defined in IFRS 12 as an entity that "*has been designed so that voting or similar rights are not the dominant factor in deciding who controls the entity, such as when any voting rights relate to administrative tasks only and the relevant activities are directed by means of contractual arrangements.*"

According to IFRS 10, control is the parent's ability to direct the financial and operating activities ("relevant activities") of a subsidiary to obtain a variable return. Control is presumed to exist whenever a parent owns, directly or indirectly, more than 50% of an entity's voting power. Control also exists when a parent has contractual rights to control the majority of the voting power or board of directors of the investee. SPEs are consolidated when the substance of the relationship between them and their investors indicates that an entity controls the SPE. To assess whether control exists, the parent entity should consider the following:

- the SPE conducts its activities on behalf of the entity (agent *vs* principal)[5];
- the entity has the decision-making power to obtain the majority of the benefits of the SPE;
- the entity has other rights to obtain the majority of the benefits of the SPE or it has the majority of the residual or ownership risks of the SPE or its assets.

To conclude, under IFRS there is no direct reference to SPEs, although IFRS 12 refers to "structured entities," which include SPEs. If an entity control a SPE, then it is required to consolidate it according to IFRS 10. Ascertaining control can be difficult and, most importantly, requires judgment, since SPEs are structured such that control is not based on voting rights but, rather, on contractual agreements and the substance of the transaction put in place.

5.2.2 Accounting Under US GAAP

Under US GAAP, there are two consolidation models (set out in ASC 810). First, all decisions regarding consolidation are evaluated under the variable interest entity (VIE) model. If the entity is a VIE, management should follow the US GAAP guidance for VIEs. The consolidation of a SPE is required by its primary beneficiary when the SPE meets the definition of a VIE and the primary beneficiary has a variable interest in the entity that will cause it to absorb a majority of the VIE's expected losses, or receive a majority of the VIE's expected residual returns, or both.[6]

Under the second model, control is evaluated based on ownership. If the parent holds, directly or indirectly, more than 50% of the voting power, control is presumed to exist. There could be situations in which an entity is consolidated under IFRS based on the notion of *de facto* control, but not under US GAAP.

[5]According to IFRS 10, an agent is a party primarily engaged to act on behalf and for the benefit of another party or parties, the principal(s), and therefore does not control the investee when it exercises its decision-making authority. Thus, sometimes a principal's power may be held and exercisable by an agent, but on behalf of the principal.

[6]The primary beneficiary is the party that has a controlling financial interest because it has both: (i) the power to direct the relevant activities of a VIE and (ii) the obligation/right to absorb/receive losses/benefits from the VIE.

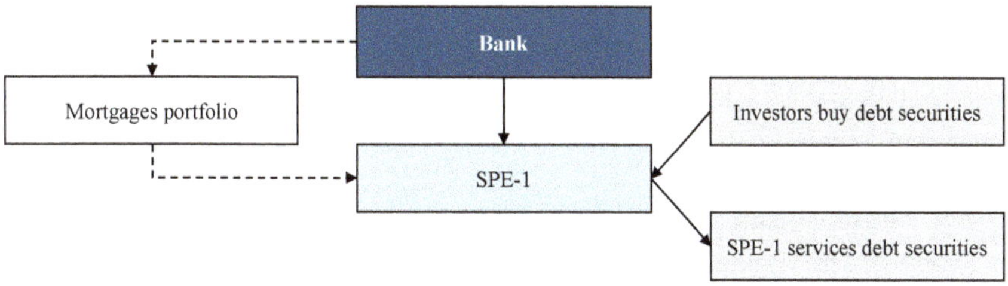

Fig. 5.1 SPE structure

5.3 Typical SPEs

Financial institutions create financial instruments and allow investors access to those instruments. While some investors wish to limit risk exposure, other investors are looking to invest in risky securities. This goal can be achieved using SPEs, since they can both mitigate and segment risks.

Example starts

Bank (a financial institution) establishes SPE-1 and transfers financial assets (mortgages) to it. Such financial assets could be, for example, a portfolio of mortgages. To fund the acquisition of financial assets from Bank, SPE-1 issues debt securities with payments linked to credit risk of the mortgage portfolio. Investors purchase the debt securities. SPE-1 uses the proceeds from the mortgage portfolio to service the debt securities (pay interest and principal). Neither Bank nor the investor in the debt securities have voting rights in SPE-1 (Fig. 5.1).

A cardinal issue is who controls SPE-1. In particular, is SPE-1 an independent entity, or is it controlled by Bank according to IFRS 10? To answer this question we need to examine whether Bank has exposure to variable risks and returns. If Bank does not have any involvement that exposes it to volatility in the mortgage portfolio held by SPE-1, including no risk of bankruptcy, then Bank probably does not control SPE-1 and hence does not have to consolidate SPE-1. However, if Bank does have exposure to variability of returns, then it would have to consolidate SPE-1.

Another important issue is whether Bank can affect the returns of SPE-1. SPEs often have some relevant activities that must be directed by a financial institution, such as Bank; decisions need to be made about managing the asset portfolio even if the investment criteria are narrowly specified. Management of the investments in the event of default may also be relevant (even if default is unlikely). Accordingly, if Bank has substantive decision-making rights over SPE-1's management activities, it probably has control and would need to consolidate SPE-1. Again, it is important to stress that this is irrespective of the fact that Bank does not have any voting rights in SPE-1.

Example ends

Example starts

Asset-backed commercial paper (i.e., ABCP) conduits are a popular way for companies to obtain financing. Here is a description of the steps involved in the development of a typical ABCP conduit.

1. A commercial bank (i.e., the sponsor) establishes a legal trust (i.e., the ABCP conduit). The trust issues a nominal amount of equity to capital-market participants (typically a hedge fund).
   a. The trust has a narrow and well-defined purpose, which is described below.
   b. The equity issued typically has a stated rate of return that does not vary with the trust performance. The equity holders, to which a fixed return is basically granted, have no voting rights, hence essentially no decision authority.
   c. The trust is a bankruptcy remote entity.
2. The trust issues commercial paper.
   a. Commercial paper is high-grade, short-term debt (maturity of up to 270 days). Commercial paper defaults are rare and its yields are usually (but not always) similar to the yield on high quality government bonds.
   b. Typically, the commercial paper sold by the trust is held by money market funds.
3. The proceeds obtained from the commercial paper issuance are used to purchase assets from companies.
   a. The purchase is considered a "true sale" from the perspective of the seller (i.e., the originator). In particular, once the sale has taken place, the sponsor has full control and ownership over the asset.
   b. For a specific trust, the assets are homogeneous and typically fall within a narrow class. For example, some trusts specialize in accounts receivable while others focus on auto loans or lease contracts.
   c. The assets purchased serve as collateral for the commercial paper issued by the conduit; hence, the name asset-backed commercial paper (ABCP).
   d. Money market funds are risk averse and face various institutional constraints; hence, they are concerned that the assets in the trust will prove worthless and, thus, they will lose their investment. To reduce these fears, the commercial bank sponsor offers the following financial services.
      (i) A careful evaluation and monitoring of the originators from which the assets were purchased.
      (ii) Liquidity guarantees, which serve to overcome timing differences. For example, suppose the conduit purchases five-year auto loans. Since commercial paper cannot (by definition) have a tenor of more than 270 days, there is a mismatch between the payments owed to the money market fund and the payments generated by the auto loans. A liquidity guarantee overcomes this mismatch by requiring the sponsor

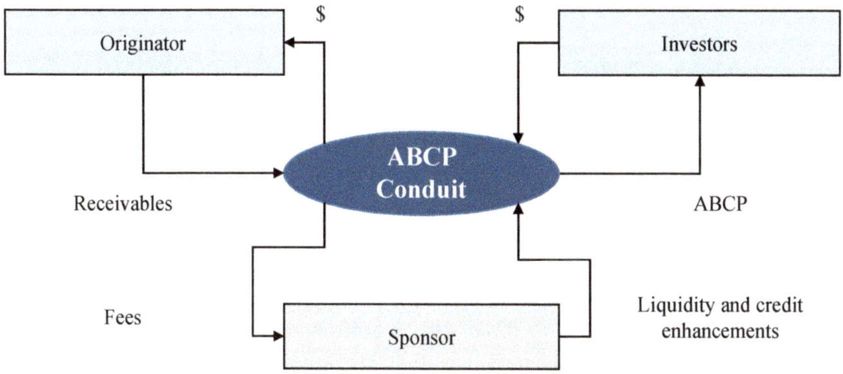

Fig. 5.2 ABCP structure

of the conduit to either: (1) issue additional commercial paper and, thus, payoff the holders of the old paper or (2) make the payment from its own funds.

(iii) Credit guarantees, which are promises to make good on assets that default. For example, if the trust holds some accounts receivable that cannot be collected, the sponsor agrees to "make good" on them (Fig. 5.2).

<u>**Example ends**</u>

<u>**Example starts**</u>

The following appeared in the notes to the 2002 annual report of the McDonalds Corporation.

> *McDonalds Corporation and six unaffiliated companies that supply the "McDonald's System" (i.e., the McDonalds Corporation, McDonald's franchisees, and suppliers to the McDonalds Corporation and its franchisees) hold equal interests in System Capital Corporation (SCC). SCC's purpose is to provide funding to McDonald's franchisees, suppliers to the McDonald's System and the McDonald's Corporation and to build equity within SCC that will benefit the McDonald's System. SCC's function is similar to that of a cooperative and its primary operating activities include: (1) providing loans to qualifying U.S. franchisees to purchase existing restaurant businesses as well as finance equipment, buildings and working capital; (2) purchasing accounts receivable and financing inventory and other needs of eligible suppliers and distributors; and (3) acquiring land and leasing it to McDonald's Corporation for new restaurants.*
>
> *The leases are generally for 20 years, provide for up to 20 additional years in renewal options and include an option for the McDonalds Corporation to purchase some or all of the real estate subject to the lease at a price equal to SCC's acquisition cost. The McDonalds Corporation's commitments under these leases are included in operating*

lease commitments and total approximately $14 million annually based on SCC's current cost of financing.

SCC funds its operations through borrowings by its wholly owned subsidiary, Golden Funding Corp (i.e., Golden Funding). Golden Funding had approximately $1.7 billion of commercial paper and medium-term notes outstanding at December 31, 2002. SCC assets included $900 million of loans to McDonald's franchisees, $500 million of land leased to the McDonalds Corporation, and $300 million of loans to McDonald's suppliers.

Under the accounting rules that existed in 2002, McDonalds Corporation did not consolidate SCC because it did not have a majority of the voting shares in SCC. Under current accounting rules, on the other hand, it is quite clear that McDonalds Corporation has the power to direct the operations of SCC (irrespective of the number of voting shares held in it) and that McDonalds Corporation is the entity that gains or loses from the profitability of SCC. Hence, McDonalds Corporation would probably consolidate SCC under current accounting rules.

Example ends

Example starts

A synthetic lease is a financing transaction whereby a financial institution establishes a SPE. The SPE then acquires property by issuing debt securities. The property is leased to the lessee (who could also be the former owner of the property). The synthetic lease transaction is generally structured with a short lease term so that the lessee accounts for it as an operating lease to keep debt off the balance sheet.[7]

The chart below describes a case where Parent establishes a Sub and transfers operations into the Sub in return for 100% of its voting shares. Clearly, Parent controls and consolidates Sub. Parent and Bank establish Property SPE and Parent transfers property into the SPE. The SPE raises debt from Bank in return for contractual interest and principal payments. The property is then leased to Sub. Sub is the lessee and SPE is the lessor (Fig. 5.3).

The lessee commits to a fixed schedule of rental payments, say for five years, so over that time, there will be a single amount for annual cash flows paid each year. The lease agreement calls for the lessor to pay the lessee any excess of the fair value of the asset, at lease termination date, over its book value plus a fixed rate of return to the lessor's owners. However, if the fair value of the asset is less than the book value plus the fixed rate of return, the lessee agrees to pay the lessor for any shortfall. Thus, there is a cash flow variability created by this residual value guarantee by the lessee.

[7]Even under IFRS 16 (effective for fiscal years beginning on or after January 1, 2019) lessees, which are required to recognize assets and liabilities for almost all leases, have the possibility not to recognized leased assets (and the related debt) on their balance sheets if the lease term is 12 months or shorter (and/or the underlying asset has a low value).

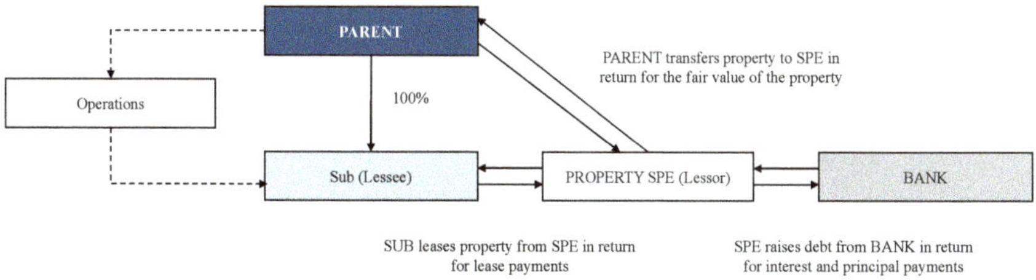

Fig. 5.3 Synthetic lease structure

1. Assume an annual rental of £50,000 for five years paid at the end of each year and a discount rate of 6%. Although there is no cash variability during the first five years (assuming the lessee does not default), the fair value of the property at the end of the fifth year is uncertain. Suppose there are three scenarios:
   a. with a probability of 40%—The asset is sold for £20,000 below book value plus fixed rate of return;
   b. with a probability of 35%—The asset is sold for a net gain, after guaranteed return to the lessor, of £10,000;
   c. with a probability of 25%—The asset is sold for a net gain of £40,000.
2. Expected residual cash flows are: [−20,000 × 0.40] + [10,000 × 0.35] + [40,000 × 0.25] = £5,500. The total expected variability is £15,244 (−7,622, 7,622). The lessee absorbs all of the variability. Note that the case here is simplified by not having variability from the rent payments. In reality, the rent may be conditional on economic events (e.g., solvency issues for the lessee).

£	A	B	C
Probability	40%	35%	25%
Annual rental	50,000	50,000	50,000
Sale proceeds	(20,000)	10,000	40,000
Expected cash flows	5,500	5,500	5,500
Gain/(loss)	(25,500)	4,500	34,500
Expected gain/(loss)	(10,200)	1,575	8,625
Present value	(7,622)	1,177	6,445

3. Accounting—The lessee will consolidate the SPE in its financial statements.[8] All assets and liabilities, except those that were transferred to the SPE from the lessee, will be valued at fair value. Assume that the SPE has the following balance sheet:

[8]While the lessee (SUB) consolidates the SPE, the lessee is consolidated by the PARENT.

	£
Total assets (property)	**1,200,000**
Mortgage debt	1,180,000
Equity	20,000
Total liabilities and equity	**1,200,000**

The fair value of the building is £1,100,000, while the fair value of the debt is £1,180,000. The lessee will consolidate the SPE based on fair values.

	£
Building	1,100,000
Goodwill	80,000
Total assets	**1,200,000**
Mortgage debt	1,180,000
Equity	20,000
Total liabilities and equity	**1,200,000**

Assume instead that the fair value of the building is £1,300,000, while the fair value of the debt is £1,180,000. The lessee will consolidate the SPE based on fair values.

	£
Total assets (property)	**1,300,000**
Mortgage debt	1,180,000
Lessor (payable)	120,000
Total liabilities and equity	**1,300,000**

This is because all the residual gains (6% guaranteed fixed return over five years) will go to the lessor.
Example ends

Example starts
Here is an excerpt from the annual financial statements of PeopleSoft for fiscal 1999:

10. CONTRIBUTION TO MOMENTUM BUSINESS APPLICATIONS

During 1998, PeopleSoft formed Momentum Business Applications, Inc. ("Momentum Business Applications"), a research and development company designed to develop eBusiness, analytical applications and industry-specific software products. All of the outstanding shares of Momentum Business Applications Class A Common Stock were transferred to a custodian on December 31, 1998 and distributed as a dividend to holders of PeopleSoft Common Stock during January 1999. Prior to the distribution, PeopleSoft contributed $250.0 million to Momentum Business Applications. The declared dividend *of $78.6 million in the accompanying consolidated financial statements represents the fair value of the Momentum Business Applications Class A Common Stock distributed based on the average market value on the day trading commenced.*

PeopleSoft consolidated the results of operations of Momentum Business Applications with the results of operations of the Company for the fourth quarter of 1998. However, during the first quarter of 1999, Momentum Business Applications no longer met the requirements for consolidation. As a result, the Company incurred a charge of $176.4 million, which represents the $250.0 million contribution less the $78.6 million dividend recorded as of December 31, 1998, investment banker fees of $2.9 million, other expenses related to the formation of Momentum Business Applications, and expenses incurred by Momentum Business Applications while consolidated with the Company. In connection with the Company's contribution to Momentum Business Applications and the distribution of Momentum Business Applications shares, Momentum Business Applications and the Company entered into a number of agreements, including a Development and License Agreement (the "Development Agreement"), a Marketing and Distribution Agreement and a Services Agreement, which are discussed below.

Momentum is a SPE established by PeopleSoft to develop software. The SPE and PeopleSoft enter several agreements. In the development agreement, Momentum hires PeopleSoft to conduct product development for Momentum (Momentum pays cost plus 10%). Momentum is required to pay for this out of the $250 million plus any interest earned and cannot use the funds for any other purposes. In the marketing and distribution agreement, PeopleSoft has exclusive rights to manage Momentum and to market its products. Finally, PeopleSoft has an option to purchase all the shares of Momentum for a maximum of the following alternatives:

- 15 times the payments made by or due from PeopleSoft as part of the marketing & distribution agreement;
- the fair value of 600,000 PeopleSoft shares;
- $300 million less all payments made by Momentum under the development agreement;
- $75 million.

The main objective of this transaction is risk segmentation. Investors can purchase securities linked only to the value of the products developed by Momentum. If the development is successful, the shareholders of Momentum will receive the value of 600,000 PeopleSoft shares. If the development fails, the shareholders will receive most of their investment back.

Example ends

Example starts

Two companies, Maj and Min, form Sub. Sub will acquire and manage two office buildings, and then sell the buildings after five years. To form Sub, Maj and Min contribute £6,000 and £4,000, respectively, and receive 60% and 40% of the shares. Soon after its formation, Sub acquires two buildings: Building A for £70,000 and Building B for £30,000.

To finance the acquisitions, Sub obtains financing from two large banks. Bank A provides credit of £65,000 to finance the acquisition of Building A, and Bank A and Bank B together provide credit of £27,000 for the acquisitions of Building B. Bank B has recourse only to the cash flows from the operations and sale of Building B for the payment of the interest and principal due. Both Banks receive interest only payments (at 5% per annum) during the five-year period; the principal will be repaid when the buildings are sold at the end of the fifth year. The buildings cannot be sold prior to the end of the five-year term without the approval of the lenders.

To secure the debt financing, Sub acquires a guarantees from Guarantor A and Guarantor B that the value of Building A and Building B in five years will be at least £64,000 and £25,000, respectively. The premium for the guarantees are £1,400 and £600, respectively.

Maj will manage the buildings, making the relevant operating decisions (selecting tenants, determine lease rates, negotiation of lease terms, and repairs and maintenance). For these services, Maj will receive fees of £150 per year. Lease terms with tenants are at market rates, and there are no fixed price purchase options, residual value guarantees or similar options attached to the lease.

Upon sale of the buildings, Sub will pay off the debt and distribute any remaining proceeds to Maj and Min, according to their equity shares.

The following table summarizes the transaction. Notice that Sub spends all the equity to buy the buildings (£5,000 for Building A and £3,000 for Building B), and to pay the guarantee premiums (£1,400 for Building A and £600 for Building B) (Fig. 5.4).

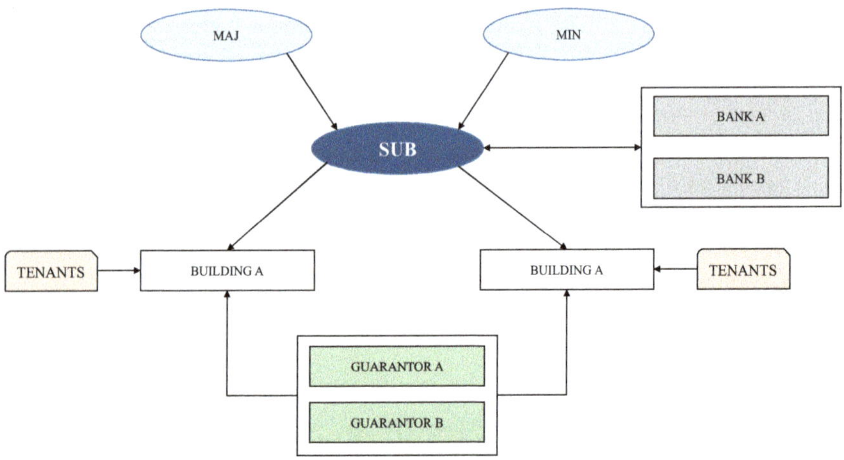

Fig. 5.4 SPE deal structure

£	Building A	Building B
Cost	70,000	30,000
Debt	65,000	27,000
Guarantee value	64,000	25,000
Guarantee premium	1,400	600

Who has the most to lose from the transaction? The answer to this question depends primarily on the selling price of the buildings after five years, because rent payments are likely to cover interest payments during the five-year term.

Maj and Min already invested £6,000 and £4,000, respectively, in the project and cannot lose more. During the next five years, Maj will manage the buildings and will collect £750 to cover salaries and other operating expenses. If the combined selling price of the buildings is more than £92,000, any excess left after paying off the debt will be divided between Maj and Min.

The banks are protected by the guarantees. The most they can lose, is £3,000 (£1,000 in Building A and £2,000 in Building B).

The guarantors will lose only if the fair value of the buildings is below £64,000 and £25,000, respectively. Factoring in the £2,000 premium they collected suggests that the likelihood of a loss is low.

Example ends

5.4 Summary

Control over an entity is often achieved when the parent holds more than 50% of the subsidiary's voting shares. However, control can be achieved through other means, for example, contractual rights, convertible securities, and guarantees. The issue of who controls whom is particularly vague in the case of special purpose entities.

A special purpose entity (SPE) or a special purpose vehicle (SPV) is an entity created by a sponsoring/originating entity to accomplish a narrow and well-defined, often temporary, objective. During the last three decades, the use of special purpose entities grew substantially. It seems that the main purpose of using special purpose entities was to keep them off the consolidated balance sheet.

SPEs are widely used in practice, mostly in securitizations and debt financing, but also in leases and project development. An interesting feature of SPEs is that, typically, voting rights do not represent the primary factor in deciding who controls them. Therefore, a new accounting model is needed to establish who controls and who should consolidate SPEs. In this chapter, we discuss the main accounting and financial reporting aspects of SPEs under IFRS and US GAAP, and provide examples of typical SPEs used in practice. The discussion in this chapter yields an important observation: The issue of who consolidates a SPE is subject to judgment and provides companies with much discretion. Hence, whether a SPE is properly consolidated depends primarily on the reporting entity's discretion.

References

Financial Accounting Standards Board (FASB), *ASC 810 Consolidation*, as updated lastly in 2018.
International Accounting Standards Board (IASB), *IFRS 3 Business Combinations*, as amended lastly in 2020).
International Accounting Standards Board (IASB), *IFRS 9 Financial Instruments*, as amended lastly in 2020.
International Accounting Standards Board (IASB), *IFRS 10 Consolidated Financial Statements*, as amended lastly in 2015.
International Accounting Standards Board (IASB), *IFRS 12 Disclosure of Interests in Other Entities*, as amended lastly in 2016.
International Accounting Standards Board (IASB), *IFRS 16 Leases*, as amended lastly in 2020.

Tax Issues in Business Combinations

6

6.1 Introduction

The term business combination (or mergers and acquisitions, M&A) refers to transactions where two or more separate businesses become part of one controlling entity (either an existing one or a newly created one). That is, business combination includes an acquisition of one company by another (acquisition), a merger of two companies into one surviving company (merger), and a consolidation of two existing companies into a new company (consolidation). Tax rules consider different types of business combinations as well (acquisitions, mergers, and consolidations). However, accounting rules both under IFRS and US GAAP, require the use of one specific accounting method—the purchase method (see Chapter 2)—for almost all types of business combinations.

Though M&A transactions generally attempt to reach the same goal, that is, to increase the strength, efficiency, and/or profitability of the companies involved, they can be carried out, as anticipated, under three major legal structures:

- in an **acquisition**, one company ("acquirer" or "parent") acquires control over another company ("target" or "subsidiary"). An acquisition could occur in one of two ways: a stock deal or an asset deal. In a stock deal, the acquirer acquires a sufficient amount of target's shares to obtain control over it. In an asset deal, the acquirer acquires substantially all the assets and liabilities of the target without buying the corporate shell[1];

[1]An acquisition usually relies on the approval of the target's board of directors. However, in a tender, which is similar to an acquisition, the acquirer approaches the target's shareholders directly to avoid the involvement of the target's board of directors.

Electronic supplementary material The online version of this chapter (https://doi.org/10.1007/978-3-030-61769-1_6) contains supplementary material, which is available to authorized users.

E. Amir and M. Ghitti, *Financial Analysis of Mergers and Acquisitions*,
https://doi.org/10.1007/978-3-030-61769-1_6

- in a **merger,** a previously existing company ("target") merges into another company ("acquirer") and it ceases to exist. Mergers are usually performed by firms which are more or less similar in size and when no one company has the financial strength to acquire the other by cash;
- in a **consolidation**, both existing companies merge and become part of a new legal entity. Therefore, both companies cease to exist as independent legal entities. In both mergers and consolidations, the surviving company directly owns the assets and liabilities of both the acquirer and the target companies.[2]

6.2 Basic Terminology

6.2.1 Taxable Versus Tax-Free Transactions

When companies structure a merger or an acquisition transaction, an important question arises as to the timing and amount of taxes. A transaction could be structured as either a taxable transaction or a tax-free transaction (there are cases of partial taxation as well). In a taxable transaction, the seller realizes a taxable gain (or incurs a deductible loss) at the completion of the transaction. The capital gain is equal to the difference between the fair value of the consideration received and the tax basis of the item sold. In a tax-free transaction (or tax-free reorganization), there is no immediate tax event, and hence, there is no immediate taxable gain or deductible loss at the completion of the transaction. Instead, the tax consequences are deferred until the seller decides to dispose of the consideration received.

Example starts
On January 1, 2010, Company A acquired all the shares of Company B for $1 million in cash. On December 31, 2018, Company A completed a sale of all the shares of Company B for $2 million in cash. Since the consideration received is in cash, the transaction is taxable and Company A will pay capital gain tax on the difference between the consideration and the tax basis of the shares, which is $1 million.
Example ends

Example starts
On January 1, 2010, Company A acquired all the shares of Company B for $1 million in cash. On December 31, 2018, Company A completed a sale of all the shares of Company B to Company C. In return for the shares of Company B, Company A received shares of Company C with a fair market value of $2 million. Since the consideration received is entirely in shares, the parties (Company A and C) could jointly structure the transaction as a tax-free transaction. Company A will not pay any capital gain tax until it decides to dispose of the shares in C. Only at

[2]This chapter refers from time to time to the US Internal Revenue Code (IRC). However, the general discussion applies, at least in part, for the UK tax code as well.

that time, Company A will have to pay capital gain tax (if there is such a gain at the time of disposal).

<u>**Example ends**</u>

As described above, the main factor in deciding whether a transaction is taxable or tax-free is the type of consideration received. In general, if most of the consideration is in cash, the transaction is taxable. However, if virtually all the consideration is in shares, the transaction could be tax-free.

The main advantage of a tax-free transaction is that both the acquirer and the target can combine their businesses, growth opportunities, risks, and market values without having to pay taxes at the acquisition date. The ability to defer taxes could have a serious effect on the acquisition price. For instance, knowing the high tax burden, the seller might insist on a higher acquisition price, whereas under a tax-free transaction the acquisition price could be lower.

The tax-free nature of the transaction could be particularly important to the founders of the target because the tax basis (cost) of their shares is often small. These founders could end up paying a high amount of taxes in case of a taxable transaction. A tax-free transaction also allows the target's shareholders to defer liquidation of their consideration to the time most suitable for them (e.g., after retirement), and hence it gives them flexibility on the timing of tax payments. Furthermore, the target's owners may defer their taxes indefinitely in case of death. The US tax code does not impose income taxes on dead people. However, inheritance taxes or death taxes may apply based on the fair value of the consideration at time of death.

Note that tax-free transactions are not always preferred to taxable transactions. If, for example, the seller expected to generate a capital loss, it would be better to structure the transaction as a taxable one. In addition, a tax-free transaction may be of less importance if the seller intends to liquidate the consideration into cash soon after the transaction. In that case, it does not really matter if the transaction is taxable or tax-free, because the seller will have to pay taxes at liquidation anyhow.

6.2.2 Tax Basis Versus Book Basis

Every asset and liability is recognized on the balance sheet using the relevant accounting principles (generally based on an accrual-basis). For example, buildings are recognized at historical cost less accumulated depreciation and any impairment losses. We refer to this value as the book value (or carrying amount) of the buildings. However, the value of an asset for tax purposes, which is called the tax basis of the asset, could be different from its book value. For example, the asset might be depreciated for financial reporting purposes using the straight-line method, while for tax purposes it might be depreciated using an accelerated method. These differences between the tax basis and the accounting basis might, in turn, generate discrepancies between the income before taxes reported on a company's income statement and the taxable income that the same company reports to the tax authorities.

Example starts

On January 1, 2008, Company A acquired a building for $1 million in cash. The company decided to depreciate the building over 40 years using the straight-line method with zero salvage value. However, for tax purposes, the building is depreciated over 35 years only with zero salvage value as well. On January 1, 2018, the fair value of the building was $600,000 and the company recognized an impairment loss. What is the book value and tax basis of the building as of January 1, 2018?

The book value of the building is $600,000 following the recognition of the impairment loss. Before the impairment loss, the book value of the building was [$1,000,000 – [($1,000,000/40) × 10]=] $750,000. The impairment loss was therefore $150,000. The tax basis of the building is ($1,000,000 – [($1,000,000/35) × 10] =) $714,285.

If the company sells the building on January 2, 2018 for $600,000, there will be no gains or losses recognized in the income statement, because the building's book value is now $600,000. However, there would be a deductible loss for tax purposes amounting to ($600,000 – $714,285 =) $114,285.

Example ends

Example starts

On January 1, 2018, Company A buys 100% of B's voting shares for $1,000,000 in cash. At that time, Company B owned only a building with a net book value of $600,000 and a tax basis of $714,285. Therefore, Company A has a tax basis in the shares of $1,000,000 and Company B has a tax basis in the building of $714,285.

Example ends

6.2.3 Step-Ups Versus Carryovers

The tax basis of an asset might change because of taxable transactions. We refer to this change as a step-up (although a change in the tax basis could go both ways). In a tax-free transaction, the tax basis of the underlying assets does not change; it is carried over. We refer to it as a carryover.

Example starts

On January 1, 2010, Company A acquired all the shares of Company B for $1 million in cash. Thus, Company A has a tax basis in the shares of $1 million. On December 31, 2018, Company A completed a sale of all the shares of Company B for $2 million in cash. Since the consideration received is in cash, the transaction is taxable and Company A will pay capital gain taxes on the difference between the consideration and the tax basis of the shares, which is $1 million. In addition, Company B now has a tax basis in the shares of $2 million. That is, Company B enjoys a step-up while Company A has a taxable capital gain.

Example ends

Example starts
On January 1, 2010, Company A acquired all the shares of Company B for $1 million in cash. Thus, Company A has a tax basis in the shares of $1 million. On December 31, 2018, Company A completed a transfer of all the shares of Company B to Company C. In return for the shares of Company B, Company A received shares of Company C with a fair market value of $2 million. Companies A and C structured the transaction as a tax-free transaction. Company C has a tax basis in B's shares of $1 million (carryover). Company A has a tax basis in C's shares of $1 million (carryover).
Example ends

6.2.4 Tax Attributes and Loss Trafficking

Net operating losses (NOL) may be carried forward and used to offset future operating income (and thus lower future tax payments).[3] Similarly, capital losses carried forward may offset future capital gains; tax credits could be used in the future to reduce tax payments as well. Tax attributes, such as NOL carried forward, tax credits and capital losses carried forward, might also serve as a motivation for profitable acquirers to acquire companies with existing tax attributes and reduce their tax liabilities going forward (if they turn profitable).[4] Such an activity is often called loss trafficking. As tax attributes are valuable, the government has a motivation to limit loss trafficking. IRC Section 382 provides the guidelines for taxable income that can be offset against NOL carried forward in cases of ownership changes.

In the event of a shift in corporate ownership, the corporation is considered to be a new loss corporation subject to the Section 382 limitations on the use of tax attributes. Basically, the limitation for the post-change year is equal to the value of the old loss-company multiplied by the long-term federal exempt rate.[5] The purpose of this rule is to limit the use of tax attributes to a fair rate of return on the value of the loss-company, but not beyond. For tax purposes, an ownership change occurs when the stock ownership owned by one or 5% of the shareholders increases by 50%.

6.2.5 Accounting Implications

The difference between the book basis and the tax basis has an important accounting implication for deferred tax recognition. Deferred taxes exist in financial statements

[3]The purpose of this tax provision is to allow some form of tax relief when a firm loses money in a tax period.

[4]Otherwise, in case of a merger or a consolidation, these tax attributes can be used to offset the taxable income of the surviving/newly created (and supposedly) profitable entity.

[5]The federal long-term tax-exempt rate for a particular month is determined by the Internal Revenue Service.

whenever the tax basis of an asset/liability is different from the book basis of that asset/liability. We can estimate deferred taxes using the following equation:

$$\text{Deferred tax liability} = (\text{Book basis} - \text{Tax basis}) \times \text{Tax rate}$$

Example starts

On January 1, 2008, Company A acquired a building for \$1 million in cash. The company decided to depreciate the building over 40 years using the straight-line method with zero salvage value. However, for tax purposes, the building was depreciated over 35 years with zero salvage value. On January 1, 2018, the fair value of the building was \$600,000 and the company recognized an impairment loss. What is the deferred tax balance on January 1, 2018 assuming that the relevant tax rate is 25%?

From the third example above, the book value of the building is \$600,000 (after the impairment loss recognition) and the tax basis of the building is \$714,285. Hence the deferred tax balance is:

$$\text{Deferred tax balance} = (600{,}000 - 714{,}285) \times 25\% = -28{,}571$$

The calculation yields a negative number, which means that the deferred tax balance is a deferred tax asset (not a deferred tax liability).[6]

Example ends

Example starts

On January 1, 2018, Company A acquired all the shares of Company B for \$1 million in cash. At the time of acquisition, the balance sheet of Company B included all the items shown in the table below ("Book value" column). In addition, Company B owns a patent with a fair value of \$250,000, which is not recognized on the balance sheet. Assume that book values are equal to their tax bases for all items and the tax rate is 25%. Use the table below to compute deferred taxes and goodwill.

$	Book values	Fair value
Buildings	600,000	800,000
Inventory	100,000	130,000
Receivable	75,000	75,000
Patent	–	90,000
Bonds	(125,000)	(125,000)
Net assets	**650,000**	**970,000**

[6]A deferred tax asset (DTA) arises because in future periods, Company A will report lower depreciation expenses and, hence, higher income before taxes although tax payables would be lower.

This transaction is a taxable stock acquisition because Company A acquired the shares of company for cash (to be discussed in more detail later). In addition, an increase in the assets' fair value will trigger a temporary difference that requires deferred tax recognition because fair values become the new book basis for accounting consolidation. So, first, we need to compute deferred taxes for each item and then goodwill.

$	Book value	Fair value	Difference	Def. taxes
Buildings	600,000	800,000	200,000	(50,000)
Inventory	100,000	130,000	30,000	(7500)
Receivable	75,000	75,000	–	–
Patent	–	90,000	90,000	(22,500)
Bonds	(125,000)	(125,000)	–	–
Net assets	**650,000**	**970,000**	**320,000**	**(80,000)**

Here is the purchase price allocation:

$	Fair value
Buildings	800,000
Inventory	130,000
Receivable	75,000
Patent	90,000
Bonds	(125,000)
Deferred tax liability	(80,000)
Total	**890,000**
Goodwill	**110,000**
Consideration	**1,000,000**

Example ends

6.3 Asset Deals, Stock Deals, and Mergers

When buying or selling a business, the seller and the buyer could structure the transaction as a purchase/sale of assets or as a purchase/sale of common stock. The buyer (acquirer) and the seller (target) can have various reasons for preferring one type of sale to the other. In an asset deal (only option if the target is a sole proprietorship or a single-member LLC treated as a sole proprietorship), the transaction is actually the sum of the sales of each of the individual assets and an assumption of agreed upon liabilities. Conversely, in a stock deal, the acquisition results in a transfer of the target's shares to the acquirer, but the target continues to be the legal owner of the same assets and liabilities.

6.3.1 Asset Deals

An asset acquisition is an acquisition realized by buying the target's assets instead of its shares (stock). In many cases, an asset acquisition also involves an assumption of certain liabilities; however, because the parties can bargain over which assets will be acquired and which liabilities will be assumed, they have more flexibility. The target company recognizes gains or losses on the difference between the sale price allocated to its assets and their tax basis on an asset-by-asset basis.

In an asset acquisition, the buyer acquires/assumes only the assets and liabilities it identifies and agrees to acquire/assume, subject to restrictions imposed by law. This is fundamentally different from a stock acquisition or a merger where the buyer acquires all the assets and assumes all the liabilities (including unknown or undisclosed ones) of the target company as a matter of law.

The ability to choose specific assets and liabilities provides the buyer with flexibility: The buyer does not need to spend resources on buying unnecessary assets; also, the risk of assuming unknown or undisclosed liabilities is lower. On the other hand, the buyer must identify the assets/liabilities it is willing to acquire/assume and receives from the seller consent to acquire/assume only those. In addition, the buyer and seller must agree on how the purchase price is to be allocated among the assets in the deal. The US IRC requires that the purchase price be allocated using the "residual method," which allocates the purchase price among the assets equal to their fair market value with any remaining balance being applied to goodwill. The acquiring and target companies both report the same agreed upon purchase price allocation.

Asset acquisitions are especially common when buyers wish to gain control of assets owned by a distressed company but are not interested in acquiring the entire business operation due to the financial state of that company. Rather than having to acquire the entire business operation, the buyer can select which assets are attractive, take steps to purchase those particular assets, and not have to deal with any other holdings that may be of no particular interest. Such an approach could be more efficient both for the buyer and for the seller.

Although less frequent, an asset acquisition can also be used to gradually gain control of a target company. Here, the buyer attempts to gain control of key assets that are important to the ongoing operation of the company. If successful, the target becomes more and more dependent on the new owner of those assets, and the opportunity to acquire the rest of the operation, by either gaining a controlling interest through stock purchases or buying the entire company, can be accomplished more easily. Use of an asset acquisition can often be productive when the target company rejects buyout offers. An asset acquisition approach is also a viable alternative when the chances of being able to purchase enough shares and gain enough support from shareholders to mount a hostile takeover are low.

In order to complete the asset deal transaction, an asset purchase agreement (APA) is used. This agreement is between the buyer and the seller, and outlines which specific assets will be purchased. The terms of an APA will also include details like the total consideration, payment structure, timing, representations, warranties, and other standard legal terms.

6.3.2 Stock Deals

In a stock acquisition, a buyer acquires the shares of the target company directly from the selling shareholders. By owning a majority of the shares, the buyer assumes control over all the assets and liabilities, including existing unknown assets and unknown liabilities (if any). The buyer is merely stepping into the shoes of the previous owner and the business continues. After the closing of the stock acquisition, the target continues, as it existed prior to the acquisition, with respect to legal ownership of its assets and liabilities.

The target company does not generally recognize any gain or loss from the sale of its own stock. Instead, its shareholders recognize gains or losses on the difference between the selling price and their tax basis in the stocks, if the consideration is paid in cash.

A stock transaction means taking control over the entire target entity, so past financial and legal liabilities are included, creating a significant risk exposure to the buyer. Thus, financial debt and legal risk could play a factor in reducing the purchase price of the sale. On the other hand, a stock acquisition is a good option if the target has a right, license, or exclusive distributorship that cannot be otherwise transferred. Further, from a tax perspective, there is no need for purchase price allocation.

In a stock acquisition, the buyer may be interested in potential growth in value of the target and in the synergies created by the transaction. Since the buyer in a stock deal takes control of all the business assets without the necessity of transferring legal ownership of each one, the buyer may prefer a stock deal if the transfer of assets may prove to be impractical or costly. For example, if the business depends heavily on certain licenses, or on key customer or distribution agreements, the buyer may prefer a stock acquisition to ensure that all of the licenses and agreements transfer with the sale. In addition, in cases involving high asset transfer fees, such as sales that involve the transfer of title to a fleet of vehicles or buildings, the buyer will generally avoid those costs by agreeing to a stock sale. Finally, in some instances, if both the buyer and seller are C corporations, the transaction may qualify for tax treatment as a tax-free reorganization. In the US IRC, a C Corporation is taxed separately from its owners (large companies traded on stock exchanges are C corporations).

6.3.3 Advantages and Disadvantages of Asset/Stock Deals

One advantage of an asset deal is that it allows the buyer to be selective in acquiring certain assets, but not others. For example, if the target has a large percentage of uncollectible accounts receivable, the buyer could decide not to buy the entire accounts receivable, but only a fraction of them, or add a contingency based on the actual collection of these receivables. In addition, an asset deal enables the buyer to avoid assuming certain liabilities, which could limit exposure to certain risks. Because the exposure to unknown liabilities is limited, the buyer needs to spend less resources on due diligence as well. In a stock deal, on the other hand, the buyer acquires all the liabilities of the seller (including undisclosed items, if any).

Asset deals also enable the buyer to integrate new assets into its operations. In an asset deal, the buyer does not engage in eliminating unnecessary functions in the target. This means that asset deals could result in larger cost cutting, all else being the same. An asset deal might require a longer preparation and negotiation of all the deal aspects (including assets allocated, employment termination and rehiring, lease assignment, contract transferability, creditor pay-outs). Lastly, minority shareholders have less power in blocking asset deals than stock deals, because their consent is not required in an asset deal.

The disadvantages of asset deals relate primarily to contracting and renegotiations. Certain contracts, for instance, with customers and suppliers, may need to be renegotiated by the new owner. Certain assets need to be retitled. Employment agreements with key employees may need to be renegotiated. Furthermore, the seller still needs to terminate existing contracts, liquidate any assets not purchased, and pay any liabilities that have not been assumed, before liquidation dividends can be paid to the target's shareholders.

There are some advantages to a stock deal. The acquirer need not bother with costly revaluations and retitles of individual assets for tax purposes, although revaluations are needed for accounting purposes in the consolidated financial statements. Buyers can typically assume nonassignable licenses and permits without having to obtain specific consent. Buyers may also be able to avoid paying asset transfer taxes.

Stock deals also have disadvantages. First, the target may remain a listed company, which means a stricter regulatory environment under securities laws. Second, a minority of shareholders could reduce the ability of the acquirer to make certain decisions. Lastly, the acquirer may be exposed to certain liabilities, which will need to be settled.

6.3.4 Merger/Consolidation

In a statutory merger (or consolidation), two or more companies combine subject to the rules set forth by the corporate laws in their jurisdictions. The only difference between mergers and consolidations, as anticipated, is that in consolidations, the companies are merged into a new corporation, whereas in mergers, one of the combining corporations survives. Going forward, we will generically refer to these transactions as "mergers".

Relative to a purchase of assets, a merger is often cheaper and easier to execute because it involves less documentation. In addition, the problem of a small minority does not exist, because in most jurisdictions, the laws require the consent of both shareholder groups; if a small minority of the target dissents, there are laws and provisions to buying out this minority for cash. Finally, there is more flexibility in designing a tax-free merger when it comes to types of consideration. That is, it is possible to structure the deal such that some shareholders enjoy a tax-free deal while others receive a taxable consideration.

6.4 The Tax-Deductibility of Goodwill

Under both US GAAP and IFRS, companies generally recognize goodwill only on their consolidated financial statements following an acquisition of a controlling interest in a target entity.[7] Specifically, goodwill may be recognized as an asset under the purchase method of accounting, as the difference between the fair value of the consideration paid and the fair value of net assets acquired. Goodwill may be recognized using the fair value method (full goodwill method) or using the partial method, as described in previous chapters. Goodwill under both US GAAP and IFRS is not amortized in the income statement, but rather tested for impairment annually. Similar requirements exist for all indefinite-lived intangibles.

What is the status of goodwill for tax purposes? Does goodwill exist for tax purposes? Under which circumstances? Is it possible to get a tax deduction for goodwill? In the US, until 1993, goodwill was not recognized for tax purposes and taxpayers did not receive any tax relief for acquiring goodwill. The main reason was that taxpayers could not obtain a reliable estimate of the useful life of goodwill. The status of goodwill for tax purposes changed in 1993 with the adoption of Section 197 to the US tax code. Section 197 allows taxpayers to amortize goodwill for tax purposes over 15 years providing it is acquired in a taxable asset acquisition.

Section 197 of the IRC considers goodwill and other intangible assets acquired after 1993 as amortizable noncapital assets. These assets can be deducted for tax purposes over 15 years using the straight-line method. Intangibles allowed under Section 197 include operating systems, customer lists, no-compete agreements, and certain intellectual property. Section 197 excludes several assets from being amortizable, for instance, an investment in sports franchise.

<u>Example starts</u>

On January 1, 2018, Company A acquired all the assets and liabilities of Company B for $1 million in cash. At the time of acquisition, Company B's balance sheet included the following items at book values: buildings, $600,000, inventory, $100,000, accounts receivable, $75,000, and bonds payable, $125,000. Assume that book values are equal to fair values, which in turn are equal to the tax basis of all assets. The tax rate is 25%.

In this example, goodwill is equal to [$1,000,000 − ($600,000 + $100,000 + $75,000 − $125,000) =] $350,000. Since this transaction is a taxable asset deal,

---

[7] An exception is pushdown accounting in which goodwill may be recognized on the Target's separate financial statements following a change-in-control event, under US GAAP (discussed in Chapter 7).

goodwill will be amortized for tax purposes over 15 years. That is, Company A will get a tax deduction of $23,333 a year over the next 15 years.

At the time of acquisition, all assets, including goodwill, have book values equal to their tax basis. Hence, there is no need to recognize deferred tax assets and liabilities. However, this will change by the end of fiscal 2018. The accounting for goodwill subsequent to acquisition depends on impairment testing. Assume that there is no impairment of goodwill during 2018, but there is an impairment charge of $50,000 in 2019.

At the end of fiscal 2018, we will need to recognize a deferred tax liability for goodwill because of the difference between tax deductions and expenses. The entry should be:

$	Dr.	Cr.
Tax receivables[a]	5,833	
Deferred tax liability		5,833

[a]Tax deduction computed as $23,333 × 25%

There is no tax expense recognition since there is no goodwill amortization or impairment.

At the end of fiscal 2019, the tax basis of goodwill is ($350,000 – $23,333 × 2=) $303,333, but the book basis is ($350,000 – $50,000=) $300,000. Hence, we will need to record a deferred tax liability/asset as follows:

$$\begin{aligned}\text{Deferred tax liability} &= \text{Book basis} - \text{Tax basis}\\ &= (\$300{,}000 - \$303{,}333) \times 25\% = -\$833\end{aligned}$$

The deferred tax liability is currently booked at $5,833, but there should be a deferred tax asset of $833. The journal entry is:

$	Dr.	Cr.
Deferred tax liability	6,666	
Tax receivable [($350,000/15) × 25%]	5,833	
Income tax expense ($50,000 × 25%)		12,500

The tax expense recognition is for impairment losses in the income statement.

Example ends

6.5 Stock Deals Turning to Asset Deals (Section 338 Election)

Section 338 of the US IRC permits a corporation that has purchased a controlling interest in another corporation, using a qualified stock purchase, to elect to have the acquisition of the target's stock to be treated as a purchase of assets rather than stocks for federal income tax purposes. Such an election is referred to as a "Deemed Asset Sale".[8] A Section 338 election is useful when the buyer has a good business reason to acquire stock rather than assets. For instance, difficulty assigning licenses or permits, but the buyer still wants the tax benefits of an asset acquisition.

Recall that in a stock deal the target's shareholders sell their stock to the acquiring company. Under Section 338 election, a stock transaction is treated like an asset deal. Specifically, the stock sale by the target's shareholders is disregarded. The target is treated as if it sold assets and distributed the proceeds in a complete liquidation. Its shareholders are taxed on gain from the deemed asset sale. The buyer receives a step-up on the basis of the target's assets. Its unused tax attributes (e.g., NOL, capital losses carried forward) survive and are transferred to the shareholders selling the target's stock.

To qualify for Section 338 election, both the acquirer and the target must be corporations. Individuals and partnerships cannot be the party that purchases the target.

In a Section 338(h)(10) election, typically only one level of tax is imposed, on the deemed asset sale; the stock sale is ignored for tax purposes and the deemed liquidation is tax-free to the selling shareholders.[9] Section 338(h)(10) elections are available only for targets who are S Corporations or members of an affiliated group of corporations (whether or not they file a consolidated federal income tax return).[10]

If the target is an S corporation and a stock purchase is desired for nontax reasons, but an asset purchase is desired for tax reasons, it is common for the target's S corporation's shareholders and the acquiring corporation to agree to make an election under section 338(h)(10). All shareholders of the target S corporation (selling and non-selling) must consent to the section 338(h)(10) election. When this election is made, for tax purposes the sale of the stock by the selling shareholders is ignored.

Further, the regulation enables a stock sale of an S Corporation to be taxed as if the transaction were an asset sale. Asset sales offer several advantages. For one, the buyer can take a "stepped-up" tax basis, which means it can significantly raise

---

[8] The section has two alternative options: Section 338(g) as a regular election and Section 338(h)(10) as an alternative election. Election under Section 338(h)(10) is much more common.

[9] The parties are treated for tax purposes as though (1) the buying corporation established a new corporation ("New Target"), (2) New Target purchased the assets of the target corporation ("Old Target") and assumed its liabilities and (3) Old Target liquidated in the hands of the seller.

[10] S Corporation is a regular corporation with 100 shareholders or less, which enables the company to enjoy the benefits of incorporation while being taxed as if it were a partnership. S Corporations typically do not pay taxes and instead file an informational return showing the net profit or loss which flows through to the shareholders. The shareholders then show the net profit or loss on their personal tax returns. All S Corporations start as a regular or professional corporation and only by requesting the S Election from the Internal Revenue Service can they act as an S Corporation.

the stated value of the seller's assets. Greater asset value, in turn, enables a buyer to claim more depreciation on its acquired assets and, therefore, to take a larger, current tax deduction. In addition, goodwill on the transaction is tax-deductible over 15 years.

6.6 Tax-Free Acquisitions

To qualify as a tax-free asset deal, a tax-free stock deal, or a tax-free merger, the parties to the transaction must follow closely the requirements of the relevant tax code. Here, we will discuss the requirement of the US tax code, and in particular, Section 368(a)(1) of the IRC Reorganizations. Section 368(a)(1) outlines a format for tax treatment to reorganizations under IRC of 1986. To qualify for favorable tax treatment, the transaction must meet certain legal requirements, and in addition, conform to certain requirements under case law. In addition to the statutory requirements, all tax-free reorganizations must satisfy three judicial requirements, which are continuity of interest, continuity of business enterprise, and business purpose.

We will focus on three subsections of Section 368(A)(1):

- subsection A focuses on Mergers or Consolidations (A Reorganization).
- subsection B of Section 368(a)(1) defines a stock-for-stock exchange, which results in B Reorganization.
- subsection C of Section 368(a)(1) defines a stock-for-asset exchange, also known as a C Reorganization.

6.6.1 A Tax-Free Stock Deal

To qualify for a tax-free stock deal (B Reorganization), the transaction must meet two basic criteria: (i) the consideration must be only in voting stock of the acquiring company; and (ii) the acquiring company must achieve statutory control of the acquired company. Any failure to comply with these two conditions will result in immediate tax on the capital gain.

While finance theory distinguishes between common stock, preferred stock, warrants, options, and convertible bonds, for tax purposes stock is stock and bonds are bonds. Options, warrants, and convertible bonds do not qualify as voting stock, but preferred stock may qualify as stock. To qualify as a voting stock, the stock must have a vote in the shareholders meeting to approve directors. It is possible to create common or preferred stock with limited voting power.

To achieve statutory control, the acquirer must obtain at least 80% of the voting power of each class of shares plus 80% of the nonvoting shares. The US tax authorities ruled that all transactions within a 12-month period will be treated as one transaction. This rule may have serious implications for step acquisitions.

Example starts

On July 1, 2018, Target had the following shares outstanding: 100,000 class A common shares with $1 par value; 60,000 class B common shares with $2 par value; and 25,000 nonvoting $5 preferred shares. On that day, Acquire acquired 85,000 class A shares, 50,000 class B shares, and 22,000 $5 preferred shares. The consideration consisted of 50,000 common shares $10 par value and 10,000 common shares with $20 par value. Each share has one vote. Does this transaction qualify as a tax-free stock acquisition?

Acquire acquired 85% of class A shares, 83.33% of class B common shares, and 88% of the $5 preferred shares. By that, Acquire obtained statutory control over Target. In addition, the consideration was solely in voting shares, even though the $20 par value shares have half the vote of the $10 par value shares. Therefore, this transaction may qualify as a tax-free stock acquisition.

The main tax implication is that Target's shareholders will not pay taxes until they liquidate their shares in Acquire. The tax basis of Target's shareholders in Acquire's shares is equal to the tax basis they previously had in Target's shares (carryover). The tax basis of Target's assets and liabilities is unchanged. The tax basis of Acquire in Target's shares is also carried over.

Goodwill in this transaction does not exist for tax purposes; however, it may be recognized on Acquire's consolidated balance sheet according to US GAAP. Note that while the tax basis of Target's assets and liabilities does not change, the fair value of these assets and liabilities is reassessed at the time of acquisition. Hence, deferred tax assets/liabilities may arise during the purchase price allocation process.

Example ends

Example starts

On February 1, 2018, Target had the following shares outstanding: 100,000 class A common shares with $1 par value; 60,000 class B common shares $2 par value; and 25,000 nonvoting $5 preferred shares. On that day, Acquire acquired all 25,000 $5 preferred stock for $98,000 in cash. On August 15, 2018, Acquire purchased 85,000 class A shares and 50,000 class B shares. The consideration consisted of 60,000 common shares $10 par value. Does this transaction qualify as a tax-free stock acquisition?

The answer is no. Since both transactions occurred in the same 12-month period, the tax authorities consider them as one single transaction for tax purposes. Consequently, the transaction is not solely for voting shares, and hence cannot qualify as a tax-free stock acquisition.

Example ends

6.6.2 A Tax-Free Asset Deal

Example starts

In an asset deal, the acquirer acquires assets and assumes liabilities from the target. In such a transaction, there could be two tax events. The first one is selling assets and liabilities to the acquirer. This transaction may result in the target paying capital gain taxes on the difference between the allocated consideration to each asset and its tax basis. The second tax event is the distribution of the consideration to the target's shareholders as dividends. Such a distribution may be subject to income taxes on dividends. Tax-free asset deals defer both tax events to a later date (liquidation of the consideration by the target's shareholders).

To qualify for a tax-free asset deal (C Reorganization), the transaction must meet two conditions: (i) the consideration must be solely in voting stock, although there are some exceptions to this rule; (ii) the buyer must take possession of substantially all of the target's assets.

Regarding the transfer of assets, there is no clear statutory condition, but guidelines issued by the US tax authorities (IRS) maintain that a transfer of 90% of the fair value of net assets, or a transfer of 70% of the gross assets owned by the target, satisfies the "substantially all" condition and the IRS will not challenge the deal.

Regarding the consideration, the restrictions on voting stock are similar to those imposed in a B Reorganization (tax-free stock transaction). Unlike a stock transaction, a tax-free asset deal allows a small portion of the consideration to be in cash (often referred to as "boot", see below).

Example ends

Example starts

On July 1, 2019, Target owns assets with fair value of $1,000,000 and liabilities with fair value of $600,000. Acquire acquired 90% of Target's assets in terms of fair values, and assumed 80% of Target's liabilities in terms of fair values. The consideration was solely in Acquire's voting stock. Does this deal qualify as a tax-free asset deal?

While the consideration is solely in voting stock, the question is whether assuming liabilities meets the condition of "solely voting stock." In essence, assuming liabilities in this case is equivalent to paying $480,000 in cash. However, this transaction qualifies as a tax-free asset deal (C Reorganization) because there is no other form of payment.

Example ends

Example starts

On July 1, 2019, Target owns assets, excluding goodwill, with fair value of $1,000,000 and financial debt with fair value of $600,000. Acquire acquired 100% of Target's assets, and assumed 20% of Target's liabilities in terms of fair values. The deal was valued at $800,000. The consideration consisted of cash payment of $25,000 and the balance in Acquire's voting stock with a fair value of $775,000. Does this deal qualify as a tax-free asset deal?

To answer the question, we need to review the rules for partial taxation in deals involving a small element of cash. If the acquirer buys at least 80% of the assets in terms of fair value by issuing solely voting stock, the acquirer can buy any of the remaining 20% for other forms of consideration (for example, cash or non-voting preferred stock). This cash element is called "boot." However, to calculate the boot, any debt assumed is considered part of it. In this example, the cash plus assumed debt has a fair value of $145,000, which is less than 20% of the total consideration. Therefore, this deal qualifies as a tax-free asset deal.

In a tax-free asset deal, the tax basis of the acquired assets and liabilities does not change and it is carried over from the seller to the buyer. The buyer cannot recognize goodwill as an amortizable asset and the seller does not pay capital gain taxes. Likely, the stock consideration (that is, acquire voting shares) is distributed to the target's shareholders in return for their shares in it; each shareholder will pay tax when liquidating the received shares on the difference between the proceeds and tax basis they had in the target's shares.

In cases with boot, there is partial taxation. If the target retains the boot and uses it for, say, paying its debt, there is taxation on the boot. If instead, the target passes the boot to its shareholders, they will pay proportional taxes on the cash element.

Example ends

Example starts

A shareholder in Target has a tax basis in Target's voting stock of $300,000. Following an acquisition of Target, the shareholder received voting stock in Acquire with a fair market value of $480,000 and nonvoting preferred stock with a fair value of $20,000. The shareholder decided to liquidate the nonvoting preferred stock. In this case, there is a total capital gain of $200,000. Note that the boot is 4% of the total consideration.

The shareholders will pay capital gain taxes on [$20,000 – (4% × $300,000) =] $8,000.[11] The tax basis of the stock consideration will be the original tax basis minus the boot and plus the gain, that is ($300,000 – $20,000 + $8000 =) $288,000 (or 300,000 × 0.96).

Example ends

6.6.3 Tax-Free Merger (a Reorganization)

To qualify as a tax-free merger/consolidation, the transaction must comply with the requirements of the US IRC, as well as with the relevant state's corporate laws.[12] In addition, a tax-free merger must satisfy the Continuing Interest Test (CIT). This test requires that the target's shareholders continue to have a substantial continuing proprietary interest in the new emerging entity, relative to the net

---

[11] If the boot is received as dividends, there will be dividends income tax.

[12] Section 368(a)(1)(A) of the IRC.

assets transferred from the target to the new entity. The CIT has emerged as one of the main tests in deciding whether a merger is taxable or tax-free. To this regard, there are two questions: what constitutes a continuing proprietary interest? In addition, what is a "substantial" interest?

Clearly, if the merger is effected solely by voting stock, both shareholders groups—acquire and target—have a continuing proprietary interest in the merged entity. In addition, nonvoting preferred stock constitutes a proprietary interest, while debt securities do not. With respect to "substantial," the guidelines are that if the shareholders of the former target receive stock with a value of at least 50% of the value of the stock they held prior to the merger, than the "substantial" test is satisfied.

As to the tax basis, the situation in a tax-free merger is similar to a tax-free asset deal, because all the assets and liabilities of the target are transferred to the new entity. That is, the assets retain their tax basis.

6.7 Summary

The purpose of this chapter is to provide the reader with a general understanding of the impact of taxes on deal structure, and in addition to explore the accounting consequences of taxes. To keep the discussion relatively simple, we adopted the terminology and general rules used in the US tax code.

Initially, we distinguished between taxable vs tax-free transactions. To construct a tax-free transaction, the consideration must be (in most cases) solely in shares. Consideration of cash or assuming liabilities virtually ensures a taxable transaction. Next, we distinguished between tax basis of an asset and its book basis. The book basis is the value of the asset on the books (financial statements); the tax basis, on the other hand, is the value of the asset for tax purposes. Furthermore, the structure of a deal as a taxable transaction or a tax-free one effects the tax basis of the acquired assets. In a taxable transaction, the tax basis of the asset is stepped-up to its fair value at the time of the deal, whereas in a tax-free transaction the tax basis is carried over, that is, does not change.

When the book basis is different than the tax basis of an asset (or liability), deferred tax assets or liabilities arise. Basically, deferred taxes are equal to the difference between the tax and book basis, multiplied by the relevant tax rate.

The tax structure of a deal has a significant impact on the accounting recognition and tax-deductibility of goodwill. If the deal is structured as a tax-free transaction, the assets and liabilities of the acquired company are consolidated at fair value, while for tax purposes, their tax basis does not change. This means that the parent company needs to recognize deferred taxes on the differences between the fair values and the tax bases, which in turn affects the amount of goodwill on the transaction. Specifically, if the fair values of the acquired net assets are larger than their existing book values, the parent company will need to recognize a deferred tax liability, which in turn will increase the goodwill on the transaction. The goodwill on a tax-free transaction cannot be amortized for tax purposes. Alternatively, if the transaction is structured as a taxable asset deal, the assets and liabilities of the acquired company are consolidated at fair values, and the tax bases are stepped-up to fair valued as well. In that case, there is no need for new deferred taxes. However, any goodwill on a taxable asset acquisition can be amortized for tax purposes over a period of 15 years.

References

US Internal Revenue Service, *Limitation on Net Operating Loss Carry Forwards and Certain Built-In Losses Following Ownership Change*, Section 382.

US Internal Revenue Service, *Definitions Relating to Corporate Reorganizations*, Section 368(a)(1).

US Internal Revenue Service, *Amortization of Goodwill and Certain Other Intangibles*, Section 197.

US Internal Revenue Service, *Certain Stock Purchases Treated as Asset Acquisitions*, Section 338.

Leveraged Buyouts and Recapitalizations

7

7.1 Introduction

Corporate reorganizations refer to cases where companies change their internal or external structure to improve efficiency or to increase revenues and income. Reorganizations often result in change of ownership, where new owners take control over the company. In this chapter, we will review two types of corporate reorganizations: Leveraged Buyouts (LBOs) and Recapitalizations (RECAPs). These transactions are often characterized by high level of debt, secured by the assets and cash flows of the acquired company. These situations raise questions about whether the assets and liabilities of the acquired company should retain their historical bases or should change the accounting basis to fair value.

7.2 Leveraged Buyouts

A leveraged buyout (LBO) is a financial transaction where one company (parent) takes over (either in a friendly or hostile deal) another company (target) using a combination of equity and a significant amount of debt financing. Many times, the assets and cash flows of the target, where the newly raised debt usually lies, are used to secure the interest and principal payments on the debt, because the parent company, being a financial investor, lacks any substantial business operations. The use of debt as a primary source of financing decreases the overall financing cost, as its cost is normally lower than the cost of equity financing, although financial leverage increases the risk of the entire deal. In addition, the seniority of debt over

Electronic supplementary material The online version of this chapter (https://doi.org/10.1007/978-3-030-61769-1_7) contains supplementary material, which is available to authorized users.

E. Amir and M. Ghitti, *Financial Analysis of Mergers and Acquisitions*,
https://doi.org/10.1007/978-3-030-61769-1_7

equity and the tax-deductibility of debt financing reduce the cost of debt financing relative to equity financing. Because of the significant amount of debt, the expected return on equity in LBOs is higher compared to other M&A deals.

While many acquisitions involve debt financing and could be regarded as a LBO, the term LBO is usually reserved for transactions where a financial investor (e.g., a private equity firm) acquires control over another company. LBOs occur in many different circumstances. On one hand, some LBOs involve target companies in distress or on the brink of insolvency, while other LBOs involve targets that operate in growing industries. Irrespective of the circumstances leading to a LBO, these deals occur primarily with private target companies, although they can also be effected with publicly listed targets.[1]

There are several forms of LBOs: Management Buyout (MBO), Management Buy-In (MBI), a secondary buyout, and a tertiary buyout. MBOs are transactions in which the existing management of the target company acquires a controlling interest in it using a large amount of debt and a relatively small amount of own funds (equity). Similarly, in MBI transactions, an external team of management (e.g., a management team of a competing company) acquires a controlling interest in the target. MBOs may occur for a variety of reasons:

- existing owners wish to exit and sell the company to experienced and trusted members of management;
- owners have lost faith in the company and are willing to sell it to management who, instead, still believe in its future;
- conflicts between management and owners: while management sees potential growth opportunities, the owners are reluctant to approve investments.

In most cases, however, management cannot raise enough funding to finance the transaction so they need the support and sponsorship of a financial investor (a private equity firm). Together, the financial investor and management execute the LBO where a key element of the negotiations relates to management's shares in the deal.[2]

A secondary buyout is a form of LBO where both the seller and the buyer are financial investors (private equity firms). That is, a buyout of a target that was previously acquired through a LBO.[3] Secondary buyouts occur because some targets

[1]A notorious case is the LBO of Dell Inc. through which the firm has been taken private in a $24 billion deal announced in February 2013.

[2]There is a conflict of interests between the owners and existing management. The owners wish to sell the company at the highest price whereas management (and the financial investor) wish to lower the price as much as possible. Since both management and the financial investor are interested in maximizing post-acquisition earnings, one way to resolve the conflict is by using contingent purchase price based on future earnings (earn-outs).

[3]This has been the case, although with discouraging financial results, of SEAT Pagine Gialle S.p.A., a former Italian listed company operating in the communications sector, which has been the subject of two LBOs (and a takeover by Telecom Italia in-between) through the second half of the 1990s and the first half of the 2000s.

are more appealing to private equity investors rather than to the public equity markets, so an exit through a public offering is not feasible. In addition, it may be easier to find a financial investor rather than to go through a lengthy IPO process, for instance, due to high legal and transaction costs. Also, it may not be feasible to sell a significant stake in a company through an IPO. Another reason why a lengthy IPO exit might not be feasible is that the first private equity fund may need a swift exit due to contractual constraints.

A tertiary LBO is a LBO where a company that was acquired through a secondary buyout is acquired by yet another financial investor.[4]

Many target companies in LBOs share several characteristics:

- high and stable cash flows to support the high debt levels involved in the deal;
- limited working capital and capital expenditures needs, so to direct the bulk of cash flows to debt repayment;
- operations in steady, noncyclical sectors;
- low operating leverage (less fixed costs relative to variable ones) to reduce operating risk and low debt levels.

In many cases, existing debt is replaced by new debt because the new debt is riskier and current debt holders are unwilling to take on additional risk or simply because change-in-control covenants might require it. LBO targets should also have strong management with vested interest in the target.[5] Finally, private equity investors will avoid targets with high valuation multiples to reduce market risk and to secure higher rates of return upon their exit.[6]

Example starts

To demonstrate the nature of a LBO, assume that Target Company has 100 outstanding shares. The carrying amount of assets and liabilities is $1,000 and $500, respectively. Therefore, the book value of net assets is $500. A buyout fund assesses the fair value of Target's equity at $1,000, $500 above the carrying amount of net assets. The fair value of all assets and liabilities are equal to their carrying amount. Hence, there are no fair value adjustments and the difference between book and fair values is attributed entirely to goodwill. That is, goodwill is equal to [$1,000 – ($1,000 – $500)=] $500.

The buyout fund forms NewCo (an acquisition vehicle), which raises both equity and debt. It wishes to hold 80% of the shares in NewCo, leaving 20% of it to Target's management. In addition, NewCo will raise $600 of high-yield debt,

[4]See Deloitte (2016).

[5]Since management has "skin in the game," the use of debt does not simply represent a financing technique, but rather a way to force changes in managerial (mis)behavior (so called "discipline of debt").

[6]One of the largest LBO ever is the acquisition of RJR Nabisco by KKR in 1989. This deal, which was valued at $31.1 billion ($109 per share), has been the largest deal on records for 17 years. The deal was described in the book and the movie "Barbarians at the Gate: The Fall of RJR Nabisco".

guaranteed by the cash flows and assets of Target. Alternatively, the shares held by the financial investor in NewCo could serve as collateral for the debt.

Debt raised by NewCo often has at least two tranches. The first one is senior debt, which is guaranteed with the cash flows and assets of the acquired company. The second one is junior or subordinated debt, which is usually not secured, thus being more risky. Sometimes, these two debt instruments are supplemented by high yield or "junk" bonds. Convertible bonds and convertible preferred shares may also be used in order to add yet more securities with different risk-reward profiles so as to appeal to a wider range of investors. In management buyouts, some of the debt is in the form of "seller notes" (loans provided by the seller) as well. In large transactions, the debt is syndicated, which means that several banks combine to provide (pool) the debt needed. Syndicated loans reduce the risk to each bank and may prevent banks from violating regulatory requirements.

In addition to raising debt, the buyout fund will inject \$320 of equity into NewCo in return for NewCo's 320 out of 400 shares (80%), and management will inject \$80 into NewCo for the remaining 80 shares.

The balance sheet of Target at acquisition includes its assets and liabilities at book value (subject to pushdown accounting to be discussed later). The consolidated balance sheet of NewCo will show the assets and liabilities of Target at fair value, including goodwill (\$500) and debt (\$600) (Fig. 7.1).

Example ends

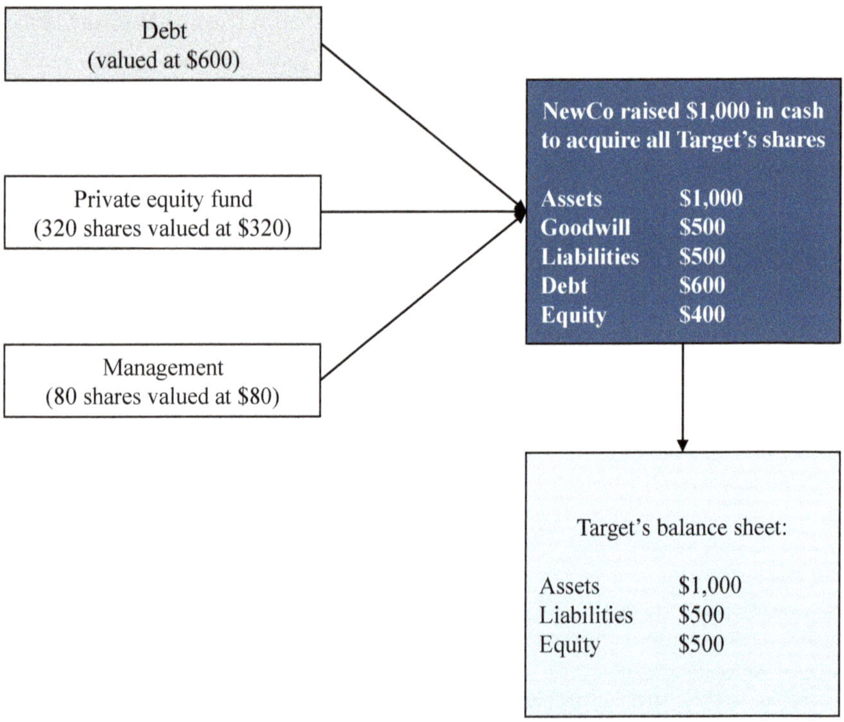

Fig. 7.1 LBO deal structure

7.3 Recapitalizations

A recapitalization (RECAP) is a corporate reorganization transaction that involves a significant change in the capital structure of the target company. One type of RECAP transaction is a leveraged RECAP, where the target company issues debt and equity and uses the funds to buy back a large amount of its own shares. In some of these transactions, current shareholders retain control but in other transactions, existing shareholders and a financial investor (private equity firm) gain control over the target.

There are several motivations for RECAP transactions. Some of the existing shareholders may wish to exit the investment in the target company. A RECAP transaction could also be a good defense against a hostile takeover. In cases where the target company loses value, or at times of poor economic performance, a RECAP transaction could be a way to induce an improvement in performance.

A financial investor, who wishes to take control over the target company, often initiates a leveraged RECAP transaction. To do so, it will raise debt, improve the target's performance, repay a substantial amount of debt, and exit through a public offering or other ways. Such transactions are quite similar to LBOs.[7]

Example starts

Consider the Target from the previous example. Recall that it is valued at $1,000. Also, recall that the former LBO transaction was effected through a new company called NewCo. Suppose now that Target raises $600 of debt. In addition, the financial investor injects $320 into Target and, in return, receives 32 new shares. Target uses the debt and equity injections ($600+$320=) of $920 to buy back 92 shares, leaving 8 shares to its existing shareholders.

The following figure presents the transaction before and after the RECAP. Before the transaction, existing shareholders hold 100 shares in Target. After the transaction, the financial investor holds 32 shares (80%) and existing shareholders hold 8 shares (20%) (Figs. 7.2 and 7.3).

If the financial investor presents consolidated financial statements, the balance sheet at the time of acquisition will look like this (assuming the partial method for goodwill and non-controlling interests):

[7]Another type of RECAP transaction is a nationalization. Here the nation where the target resides takes it over by buying a large amount of its equity. Existing equity holders usually lose control. Nationalization occurs when the nation would like to protect important national resources from being controlled by outside shareholders.

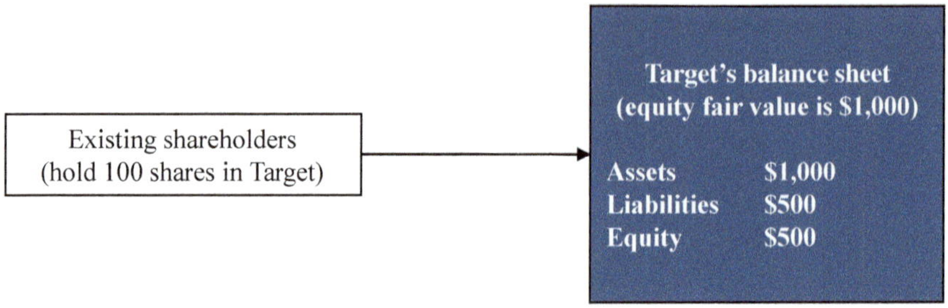

Fig. 7.2 Target's structure before the RECAP transaction

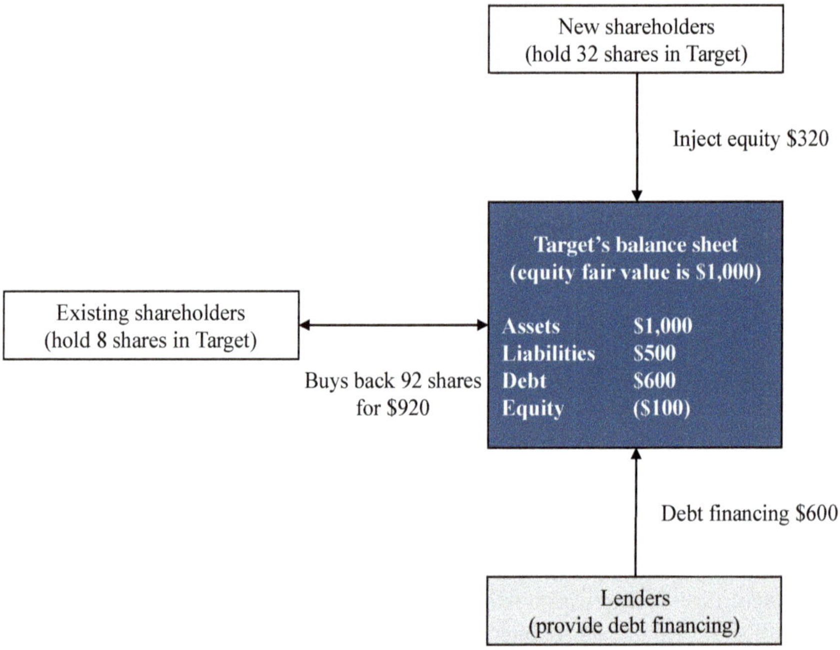

Fig. 7.3 Target's structure after the RECAP transaction (1st version)

Balance sheet	$	Comments
Target's assets at fair value	1,000	
Goodwill	400	$800 – 0.8 × ($1000 – $500)
Total assets	**1,400**	
Target's liabilities at fair values	500	
Debt	600	Raised at acquisition
Non-controlling interests	100	0.2 × ($1000 – $500)

Balance sheet	$	Comments
Shareholders' equity	200	
Liabilities and equity	**1,400**	

Target's balance sheet includes assets and liabilities at historical figures and does not include goodwill. Target's shareholders' equity is equal to the beginning balance, $500, plus the new equity injection, $320, minus the share buyback, $920, a total of −$100.

Essentially, the same RECAP could be effected in a different way: instead of a share buyback, the financial investor could form NewCo, NewCo could raise $600 of debt and, together with $200 of equity, buy 80% of Target's shares directly from the existing shareholders. In this case, Target's balance sheet will not include the debt, although its assets and cash flows will most likely guarantee the debt payments (Fig. 7.4).

In this case, the consolidated balance sheet of NewCo at the time of the RECAP (assuming the partial method for goodwill and non-controlling interests) will be identical to that presented in the previous version of the RECAP. However, Target's balance sheet will be different because the debt now resides in NewCo and Target did not engage in a share buyback.

A third possible structure is that the financial investor forms NewCo and raises debt of $600 and equity of $320. NewCo then injects $920 into Target in return for

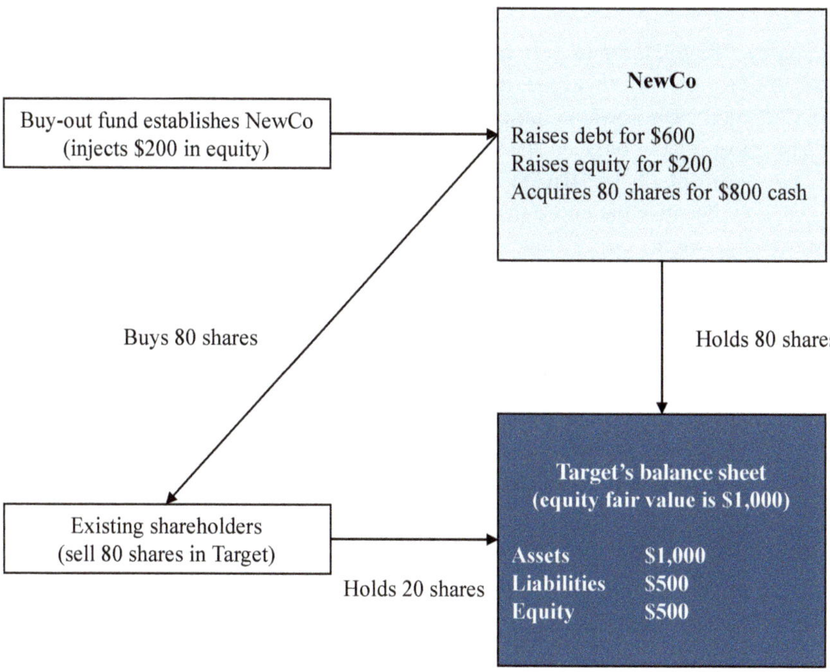

Fig. 7.4 Target's structure after the RECAP transaction (2nd version)

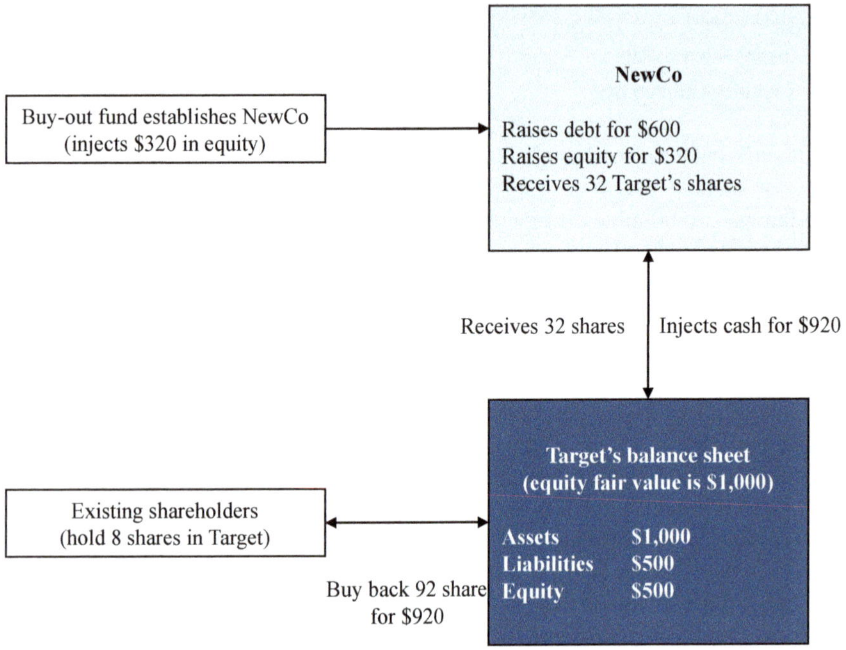

Fig. 7.5 Target's structure after the RECAP transaction (3rd version)

32 shares. The $920 are used to buy back 92 shares from existing shareholders and retire these shares. In this case, the debt resides in NewCo, but it is guaranteed by the assets and cash flows of Target (Fig. 7.5).

The consolidated balance sheet of NewCo will be identical to that in the previous two versions of the RECAP. However, in this case, Target's balance sheet is unchanged, because the entire proceeds from NewCo are used to buy back shares. Specifically, when Target issues 32 shares to NewCo, it records the following accounting entry:

$	Dr.	Cr.
Cash	920	
Shareholders' equity		920

When Target buys back shares, it records the following accounting entry:

$	Dr.	Cr.
Shareholders' equity	920	
Cash		920

Example ends

To summarize, in all LBOs and RECAPs, the financial statements of NewCo and the financial investor, if consolidated financial statements are prepared, include Target's assets and liabilities at fair value, goodwill, debt raised in the transaction and non-controlling interests (if any). Thus, these financial statements are similar to any acquirer's consolidated financial statements. However, most likely, these financial statements are not released to the public, because both the financial investor and NewCo are often private companies.

Consider for example, a RECAP transaction where the target company buys back a large number of shares and, in addition, guarantees the debt of NewCo. Since the debt is off Target's balance sheet, and since Target's financial statements show historical figures and no goodwill, it is difficult for outside investors to properly analyze Target's financial statements. To overcome this problem, US GAAP currently includes the option of pushdown accounting (not allowed under IFRS). This accounting procedure is discussed next.

7.4 Pushdown Accounting

7.4.1 Introduction

When a parent company obtains control over a target company, the parent must recognize all of the target's assets and liabilities at fair value in its consolidated financial statements. That is, as a result of obtaining control, the assets and liabilities of the target are stepped-up from historical values to fair values, but only in the consolidated financial statements.

The question that arises is whether the financial statements of the target company should remain the same, or be adjusted to reflect the new fair value information from the transaction. Normally, the target continues using historical figures in its own financial statements; but is it possible for it to use fair values in its separate financial statements? Under current US GAAP (since November 2014), if the target issues separate financial statements, it can elect to use the new basis of accounting, fair values, in its separate financial statements. This accounting procedure of changing the basis of accounting in the target is called Pushdown Accounting.

Pushdown accounting means establishing a new basis for the assets and liabilities of the acquired company based on a "pushdown" of the acquirer's stepped-up basis. In effect, the total amount paid to acquire the target becomes its new book value on its separate financial statements. This accounting procedure is allowed only if the target issues separate financial statements and it elects to do so. If the target itself is a parent company that issues consolidated financial statements, pushdown accounting is not allowed.

7.4.2 Background

Pushdown accounting has been in practice since the 1970s, but only for companies under the supervision of the Securities and Exchange Commission (SEC) in the US. SEC registrants (mostly companies with publicly traded equity or debt) had to apply pushdown accounting according to highly restrictive guidance issued by the SEC. The SEC justified the use of pushdown accounting with the need to protect the interests of lenders in transactions that often involved large amounts of debt and where the assets and cash flows of the target company often guaranteed that debt.

In November 2014, the Financial Accounting Standards Board (FASB) issued Accounting Standard Update (ASU) 2014–17, Business Combinations (Topic 805), Pushdown Accounting (FASB, 2014). This document, which represents a consensus opinion of the FASB's Emerging Issues Task Force (EITF), became effective upon issuance. The ASU allows an acquiree the option to apply pushdown accounting in its separate financial statements at the event of a change in control. The application of pushdown accounting is allowed to all companies, SEC registrants or not.

Prior to ASU 2014–17, SEC registrants applied pushdown accounting based on guidance issued by the SEC in the Staff Accounting Bulletin (SAB) Topic 5.J, and EITF Topic D-97, as well as comments made by the SEC observer at EITF meetings. In addition, pushdown accounting practice developed over the years based on SEC staff speeches; papers issued by the American Institute of Certified Public Accountants (AICPA), and a discussion memorandum on pushdown accounting issued by FASB in 1991. However, the pushdown accounting guidance was complicated and incomplete. In addition, the guidance was relevant only to SEC registrants, and was based on quantitative measures that provided registrants with the ability to avoid pushdown accounting. For example, previous SEC guidance prohibited the use of pushdown accounting in situations where the acquirer held less than 80% of the acquiree's stock, and required pushdown accounting when the ownership in the acquiree was above 95%. Between 80 and 95%, application of pushdown depended on certain deal-specific circumstances.

Under the new guidance, an entity has the option to apply pushdown accounting in situations where there is a change in control, as defined in existing consolidation rules. Following the issuance of the new guidance by the FASB, the SEC staff issued SAB 115 (SEC, 2014) to rescind the guidance in SAB Topic 5.J, and the FASB issued ASU 2015–08 to rescind the remaining guidance on pushdown accounting. ASU 2014–17, which was codified into the pushdown accounting subsections of ASC 805–50, now provides both public and nonpublic entities with authoritative guidance on applying pushdown accounting.

7.4.3 Application

Pushdown accounting is applied only when there is a change-in-control event. A change-in-control event is one in which an acquirer obtains control of a company (guidance is provided by ASC 805). Control could be achieved by transferring cash or other assets to the target; alternatively, by acquiring a controlling interest in the open market, or by assuming the target's liabilities, or by issuing shares, or a combination thereof. In some cases, the acquirer obtains control without any transfer (e.g., contractual arrangements). Change-in-control events often occur in LBOs and RECAPs.[8]

Example starts

Recall that in a RECAP transaction the company undergoes a major restructuring of its financial position. In some cases, a RECAP constitutes a change-in-control event, whereas in other cases, there is no change-in-control. Suppose, Companies A1, A2, A3, and A4 each hold 25% of the voting shares of Company B. Suppose further that Company B raises debt and buys back all the shares held by Company A4. This is a RECAP transaction for Company B, but there is no change-in-control event. Therefore, Company B cannot elect to use pushdown accounting.

Suppose now that before the RECAP, Company A1 holds 35% of the voting shares, and Company A2 also holds 35% of the voting shares. In addition, Companies A3 and A4 each hold 15% of the voting shares in company B. Company B raises new debt and buys back all the shares of Company A2. Now, Company A1 controls Company B with 53.85% of the voting shares (35/65 = 53.85%). This is a transaction with a change-in-control event, and Company B may elect to use pushdown accounting in its separate financial statements.

Example ends

Pushdown accounting is optional under US GAAP. The target must decide in the period of the acquisition (change-in-control event) whether to apply pushdown accounting in its separate financial statements or not. The decision to apply pushdown accounting must be made until the financial statements for the acquisition period are issued. Once the target decides to use pushdown accounting, this decision is irrevocable. However, if the target decides not to apply pushdown accounting upon the change-in-control event, it may decide to adopt it later as a change in accounting principle, and retrospectively adjust its financial statements to the new accounting method. In addition, the decision to apply pushdown accounting could vary across subsidiaries. The parent could decide to apply pushdown accounting in one subsidiary but not in another. Each change-in-control event is independently assessed, providing the subsidiary issues separate financial statements.

The election of pushdown accounting is available to the acquired company, as well as to any direct or indirect subsidiaries of the acquired company. Each acquired company or any of its subsidiaries can make its own election independently.

[8]Some acquirers, for example, an investment company or a private equity company, do not present consolidated financial statements. In these cases, the target could still apply pushdown accounting as if the acquirer had applied business combination accounting under ASC 805.

Pushdown accounting is not allowed under IFRS. Business combination transactions are subject to IFRS 3, which means that assets and liabilities of the target are measured at fair value in the consolidated financial statements, and goodwill is assessed. If a US company is acquired by an IFRS company, the US company may still use pushdown accounting on a standalone basis. Therefore, the US company would probably have to maintain a set of financial statements for the purpose of pushdown accounting and another set for the purpose of the consolidated financial statements under IFRS.

The potential impact of pushdown accounting on the target's financial statements varies, but typically, due to fair value adjustments, recognition of intangible assets and goodwill, the accounting values of its assets increase substantially. If there are additional liabilities identified at acquisition, such as onerous contracts and provisions, the accounting values of its liabilities could also increase. In addition, reported income subsequent to applying pushdown accounting is likely to decrease due to higher depreciation, amortization, and potential impairment losses.

Before electing pushdown accounting, the acquiree should consider the user's needs of an acquired company's financial statements. While some users may prefer the historical basis, others may prefer the "stepped-up" basis of pushdown accounting, and in particular, the lower income resulting from higher amortization and depreciation expenses. Those users that focus on cash flows may be indifferent, because pushdown accounting is an accrual procedure (ignoring tax effects). In many cases, there are multiple users of the financial statements with conflicting needs, which makes the election of pushdown accounting more challenging.

For example, private equity acquirers may prefer avoiding pushdown accounting to maximize income subsequent to acquisition and thus increase the probability of existing sooner and at higher valuations. Debt holders may prefer pushdown accounting because financial statements are based more on fair values. Analysts may prefer to apply pushdown accounting to avoid analyzing certain assets (goodwill and fixed assets), at two different values (historical and fair values). Acquirers involved in tax-free acquisitions (carryover) may want to avoid pushdown accounting to ensure consistency between tax and financial reporting.

7.4.3.1 Initial Measurement

When a change-in-control event occurs and pushdown accounting is elected, the target records its assets and liabilities on the same basis as the parent company does in its consolidated financial statements, namely at fair values according to ASC 805. In addition, the target will disclose sufficient information to enable users to evaluate the impact of pushdown accounting. If the acquirer is not required to apply ASC 805 in its financial statements (because the parent is an individual or an investment company), the acquiree may still elect to use pushdown accounting, as if the acquirer were subject to business combination accounting under ASC 805. If the acquiree elects to apply pushdown accounting, full pushdown accounting must be used. There is no such thing as partial pushdown accounting. Moreover, the acquiree cannot use pushdown accounting for some assets/liabilities but not for others.[9]

Example starts

Tal Company acquires all the voting common shares of Adi Company for $100,000 in cash. The transaction is an acquisition subject to business combination accounting rules under ASC 805. Adi issues separate financial statements and has elected to use pushdown accounting. Below is Adi's balance sheet at the time of acquisition. Note that the fair value of Adi's identifiable net assets is $80,000. Therefore, goodwill is equal to $20,000.

Balance sheet ($)	Book values	Fair values
Current assets	40,000	40,000
Property, plant, and equipment	85,000	105,000
Total assets	**125,000**	**145,000**
Current liabilities	25,000	25,000
Long-term debt	35,000	40,000
Total liabilities	**60,000**	**65,000**
Common stock	10,000	–
Additional paid-in capital	20,000	–
Retained earnings	35,000	–
Shareholders' equity	**65,000**	**80,000**
Total liabilities and equity	**125,000**	**145,000**

Adi will record the following accounting entry:

$	Dr.	Cr.
Property, plant, and equipment	20,000	
Goodwill	20,000	
Retained earnings	35,000	
Long-term liabilities		5,000
Additional paid-in capital		70,000

Here are Adi's balance sheets before and after pushdown accounting.

Balance sheet ($)	Pre pushdown	Post pushdown
Current assets	40,000	40,000
Property, plant, and equipment	85,000	105,000

[9]Refer to FASB ASC 810–10.

Balance sheet ($)	Pre pushdown	Post pushdown
Total assets	**125,000**	**145,000**
Current liabilities	25,000	25,000
Long-term debt	35,000	40,000
Total liabilities	**60,000**	**65,000**
Common stock	10,000	10,000
Additional paid-in capital	20,000	70,000
Retained earnings	35,000	–
Shareholders' equity	**65,000**	**80,000**
Total liabilities and equity	**125,000**	**145,000**

Pushdown accounting represents a new basis of accounting and thus, the accounting reflects a new start. This is why retained earnings start from zero, to reflect the beginning of Adi.

Example ends

Example starts

Consider the LBO example above. In this new example, NewCo, a newly established company raises equity and debt to acquire all the shares of Target for $1,000. Following the transaction, the situation is as follows (Fig. 7.6):

Fig. 7.6 LBO deal structure

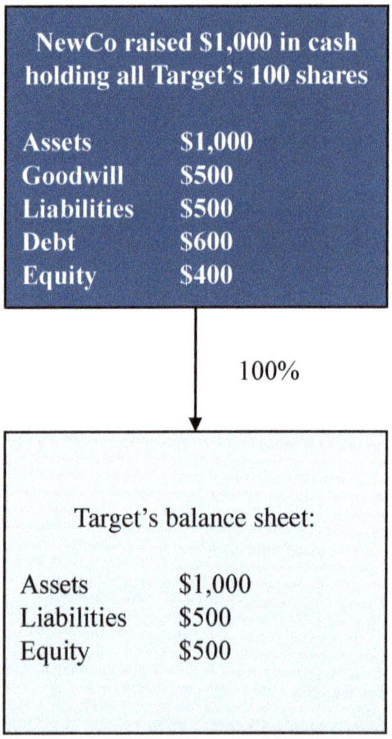

If Target issues separate financial statements and elects to use pushdown accounting, and is obligated to repay the debt, then its balance sheet will be as follows:

Balance sheet	$
Assets at fair value	1,000
Goodwill	500
Total assets	**1,500**
Liabilities	500
Debt	600
Total liabilities	**1,100**
Shareholders' equity	400
Total liabilities and equity	**1,500**

Example ends

Example starts

Consider the RECAP transaction described above (3rd version) (Fig. 7.7).

If Target elects to use pushdown accounting in its separate financial statements, and if it is named as an obligor in the debt raised by NewCo, then its balance sheet under pushdown accounting will be as follows:

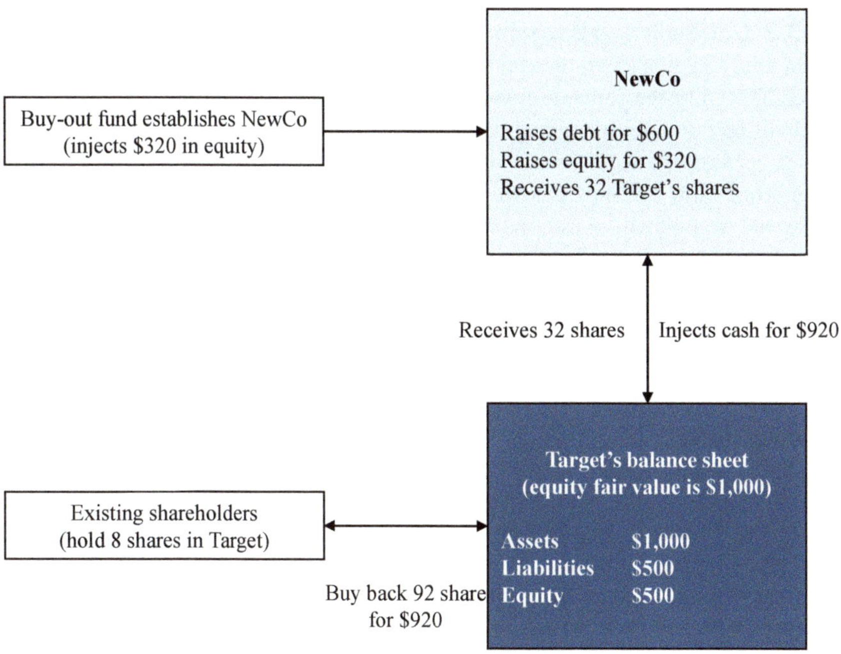

Fig. 7.7 Target's structure after the RECAP transaction (3rd version)

Balance sheet	$
Assets at fair value	1,000
Goodwill	500
Total assets	**1,500**
Liabilities	500
Debt	600
Total liabilities	**1,100**
Shareholders' equity	400
Total liabilities and equity	**1,500**

The pushdown entry in Target's financial statements will be:

$	Dr.	Cr.
Goodwill	500	
Additional paid-in capital	100	
Debt		600

Note that Target's balance sheet under pushdown accounting in the RECAP transaction is the same as its balance sheet under pushdown accounting in the LBO transaction.

Example ends

7.4.3.2 Goodwill and Bargain Purchase Gains

When applying pushdown accounting, goodwill arising from the transaction must be recognized in the separate financial statements of the acquiree. The amount of goodwill recorded by the acquirer and the acquiree does not have to be identical. This is because the acquirer may assign some of the goodwill to other subsidiaries or reporting units that may benefit from the acquisition.

Instead of goodwill, a transaction could result in bargain purchase gains (negative goodwill). Such a gain is recognized by the acquirer in its income statement (under ASC 805), but is not recognized in the acquiree's income statement in case of pushdown accounting. Instead, the acquiree recognizes a bargain purchase gain as an adjustment to equity (additional paid-in capital) in its separate financial statements.

Example starts

On April 1, 2014, MG Company acquires 80% of the voting shares of the Islanders Corporations for $2,000,000 in cash. Islanders elects to apply pushdown accounting. Goodwill arising from the transaction is $400,000. According to ASC 350, MG Company allocates goodwill to three reporting units: SEG1 (which is expected to benefit from the synergies with Islanders)—$50,000, SEG2 (which is expected to benefit from the synergies with Islanders)—$100,000, and SEG3, which includes the Islanders Corporations—$250,000. While MG allocates goodwill to three reporting units, the Islanders Corporations recognizes the $400,000 goodwill in its separate financial statements. Furthermore, according to US GAAP, the Islanders Corporation must test goodwill for impairment on an annual basis. However, even if the Islanders Corporation recognizes an impairment loss, this loss may not necessarily be recognized in the consolidated financial statements of MG Company, unless the impairments at the parent level is identical to that used by the Islanders Corporation.

Example ends

7.4.3.3 Acquisition-Related Liabilities

Acquisition-related liabilities, including debt incurred by an acquirer, are recognized in the acquiree's separate financial statements only if it is required to do so under other US GAAP. For example, if the obligations result from joint and several liability arrangements, or if the acquiree is a legal obligor for the debt.

Prior to the issuance of ASU 2014–17 by FASB in 2014, SEC rules regarding pushdown accounting required that if the acquiree's assets were pledged as collateral for the acquirer's debt, the debt be pushed down to the acquiree's separate financial statements. The requirement to push down such collateralized debt was rescinded by SAB 115. If an acquiree's assets or equity is pledged as collateral against the acquirer's debt, there is no longer a requirement to reflect that debt in the acquiree's separate financial statements. However, disclosures of such arrangements may be appropriate under other requirements.

If the acquiree elects to use pushdown accounting in its separate financial statements, and debt incurred by the acquirer is not pushed down, the acquiree records additional paid-in capital in its separate financial statements instead.

Example starts

On June 1, 2019, LBS Company forms NewCo and contributes to it $100,000 in cash for all the 1,000 shares issued by NewCo. In addition, NewCo borrows $50,000 from the bank. On June 15, 2019, NewCo acquires all the shares of Gal Corporation for $150,000 in cash. The bank requires that Gal be named as a legal obligor for the debt. Should Gal record the debt on its balance sheet?

Gal should record the debt on its separate balance sheet and recognize the interest expense on its income statement regardless of whether it uses pushdown accounting or not (based on guidance in ASC 405–40). That is, if LBS Company raises debt with Gal being named as the legal obligor, that debt would need to be presented in Gal's financial statements even if Gal does not apply pushdown accounting.

Example ends

Example starts

On June 1, 2019, LBS Company forms NewCo and contributes to it $100,000 in cash for all the 1,000 shares issued by NewCo. In addition, NewCo borrows $50,000 from the bank. On June 15, 2019, NewCo acquires all the shares of Gal Corporation for $150,000 in cash. The bank requires that Gal's buildings and inventory be pledged as a collateral for the loan. Should Gal record the debt on its balance sheet?

If Gal elects to use pushdown accounting, the debt incurred by LBS Company is not pushed down to Gal. Instead, Gal records additional paid-in capital instead of debt.

Example ends

7.4.3.4 Transaction Costs and Income Taxes

Transaction costs incurred by the acquirer in effecting the transaction pertain to it and not to the acquiree. Therefore, such costs are not part of the pushdown accounting procedure and should not be recognized in the acquiree's separate financial statements.

If the transaction is structured as a taxable asset transaction for tax purposes (see Chapter 6), most likely, there is a change in the tax bases of assets and liabilities of the acquired company. If the acquired company elects not to apply pushdown accounting in its separate financial statements, its assets and liabilities keep their book basis. Hence, there is a difference between the book bases and the stepped-up tax bases of the acquired company's assets and liabilities. In this situation, deferred taxes would be recognized for the book-tax differences resulting from the transaction. The initial deferred tax balances resulting from the transaction would be recorded in equity. If, however, the acquired company elects to use pushdown accounting, no such deferred taxes are needed.

7.5 Summary

This chapter is about corporate reorganization—cases where a company changes its structure to improve efficiency or to increase revenues and income. Corporate reorganizations often result in a change of control. We begin by reviewing two types of corporate reorganizations: Leveraged Buyouts (LBOs) and Recapitalizations (RECAPs). These transactions often involve high levels of debt, secured by the assets and cash flows of the acquired company.

Transactions that involve a change in control, raise questions about whether the assets and liabilities of the acquired company should retain their historical accounting basis, or should these assets and liabilities change their accounting basis to fair value. This question becomes particularly important in cases where the parent company is a private investment vehicle and the target company has public debt or equity.

In the first part of this chapter, we discuss several forms of LBOs and RECAPs. In the second part, we introduce a new accounting procedure called pushdown accounting. Pushdown accounting is optional whenever there is a change-in-control event. The acquired company that issues separate financial statements may elect pushdown accounting and present its assets and liabilities, including goodwill, at fair valued at the time of acquisition. We review this accounting procedure and provide some useful examples.

References

Financial Accounting Standards Board (FASB), *ASC 350 Intangibles—Goodwill and Other*, as updated lastly in 2019.

Financial Accounting Standards Board (FASB), *ASC 405 Liabilities*, as updated lastly in 2016.

Financial Accounting Standards Board (FASB), *ASC 805 Business Combinations*, as updated lastly in 2019.

Financial Accounting Standards Board (FASB), *ASC 810 Consolidation*, as updated lastly in 2018.

Financial Accounting Standards Board (FASB), *ASU 2014–17 Business Combinations (805): Pushdown Accounting.*

Financial Accounting Standards Board (FASB), *ASU 2014–17, Business Combinations (805), Pushdown Accounting, a consensus of the FASB Emerging Issues Task Force.*

Financial Accounting Standards Board (FASB), *ASU 2015–08 Business Combinations (805): Pushdown Accounting: Amendments to SEC Paragraphs Pursuant to Staff Accounting Bulletin No. 115.*

Deloitte, *A Roadmap to Pushdown Accounting*, 2016.

International Accounting Standards Board (IASB), *IFRS 3 Business Combinations*, 2008 (as amended lastly in 2020).

KPMG, *Issues In-Depth, Pushdown Accounting*, 2015.

PWC, *Pushdown Accounting Now Optional: New Guidance Applicable to All Companies*, 2014.

SEC Staff Accounting Bulletin, *New Basis of Accounting Required in Certain Circumstances (Topic 5.J)*, 2014.

SEC, *Staff Accounting Bulletin No. 115*, 2014.

Financial Analysis of Business Combinations (Ratios)

8

8.1 Introduction

The objective of financial statement analysis (FSA) is using financial statements, combined with other sources of information, to form expectations about a company's future financial performance so that financial statement users will be able to make informed investment, credit, and other pivotal economic decisions.[1] Market operators might be interested in evaluating equity investments to be included in a broader portfolio of securities or to make investment recommendations, assigning ratings to bond issuances, determining the creditworthiness of companies, and scouting potential targets for M&A deals, among others. All these decisions rely, at least in part, on FSA techniques.[2]

While accounting and financial reporting are closely regulated by accounting standards, and security regulations, there are no rigid rules or standards governing FSA. It is thus crucial to perform FSA consistently over time and across companies, in order to achieve reliable and meaningful results. As a rule, it is essential to compare companies using the same accounting standards, or to adjust financial measures for differences between sets of standards. If not, different accounting policies might distort the comparability all together.

To achieve its objective, FSA primarily relies, as a source of data, on financial reports prepared by companies although very different types of inputs can, and

[1]Robinson T.R. (2020) and Penman S. (2012).

[2]Robinson T.R. et al. (2003).

Electronic supplementary material The online version of this chapter (https://doi.org/10.1007/978-3-030-61769-1_8) contains supplementary material, which is available to authorized users.

E. Amir and M. Ghitti, *Financial Analysis of Mergers and Acquisitions*,
https://doi.org/10.1007/978-3-030-61769-1_8

usually are, put into use.[3] Once the (raw) data are available, it is necessary to perform some kind of analysis by arranging them in a useful way. To this end, the main tools and techniques are financial statement reformulation, ratio, and common size analysis.

Basic FSA is, usually, performed through the following steps:

(a) *Define the scope of work.* What is the purpose of the analysis (analyzing management performance, evaluating the quality of reported income, evaluating the ability of a company to pay its obligations, etc.)?
(b) *Collect the relevant data.* Identify useful information that is required by the scope of work (financial statements, industry and analysts' reports, economic bulletins, filings with the government, financial information of main competitors, etc.).
(c) *Process the data.* Work on the collected (raw) data by applying FSA tools and techniques, such as reformulations, ratio, and common size analysis;
(d) *Interpret your findings.* Produce and present analytical conclusions from the analysis.

FSA becomes more challenging in the presence of business combinations and corporate restructurings. An acquisition "distorts" financial statements, because once the acquisition is completed, there is a shock to the balance sheet (assets and liabilities enter the balance sheet as part of the consolidation process and are (usually) recognized at fair values). The consolidation process also distorts the intertemporal comparability of income statements and cash flow statements. To mitigate the loss of comparability, accounting regulation requires certain disclosures when acquisitions occur.[4] Such disclosures include, for example, information on purchase price allocations and on income "as if" the acquisition occurred at the beginning of the period.

8.2 Financial Statement Reformulation

Financial statement reformulation is a way to regroup accounting items as presented in financial reports so that useful metrics may be identified. For instance, income statements may be rearranged to show non-GAAP measures such as EBITDA or EBITDAR, or to highlight core and noncore items.[5] Balance sheets may be rearranged based on liquidity/maturity levels of assets and liabilities, or based on whether the assets/liabilities are operating or financial in nature.

[3]Such inputs might include economic variables (e.g., inflation, interest rates), industry reports, press releases, and regulatory filings, among many others.

[4]Throughout this chapter, the terms "acquisition" and "purchase" will be used interchangeably.

[5]EBITDA stands for "earnings before interest, taxes, depreciation, and amortization," while EBITDAR stands for "earnings before interest, taxes, depreciation, amortization, and rent".

8.2.1 Income Statement Reformulations

There are three broad reformulation schemes to rearrange the income statement. Each one of these reformulations highlights an important economic aspect of the entity being analyzed. These schemes are: (i) the income statement at added value; (ii) the income statement with functional cost aggregation; (iii) the income statement at variable costs.

These reclassifications look the same below the operating profit line. They only differ in the way operating revenues and expenses are reclassified.

The added value scheme allows analysts to focus on how much value a firm is able to "extract" from the products it makes compared to the costs of production components used and acquired from third parties (i.e., costs of raw materials and services, such as electricity and energy, insurance premiums, maintenance costs, etc.). This value, which is added to materials and services acquired from outside, through the internal production process of a firm, needs to cover for the remaining internal production factors. This analysis allows to draw some important conclusions about a company's business. If, for instance, added value is positive, but operating profit is negative, this might mean that the core business operations, although profitable per se, are implemented within a structure that is too big and costly either in terms of personnel, or assets in place, or both.

Income statement at added value
Total revenues
– Raw materials (external costs)
– Costs of services (external costs)
Added value
– Personnel costs (internal costs)
EBITDA
– Depreciation and amortization (internal costs)
Operating profit
– Net financial charges
Profit before taxes
– Income taxes
Net profit

The income statement with functional costs aggregation classifies costs according to their different function (i.e., trading costs, administrative costs, commercial costs, etc.). This, in turn, allows analysts to identify which of these areas are managed more or less efficiently. This reclassification scheme might be harder to implement for external analysts, because the information required to classify each cost according to its function is not always available. For example, if an income statement shows a large "other operating costs" line item without any additional information, it will be impossible to use this reclassification scheme in a productive manner. Lastly, it may be harder to identify EBITDA because depreciation and amortization charges are spread among all the different business areas identified.

Income statement with functional costs
Total revenues
– Cost of goods sold
Gross profit
– Trading costs
– Transportation costs
– Administrative costs
– General costs
Operating profit
Net financial charges
Profit before taxes
Income taxes
Net profit

The income statement reformulation at variable costs distinguishes between variable and fixed costs. This reformulation allows analysts to assess the structural flexibility of the company as well as the impact of changes in production volume on profitability. It is paramount to have access to internal information about the nature of every single cost a company incurs to properly classify it either as variable or fixed. The requirement for further internal information makes this scheme less useful for external analysts because of lack of information.

The difference between total revenues and variable costs is called "contribution margin". Dividing the contribution margin by revenues yields the percentage margin available to cover fixed costs. Dividing the fixed costs by the contribution margin yields the break-even point in terms of sales, that is, the sales level necessary to cover both variable and fixed costs.

Income statement at variable costs
Total revenues
– Variable costs
Contribution margin
– Fixed costs
Operating profit
Net financial charges
Profit before taxes
Income taxes
Net profit

8.2.2 Balance Sheet Reformulations

There are two common balance sheet reformulations. The first one is based on the level of liquidity/maturity of assets and liabilities (financial balance sheet). This is the balance sheet usually reported in financial statements. The second one is based on the "type" of assets and liabilities (operating *versus* financial items).

The financial balance sheet groups assets and liabilities according to their liquidity level (when they will become cash) and maturity level (when they will become collectable), respectively. Assets and liabilities are, thus, divided into short- and long-term items. They are classified as short-term if they will become cash, in case of assets, or collectable, in case of liabilities, within the next 12 months (or one business cycle). If it will take longer than that, assets and liabilities are commonly classified as long-term. This classification allows gauging the financial viability of the company, at least in the short term, by comparing current assets to current liabilities.

Financial balance sheet
Cash and equivalents
Trade receivables
Inventories
Other current assets
Total current assets
Property, plant and equipment
Investment property
Intangible assets
Other non-current assets
Total assets
Trade payables
Short-term debt
Other current liabilities
Total current liabilities
Long-term debt
Employee benefits
Provisions
Other non-current liabilities
Total liabilities
Share capital
Reserves
Total shareholders' equity

The operating balance sheet groups assets and liabilities according to whether they are operating or nonoperating (i.e., financial). Within the operating section, assets and liabilities are subdivided into core business operations (e.g., tangible fixed assets, inventory, or accounts receivable) and those pertaining to ancillary operations (e.g., investment property, tax assets, and liabilities). The nonoperating section includes financial assets and liabilities (e.g., cash and equivalents, financial investments, short- and long-term debts, and shareholders' equity). This reclassification scheme offers a view on a company's overall financial indebtedness (short- and long-term). Last, assets and liabilities are usually expressed on a "net basis" since we are now grouping them based on the business area they belong to, irrespective of whether they are assets or liabilities. This allows to identify important metrics (discussed later), such as net operating working capital and net financial position.

Operating balance sheet
Property, plant, and equipment
Intangible assets
Fixed assets
Inventories
Trade receivables/(payables)
Net operating working capital
Investment property
Other accessory assets/(liabilities)
Net noncore assets
Deferred tax assets/(liabilities)
Other tax receivables/(payables)
Net tax position
Net invested capital
Financial debt (short- and long-term)
Financial investments (including cash)
Net financial position
Share capital
Reserves
Total shareholders' equity
Total funds

Example starts

The following is the consolidated income statement for fiscal 2018 of Salvatore Ferragamo S.p.A., an Italian luxury firm, as included in its financial statements. We also added a common size income statement.

This income statement is actually the income statement with functional costs aggregation, mentioned above. We reformulate the reported income statement to obtain the income statement at added value and at variable costs.

Reviewing the notes, it is possible to rearrange all the operating costs shown below (cost of goods sold, style, product development, and logistics costs) in the way needed to construct the income statement at added value. Moreover, it is possible to isolate noncash charges (depreciation, amortization, and write-downs) so that we can identify EBITDA, a key non-GAAP measure, which serves as a measure, although an imprecise one, of unlevered operating cash flows. For instance, the ratio of net financial debt (financial debt net of cash and equivalents) to EBITDA is often examined in M&A deals to evaluate their feasibility from a financial viewpoint.[6]

Income statement (€/000)	2017	%	2018	%
Revenues	1,393,472	100.0	1,346,842	100.0
Cost of goods sold	(494,755)	(35.5)	(484,862)	(36.0)
Gross profit	**898,717**	**64.5**	**861,980**	**64.0**
Style, and logistics costs	(44,151)	(3.2)	(48,376)	(3.6)
Sales and distribution costs	(474,674)	(34.1)	(456,803)	(33.9)
Marketing costs	(70,708)	(5.1)	(73,326)	(5.4)
General costs	(115,682)	(8.3)	(124,565)	(9.2)
Other operating costs	(19,183)	(1.4)	(19,341)	(1.4)
Other income	11,735	0.8	10,200	0.7
Operating profit	**186,054**	**13.4**	**149,769**	**11.2**
Financial charges	(52,079)	(3.7)	(53,432)	(4.0)
Financial income	39,370	2.8	39,575	2.9
Profit before tax	**173,345**	**12.4**	**135,912**	**10.1**
Income taxes	(59,062)	(4.2)	(45,725)	(3.4)
Net profit	**114,283**	**8.2**	**90,187**	**6.7**
Group profit	118,641	8.5	88,361	6.6
Non-controlling interests	(4,358)	(0.3)	1,826	0.1

Income statement at added value (€/000)	2017	2018
Revenues	1,393,472	1,346,842
Raw materials	(302,929)	(282,472)
Cost of services	(616,163)	(624,298)
Other operating charges (net)	(7,448)	(9,141)

[6]This ratio gauges the debt capacity of the post-deal company by showing how many "years" of current EBITDA are necessary to pay back all the debt outstanding.

Income statement at added value (€/000)	2017	2018
Added value	**466,932**	**430,931**
Personnel costs	(218,424)	(216,710)
EBITDA	**248,508**	**214,221**
Depreciation, amortization, write-downs	(62,454)	(64,452)
Operating profit	**186,054**	**149,769**
Net financial charges	(12,709)	(13,857)
Profit before taxes	**173,345**	**135,912**
Income taxes	(59,062)	(45,725)
Net profit	**114,283**	**90,187**
Group profit	118,641	88,361
Non-controlling interests	(4,358)	1,826

Salvatore Ferragamo does not disclose which costs are variable or fixed. Hence, it is impossible for us, as external analysts, to construct an accurate income statement at variable costs. We will proceed by making the following assumptions: raw materials costs are 100% variable, cost for services are 20% variable, other operating charges are 10% variable, personnel costs are 60% variable, depreciation and amortization are 100% fixed.

Income statement at variable costs (€/000)	2017	2018
Revenues	1,393,472	1,346,842
Raw materials (100%)	(302,929)	(282,472)
Cost of services (20%)	(123,233)	(124,860)
Other operating charges (10%)	(745)	(914)
Personnel costs (60%)	(131,054)	(130,026)
Contribution margin	**835,511**	**808,570**
Cost of services (80%)	(492,930)	(499,438)
Other operating charges (90%)	(6,703)	(8,227)
Personnel costs (40%)	(87,370)	(86,684)
Depreciation and amortization (100%)	(62,454)	(64,452)
Operating profit	**186,054**	**149,769**
Net financial charges	(12,709)	(13,857)
Profit before taxes	**173,345**	**135,912**
Income taxes	(59,062)	(45,725)
Net profit	**114,283**	**90,187**
Group profit	118,641	88,361
Non-controlling interests	(4,358)	1,826

Based on this reclassified income statement, for fiscal 2018 the contribution margin is 60% of sales ($808,570/$1,346,842). Dividing operating fixed costs, amounting to $658,801, by this amount, we see that the sales volume required to break-even at the operating profit level, is $1,097,370 ($658,801/60%). At this sales level, variable costs are $438,948 ($1,097,370 × 40%), fixed costs, by definition, do not change and are equal to $658,801. The sum of variable and fixed costs is exactly equal to the break-even point we found ($1,097,370 = $438,948 + $658, 801).

A similar analysis may be performed with the balance sheet. The following is Salvatore Ferragamo's consolidated balance sheet for fiscal 2018. This is actually the financial balance sheet mentioned above. We will reformulate it to obtain an operating balance sheet.

The key insight is that a company has to fund primarily two types of investments: fixed assets and working capital. The operating assets are financed primarily by interest-bearing debt and equity. The reformulation choice proposed presents the net operating assets and the sources of funding.

Balance sheet (€/000)	2017	2018
Inventories	325,516	365,779
Trade receivable	148,583	142,905
Tax receivable	27,654	21,851
Other current assets	68,546	42,166
Other current financial assets	341	1,080
Cash and equivalents	212,088	207,710
Total current assets	**787,728**	**781,491**
Property, plant, and equipment	249,600	259,821
Investment property	6,139	6,094
Intangible assets	43,593	42,879
Other non-current assets	4,963	3,331
Other non-current financial assets	15,981	16,646
Deferred tax assets	79,624	76,869
Total assets	**1,182,628**	**1,187,131**
Trade payables	203,613	215,125
Current debt	66,529	20,939
Tax payables	19,772	19,507
Other current liabilities	33,269	38,279
Other current financial liabilities	3,595	2,963
Total current liabilities	**326,778**	**296,813**
Non-current debt	14,814	15,892
Provisions	13,794	19,491
Employee benefits	11,509	11,392

Balance sheet (€/000)	2017	2018
Other non-current liabilities	59,067	57,681
Deferred tax liabilities	8,235	5,524
Total liabilities	**434,197**	**406,793**
Share capital	16,879	16,879
Reserves	586,730	648,451
Retained profit	118,641	88,361
Non-controlling interests	26,181	26,647
Total shareholders' equity	**748,431**	**780,338**
Total liabilities and equity	**1,182,628**	**1,187,131**

Balance sheet (€/000)	2017	2018
Property, plant, and equipment	249,600	259,821
Investment property	6,139	6,094
Intangible assets	43,593	42,879
Fixed assets	**299,332**	**308,794**
Inventories	325,516	365,779
Trade receivables	148,583	142,905
Trade payables	(203,613)	(215,125)
Net operating working capital	**270,486**	**293,559**
Deferred tax assets	79,624	76,869
Deferred tax liabilities	(8,235)	(5,524)
Tax receivables (net)	7,882	2,344
Tax position	**79,271**	**73,689**
Other current/non-current assets/liabilities	(28,149)	(64,700)
Net invested capital (net operating assets)	**620,940**	**611,342**
Shareholder's equity	722,250	753,691
Non-controlling interests	26,181	26,647
Total equity	**748,431**	**780,338**
Cash and equivalents	(212,088)	(207,710)
Financial debt (net)	84,597	38,714
Net financial position	**(127,491)**	**(168,996)**
Total funds	**620,940**	**611,342**

This scheme highlights key figures often used in financial statement analysis:

- net operating working capital, which is the net investment required to run current operations (inventories, receivables, net of operating payables). It represents the extent to which the acquisition-transformation-sales cycle generates financial needs to be covered by external funding;

- net invested capital (also, net operating assets), which is the total capital investments to be funded by debt and/or equity;
- net financial position (or net debt), which measures the net interest-bearing debt;
- total funds, equal to equity plus net debt, which is also equal to net operating assets.

Example ends

8.3 Ratio Analysis

Ratio analysis is useful in identifying relationships between financial items by expressing them as ratios or quotients. For instance, dividing net income, a measure of performance, by shareholders' equity, the capital provided by equity investors, yields the return on equity (ROE), which is the accounting rate of return on shareholders' equity. Ratios are unit-free and they remove the size effect, thus facilitating comparability over time and across companies.

There are four main categories of financial ratios: (i) profitability, (ii) activity (efficiency), (iii) liquidity, and (iv) solvency ratios.

Profitability ratios are divided into two groups—return ratios and margin ratios. Return ratios measure a company's ability to generate profit from its resources (e.g., how many units of profit are generated by the assets in place). Usually, the numerator will include an item from the income statement and the denominator will include an item from the balance sheet.

Main return ratios	Numerator	Denominator
Return on assets (ROA)	Net income	Total assets
Return on investments (ROI)	Net operating income	Net invested capital
Return on equity (ROE)	Net income	Equity

These ratios provide a measure of (after-tax) accounting returns earned by a company. ROA measures return on total assets in place.[7] ROI measures return on net invested capital (or net operating assets). Contrary to ROA, this ratio measures returns from net resources. ROE measures return relative to shareholders' equity. It is possible to measure this ratio with or without non-controlling interests. However, one must be consistent in excluding non-controlling interests from both the numerator and the denominator.

[7]The numerator (net income) measures dollar return to equity holders, while the denominator (total assets) includes assets available to both equity and debt holders. For this reason, we find more consistent ROI.

Margin ratios measure the ability of the company to generate profit from sales. These ratios provide insights as to the cost structure of a company. Most margin ratios will include a profit measure in the numerator and sales (or revenues) in the denominator.

Main margin ratios	Numerator	Denominator
Net profit margin (NPM)	Net income	Sales
Operating profit margin (OPM)	Operating income	Sales
Gross profit margin (GPM)	Gross profit	Sales
Effective tax rate	Income tax expense	Income before tax

Efficiency ratios, also known as turnovers, measure how efficient a company is in using operating assets in day-to-day activities (e.g., managing inventories, collect receivables).

Main activity ratios	Numerator	Denominator
Receivables turnover	Sales	Accounts receivable
Days of sales (DSO)	Receivables	Daily sales (Sales/365)
Inventory turnover	Cost of sales	Inventory
Days of inventory (DOI)	Inventory	Daily cost of sales (Cost of sales/365)
Payables turnover	Purchases	Accounts payable
Days of payables (DOP)	Payables	Daily purchases (Purchases/365)
Working capital turnover	Sales	Working capital
Fixed assets turnover	Sales	Fixed assets
Total assets turnover	Sales	Total assets

The receivables turnover measures how many times, on average, a company collects its receivables during a period (quarter or year). Similarly, the inventory turnover measures how many times a company sells the inventory during a period. The payables turnover is a measure of how many times per period, on average, a company pays for purchases from suppliers.

DSO measures how many days, on average, it takes a company to collect cash from customers. Similarly, DOI is a measure of the number of days it takes a company to deliver the inventory, and DOP is the average number of days it takes to pay the trade payables. Working capital, fixed assets, and total assets turnovers are measures of efficiency—how efficient the company in generating revenues from its working capital, fixed assets, and total assets, respectively. For example, a fixed assets turnover ratio of 2 means that a company generates, on average $2 of revenue for every $1 of fixed assets.

Liquidity ratios measure a company's ability to meet its short-term obligations, that is, whether the company has enough short-term assets to pay for its short-term liabilities. Liquidity ratios mostly reflect how efficient a company is in managing its assets to meet payables as they become due. An important factor is managing working capital. Efficient management of working capital (avoid overinvestment in inventory and receivables) increases the likelihood of generating sufficient amounts of cash from operations to meet current liabilities.

There are two subgroups of liquidity ratios: balance sheet ratios and coverage ratios. The balance sheet ones are based on stock measures obtained from the balance sheet, while the latter combines stock measures with flow measures obtained from thelow statement.

Main balance sheet ratios	Numerator	Denominator
Current ratio	Current assets	Current liabilities
Quick ratio	Cash + STMI + AR	Current liabilities
Cash ratio	Cash + STMI	Current liabilities

STMI = Short-term marketable investments (investments with a very short duration and readily convertible in cash, such as cash invested in money market funds)
AR = Accounts receivable

The three balance sheet ratios shown above measure by how much current assets cover (or fall short of) current liabilities. Current ratio considers all the current assets a company has, even though they might not be truly easily convertible into cash (for instance, bad loans or "out of fashion" inventory). The quick ratio and cash ratio exclude the less liquid assets and focus only on assets that are easily converted into cash.

Coverage ratios are useful in assessing whether a company has excess debt. Since a default on debt could be fatal for a company, it is important to gauge whether the company is over-leveraged. Also, too much debt could force companies to liquidate assets, thus reducing their ability to generate operating cash flows. Given their importance, coverage ratios are often included in bankruptcy prediction models and models used by rating agencies.

The most widely used coverage ratios include the interest, debt-service, and asset coverage ratios.

Main coverage ratios	Numerator	Denominator
Interest coverage ratio (ICR)	Operating profit	Net interest expenses
Interest coverage (cash flows)	CFO	Net interest payments
Debt-service coverage ratio (DSCR)	CFO	Debt principal and interest
Asset coverage ratio (ACR)	Net tangibles assets	Debt outstanding

CFO = Cash flows from operations

ICR measures how many times the operating profit could potentially cover interest charges. This ratio comes in two forms: accrual form and cash flow form. The accrual form is defined as earnings before interest and taxes divided by net interest expenses. The cash flow form is defined as cash from operations (excluding interest and taxes) divided by net interest payments. A more precise measure of a company's ability to service its debt is provided by the DSCR, which, unlike the ICR, takes into account principal debt repayments in addition to interest charges. The cash available to service these payments is defined as cash from operations (CFO), that is the resources a company is able to raise through its day-to-day operations before paying for new investments.

The idea underlying the ACR is that, in general, the more assets a company has compared to its total borrowings, the more likely it will be to meet its payments. As such, the ACR takes a company's net tangible assets (total assets net of intangibles and short-term liabilities) and divides the remaining number by the total debt outstanding. Clearly, the greater this ratio turns out to be, the larger the asset base of a company will be to service its debt outstanding.

Solvency ratios measure a company's ability to meet its long-term obligations. They also provide information about the relative amount of debt in a company's capital structure.

Main solvency ratios	Numerator	Denominator
Leverage ratio	Total assets	Total equity
Debt-to-equity ratio	Total debt	Total equity
Debt-to-capital ratio	Total debt	Total debt + equity

The leverage ratio measures the amount of total assets per each unit of equity. Therefore, this ratio speaks to how much a company relies on external funding (debt and other liabilities). The debt-to-equity ratio measures the amount of debt capital (interest-bearing) per one unit of equity, with focus on interest-bearing debt instead of total liabilities. This ratio is especially important for business valuation analysis since debt and equity are the two main variable of interest therein. Similarly, the debt-to-capital ratio measures the amount of debt capital as a percentage of the total funding sources (debt and equity). This ratio provides an indication about the weights of debt and equity in measuring the weighted average cost of capital (WACC); although these weights are book-based instead of market-based.

Example starts

Here are the ratios for Salvatore Ferragamo based on its consolidated financial statements (provided above).

Profitability ratio—To examine Ferragamo's operating profitability, we compute ROI dividing after-tax operating profit (NOPAT) by net invested capital.

Profitability ratio	ROI
NOPAT (33.6% tax rate)	99,382
Net invested capital (average)	616,141
ROI	**16.13%**

To assess Ferragamo's profitability, we should compare the ROI with that of other companies in the industry or with Ferragamo's ROI in prior periods. We could also compare the ROI with Ferragamo's estimated weighted average cost of capital (WACC). Generating ROI above WACC is a positive indication about whether the company uses its invested capital effectively.

Margin ratio—To gain insights as to the company's cost structure, we often examine margin ratios. Here is the operating profit margin:

Operating profit margin	OPM
Operating profit	149,769
Sales	1,346,842
OPM	**11.12%**

This figure tells us that Ferragamo is able to generate €11.12 in operating profit for each €100 of sales. This means that operating expenses account for the remaining €88.88. We should compare this ratio to the company's main competitors or the industry average to see whether Ferragamo's cost structure is efficient.

Efficiency ratios—To assess how fast Ferragamo collects cash from its customers, we compute the days of receivables (or Days Sales Outstanding, DSO) by dividing the accounts receivable balance by the daily sales of the company.[8]

Activity ratio	DSO
Account receivables (average)	145,744
Daily sales (360 base)	3,741
DSO	**39 days**

This figure suggests that, on average, it takes Ferragamo 39 days to collect its receivables. Similar ratios could be computed for the days of inventory (DOI) and days of payables (DPO). By combining DSO and DOI net of DPO we estimate the "cash conversion cycle," which measures the length of time it takes, on average, to collect cash from its operations. The cash conversion cycle is equal to DSO + DOI – DPO (days of inventory plus days of receivables and minus days of payables).

Liquidity ratios—To examine whether Ferragamo is well positioned to meet its short-term obligations, we can compute the current ratio, dividing current assets by current liabilities.

[8]When a ratio is constructed using a balance sheet item (such as receivables) and an income statement item (such as sales), it generally makes sense to average out the balance sheet item. This is reasonable since the income statement item accrues over the entire period whereas the balance sheet item is at a point in time. In practice, the average is computed as: average = (beginning balance + ending balance)/2. Also, note that receivables could include Value Added Tax (VAT), but we ignored this issue for simplicity.

Liquidity ratio	Current ratio
Current assets	781,491
Current liabilities	296,813
Current ratio	**2.63**

This figure tells us that Ferragamo's current assets are well in excess of its current liabilities. According to this ratio, the company should have no problem meeting its short-term liabilities. This ratio implicitly assumes that inventories and receivables are indeed liquid which might not be the case if DSO and DOI exceed 360 days.

To assess whether Ferragamo will be able to serve its debt outstanding, we can compute the ICR by dividing the operating profit by total interest charges.

Coverage ratio	ICR
Operating profit	149,769
Interest charges	13,857
ICR	**10.81**

This figure tells us that Ferragamo should not face any difficulty servicing its outstanding debt, since its operating profit is ten times the interest charges. A more precise way to gauge Ferragamo's ability to service its debt would be to use the DSCR ratio, that is, substituting the operating profit with the CFO (a measure of the cash flows generated by the company's operations) and adding together interest and principal payments on debt.

Solvency ratios—To examine whether Ferragamo is able to meet its long-term obligations, we compute the leverage ratio, by dividing total assets by shareholders' equity.

Solvency ratio	Leverage
Total assets	1,187,131
Shareholders' equity	780,338
Leverage	**1.52**

According to this ratio, each €1 of equity supports, on average, €1.52 of assets (€0.52 being funded externally by liabilities). Higher ratios suggest a more leveraged company (i.e., using more debt to finance assets). There are other commonly used leverage ratios, such as Debt/Equity, Equity to Total assets, and Long-term Debt to Equity. These ratios are highly correlated with each other. Another important ratio is the asset coverage ratio (total assets divided by the sum of principal and interest payments on debt), which provides an indication on whether the company has sufficient assets to cover debt-related payments.

Example ends

8.4 Ratio Analysis in the Presence of Intercorporate Investments

The diversity of accounting methods for intercorporate investments may have a significant effect on financial ratios. For example, passive investments are typically presented on the balance sheet at fair value or at cost. Investments with significant influence on the investee are presented under the equity method and controlled investments are consolidated under the purchase (acquisition) method. Therefore, the choice of the accounting method could have a significant effect on the financial ratios as well as on valuation multiples. The following example demonstrates the effect of accounting methods for intercorporate investments on ratios and valuation multiples, if not properly adjusted.

<u>Example starts</u>

On January 1, 2019, Company A acquires 75% of the common stock of Company B for $15,000 in cash. The pre-acquisition balance sheets and income statements of Company A and B are shown below. Assume for simplicity that book values of the items on B's balance sheet are equal to their fair values.

Next we prepare the post-acquisition balance sheet and income statement of Company A assuming that the investment in Company B is accounted for under (i) the purchase method; (ii) the equity method; and (iii) the proportionate consolidation method.

In addition, we examine how ROE, ROA, net profit margin, ICR, and leverage change under each accounting method.

Pre-acquisition ($/000)	Company A	Company B
Cash	20,000	25,000
Other current assets	35,000	10,000
Non-current assets	20,000	5,000
Total assets	**75,000**	**40,000**
Current liabilities	20,000	20,000
Share capital	50,000	15,000
Retained earnings	5,000	5,000
Total liabilities and equity	**75,000**	**40,000**

Pre-acquisition ($/000)	Company A	Company B
Revenue	100,000	25,000
Operating expenses	(55,000)	(15,000)
Operating profit	**45,000**	**10,000**
Interest charges	(10,000)	(5,000)
Net income	**35,000**	**5,000**

Recall that the purchase method reflects the control of the parent company over all the resources of the subsidiary. In contrast, both the equity and proportionate consolidation methods reflect ownership of a part of the investee.

Under the purchase method, assets and liabilities of Companies A and B are consolidated, and the stockholders' equity of B is eliminated. In addition, non-controlling interests are recognized as part of equity (25% of Company B's equity not owned by Company A). Under the equity method, Company A reports its 75% interest in B in a one-line item on its balance sheet; there is no non-controlling interests line item under this method. Under the proportionate consolidation method, Company A includes the proportion owned in each asset and liability; again, there is no non-controlling interests line item.

As for the income statement, under the purchase method, revenues and expenses of Company A and B are consolidated in full. Non-controlling interests account for the portion of Company B's net income not owned by A. Under the equity method, Company A will report its 75% share in B's net income in a one-line item in the income statement; there are no non-controlling interests. Under the proportionate consolidation, Company A reports its 75% share in B's revenues and expenses; again, there are no non-controlling interests. proportionate consolidation yields higher revenues and expense than the equity method, but net income should be the same.

Post-acquisition ($/000)	Purchase	Equity	Proportionate
Cash[a]	30,000	5,000	23,750
Current assets	45,000	35,000	42,500
Non-current assets	25,000	20,000	23,750
Investment in B	–	15,000	–
Total assets	**100,000**	**75,000**	**90,000**
Current liabilities	40,000	20,000	45,000
Share capital	50,000	50,000	50,000
Retained earnings	5,000	5,000	5,000
Non-controlling interests	5,000	–	–
Total liabilities and equity	**100,000**	**75,000**	**90,000**

[a]Under the purchase method, cash is $30,000 ($20,000A + $25,000B – $15,000). Under the equity method, cash is $5,000 ($20,000A – $15,000). Under proportionate consolidation, cash is $23,750 [$20,000A + ($25,000 × 75%) – $15,000]

Post-acquisition ($/000)	Purchase	Equity	Proportionate
Revenue	125,000	100,000	118,750
Operating expenses	(70,000)	(55,000)	(66,250)
Operating profit	**55,000**	**45,000**	**52,500**
Interest charges	(15,000)	(10,000)	(13,750)

Post-acquisition ($/000)	Purchase	Equity	Proportionate
Equity income from B	–	3,750	–
Non-controlling interests	(1,250)	–	–
Net income	**38,750**	**38,750**	**38,750**

There are four important effects that result from the choice of accounting method:

- All three methods report the same net income;
- Excluding NCIs, all methods report the same shareholders' equity;
- Assets and liabilities are highest under the purchase method and lowest under the equity method; proportionate consolidation is in-between;
- Sales are highest under the purchase method and lowest under the equity method; proportionate consolidation is in-between;

Using the following five common ratios, we demonstrate the differences among the three methods:

- *ROE*—Computed in two ways. The first one is at the group level (income is before non-controlling interests and equity includes non-controlling interests). The second one is at the parent company's level (income is after subtracting the share of non-controlling interests, and equity excludes non-controlling interests).
- *ROA*—Computed as net income, after subtracting the share of non-controlling interests, divided by total assets.
- Net income margin—Computed as net income after subtracting the share of non-controlling interests, divided by revenues.
- *ICR*—Computed as operating profit divided by interest charges.
- *Assets-to-equity (leverage)*—Computed as total assets divided by total equity (including non-controlling interests).

As the following table shows, the equity method presents the most favorable results, the purchase method the least favorable, with proportionate consolidation in-between.

Post-acquisition	Purchase	Equity	Proportionate
ROE (before NCI)	66.67%	70.45%	70.45%
ROE (after NCI)	70.45%	NA	NA
ROA	38.75%	51.67%	43.06%
Net income margin	31.00%	38.75%	32.63%
ICR	3.67	4.50	3.81
Leverage	166.67%	136.36%	163.64%

Example ends

Another important point relates to valuation multiples (e.g., price-to-earnings, market-to-book ratio, enterprise value-to-EBITDA) when a company holds a non-controlling interest in equity investments. The critical issue here is to construct comparable ratios by assuring that both the numerator and the denominator refer to comparable figures.[9]

Recall that when an investment is categorized as "non-controlling" (unconsolidated), line items above operating profit do not reflect any contribution of the holding (the share of net result coming from the investment is shown in a single line item below operating profit). However, when an investment is categorized as "controlling" (full consolidation), every line item above as well as below operating profit reflects 100% of the investment's results.

The numerator of valuation multiples shows either the equity value (equity side multiple) or the enterprise value (asset side multiple) of a company. These metrics include the company's market capitalization, which represents the market value of its equity including the value of all investments based on the effective percentage owned. Therefore, if Company A has a 30% stake in Company B, A's market capitalization will incorporate the fair value of the 30% stake in B (this is true for any stake A may hold in B). The problem with valuation multiples (asset side) then arises: For minority holdings, since the numerator includes the market value of these holdings while the denominator does not include any contribution from them; the multiple will be biased upward. For majority holdings, since the numerator includes their market values, but only for the effective percentage owned, while the denominator includes the results coming from them in full; the multiple will be biased downwards.

There are two ways to fix the problem:

- for minority holdings, by either subtracting the estimated value of the holdings from the numerator or by adding to the denominator the portion of revenues, EBITDA, operating profit, or any other metric we are using coming from the holding;
- for majority holdings, by either adding the estimated value of non-controlling interests to the numerator or by subtracting from the denominator the non-controlling interests portion of revenues, EBITDA, operating profit, or any other metric we are using.

Example starts

On December 31, 2019, Parent Company had 300 ordinary shares outstanding with a fair value of £1 each. Parent also had a 25% stake in Associate Company who, in turn, had 1,000 ordinary shares outstanding with a fair value of £0.1 each. Lastly, Parent had a cash balance of £25 and long-term financial debt amounting to £250, with a fair value of £250. Associate does not have any debt outstanding. Below are the separate income statements of the two companies.

[9] Palepu K. G. et al. (2019).

£ Thousand	Parent	Associate
Revenues	500	100
Expenses	(450)	(75)
Operating profit	**50**	**25**
Interest charges	(15)	–
Income taxes	(10)	(5)
Net income	**25**	**20**

To compute EV/EBIT (enterprise value divided by operating profit) and P/E (market capitalization divided by net earnings) multiples for Parent Company, we need to account for Parent's investment in Associate and incorporate the income from Associate into Parent's income statement.

£ Thousand	Parent
Revenues	500
Expenses	(450)
Operating profit	**50**
Equity income	5
Interest charges	(15)
Income taxes	(10)
Net income	**30**

Next, we compute Parent's enterprise value, which is equal to the value of equity plus the value of debt minus the value of financial assets (cash). Equity value is £300 (300 share * £1 each). The cash balance is £25 and the value of debt is £250. The resulting enterprise value is (£300 + £250 – £25 =) £525. The critical point is to recognize that this value also includes the 25% stake Parent holds in Associate. Associate's value of equity £100 (1000 share * £0.1), therefore Parent's standalone equity value and enterprise value are £275 (£300 – £100 * 25%) and £500 (£275 – £ 25 + £250), respectively.

Next, we compute Parent's EV/EBIT multiple; this multiple is equal to 10. Had we not adjusted the multiple as shown above, it would have been equal to (525/50 =) 10.5.

£ Thousand	Parent
Equity value	300
Cash	(25)
Debt	250
Associates	(25)
Standalone EV	**500**
EBIT	50
EV/EBIT	**10.5**

To compute the P/E ratio, we do not need to make any adjustment to the numerator of our ratio since it is already consistent with the denominator, as both figures take into account Associate for the effective percentage owned by Parent. The numerator includes its fair value, while the denominator includes the share in the net income of Associate.

£ Thousand	Parent
Equity value	300
Net income	30
P/E	**10**

How would these two valuation multiples change if Parent's stake in Associate (which we will now call Subsidiary) was 75% rather than 25%, assuming the price paid is now £75 and the market cap of Parent remains £300?

Now Parent has a controlling investment in Subsidiary, which is consolidated. Parent's consolidated income statement is shown below.

£ Thousand	Parent
Revenues	600
Expenses	(525)
Operating profit	**75**
Interest charges	(15)
Income taxes	(15)
Non-controlling interests	(5)
Net income	**40**

Since the consolidated operating profit now includes 100% of Subsidiary's operating profit (£25), but Parent's equity value only includes 75% of Subsidiary's fair value, we need to adjust it by adding the fair value of the remaining 25% of Subsidiary (non-controlling interests). Ignoring any premium or discount, the fair value of Subsidiary's 25% is £25 (1000 * £0.1 * 25%). Now we can compute the Parent's EV/EBIT multiple, which turns out to be (550/75 =) 7.3.

£ Thousand	Parent
Equity value	300
Cash	(25)
Debt	250
NCI	25
Enterprise value (EV)	**550**
Operating profit	75
EV/EBIT	**7.3**

Had we not adjusted the multiple as shown above, it would have been equal to (525/75 =) 7.0. The new multiple is lower than before because we assume constant market capitalization of Parent throughout the example.

To compute the P/E ratio, we do not need to make any adjustment to earnings since both the Parent's market capitalization and net income include the Subsidiary's fair value and income for the effective percentage owned.

£ Thousand	Parent
Equity value	300
Net income	40
P/E	**7.5**

The new multiple is lower than before because we assume constant market capitalization of Parent throughout the example.

Example ends

8.5 Summary

We started this chapter with an introduction to basic FSA, focusing on ratio analysis. Ratios are often used in financial analysis because they are unit-free and unaffected by size. As such, ratios are comparable across companies and over time. For example, being unit-free, it is possible to compare ratios of companies that report in different currencies.

The main goal of this chapter was to examine the effect of different accounting methods for intercorporate investments on key financial ratios. First, we identified a set of key ratios in four different categories: profitability, efficiency, liquidity, and solvency ratios. In each category, we defined a small number of ratios. Then, we computed the ratios under three methods for intercorporate investments—Equity method, Purchase method, and Proportionate Consolidation.

We also examined the sensitivity of valuation multiples to different accounting methods for intercorporate investments. We defined two valuation multiples: The enterprise value (EV) to earnings before interest and taxes, the price–earnings ratio. We demonstrated the bias in these multiples caused by different accounting methods for intercorporate investments and propose ways to correct the bias.

In the next chapter, we will examine other issues related to financial analysis in the presence of mergers and acquisitions.

References

Palepu K. G., Healy P. M., Bernard V. L., Peek E., *Business Analysis and Valuation*, 5th edition, 2019, Thomson Learning.

Penman S., *Financial Statement Analysis and Security Valuation*, 2012, 5th edition, McGraw Hill.

Robinson T. R., *International Financial Statement Analysis*, 4th edition, 2020, Wiley (CFA Institute).

Robinson T. R., Munter P., Grant J., *Financial Statement Analysis: A Global Perspective*, 2003, Prentice Hall.

Financial Analysis of Business Combinations (Advanced Issues)

9

9.1 Equity Method—Off Balance Sheet Financing

The equity method is a single-line consolidation method, which means that the investee's liabilities are netted against its assets, and hence, the investee's debt is not shown explicitly on the investor's balance sheet. In contrast, proportionate consolidation presents the investor's share in the investee's assets and liabilities on the investor's balance sheet. This is why many argue that proportionate consolidation provides more useful information than the equity method. Under proportionate consolidation, information on assets, liabilities, revenues, and expenses is more transparent, and in particular, there is less off the balance sheet.[1]

The choice of an accounting method is especially important if the investor retrieves a significant part of its profits from investments in other companies. The accounting method choice is also important in case of debt covenants, used by lenders to monitor the borrower.[2] Violating debt covenants is costly to the borrower because it requires lengthy renegotiations of debt agreements with lenders and, in extreme cases, could lead to immediate default. Since accounting methods affect reported figures and ratios, the choice of an accounting method could result in either violating or not violating debt covenants.

Given the structure of an investment, investors do not always have complete freedom to choose the accounting method to account for it. However, the investor

[1]The argument against proportionate consolidation is that the investor does not normally have access to its share of assets and liabilities, and therefore, a balance sheet under proportionate consolidation is somewhat misleading.

[2]Debt covenants are often defined in terms of accounting ratios.

Electronic supplementary material The online version of this chapter (https://doi.org/10.1007/978-3-030-61769-1_9) contains supplementary material, which is available to authorized users.

E. Amir and M. Ghitti, *Financial Analysis of Mergers and Acquisitions*,
https://doi.org/10.1007/978-3-030-61769-1_9

has the power to structure a transaction such that it meets the criteria for a certain accounting method. For example, the investor could acquire 50% of the voting shares of a company and choose the equity method, or it could acquire 51% of the voting shares and use the purchase method.[3]

Example starts

On January 1, 2019, Company A acquires 30% of the common stock of Company B from its existing shareholders for £24,000 in cash (there are no fair value adjustments or goodwill in this deal). Company A wishes to maintain some financial flexibility and, therefore, decides not to use its available cash balance of £25,000 to fund the deal. Instead, it borrows the acquisition cost (£24,000) from BANK paying a 5% annual interest. The borrowed funds will be added to the long-term debt Company A already has on its balance sheet (£15,000). BANK agrees to lend the money but sets up a couple of covenants to closely monitor the lender. The two covenants, to be calculated on the post-deal balance sheet of Company A, are:

- interest coverage ratio (ICR) > 2.25 (calculated as operating profit/interest charges);
- leverage ratio < 4.0 (calculated as total assets/equity).

Company B's cost of debt is 7.5%. Both Company A and B face an effective tax rate of 30%.

Company A wishes to assess if different accounting methods for its investment in Company B can lead to violating debt covenants. Suppose Company A can either account for the investment by using the equity method or the proportionate consolidation method.[4] Below are the pre-deal balance sheets and income statements of the two companies. If needed, complete them with any missing data.

Irrespective of the choice of the accounting method, Company A raises £24,000 in new debt to fund the deal. Therefore, its long-term debt will increase to £39,000 (£15,000 + £24,000), and its cash balance will temporarily increase to £49,000 (£25,000 + £24,000), although after the deal is completed and the consideration is paid, the cash balance will revert back to £25,000. The additional debt leads to additional interest charges that, for simplicity, are already considered in the income statement below.

---

[3]The academic literature distinguishes between two types of financial reporting management: accrual management and real earnings management. Accrual management is achieved by selecting certain accrual accounting parameters. For example, a company may select a shorter useful life for a depreciable asset, thus reducing depreciation expenses. Real earnings management means executing a certain set of transactions in order to affect reported income. For example, selling a subsidiary in order to recognize a gain in the income statement.

[4]Normally, the proportionate consolidation method would not be allowed under the circumstances described in this example. We use it here to demonstrate the effect of different accounting methods on ratios and debt covenants.

Pre-deal (£/000)	Company A	Company B
Cash	25.0	40.0
Other current assets	5.0	120.0
Non-current assets	10.0	90.0
Total assets	**40.0**	**250.0**
Current liabilities	5.0	70.0
Long-term debt	15.0	100.0
Total liabilities	**20.0**	**170.0**
Share capital	10.0	50.0
Retained earnings	10.0	30.0
Total liabilities and equity	**40.0**	**250.0**

Pre-deal (£000)	Company A	Company B
Revenue	40.0	130.0
Operating expenses	(25.0)	(100.0)
EBITDA	**15.0**	**30.0**
Depreciation & amortization	(10.0)	(17.5)
Operating profit	**5.0**	**12.5**
Interest charges	(2.0)	(7.5)
Profit before taxes	**3.0**	**5.0**
Income taxes	(0.9)	(1.5)
Net Income	**2.1**	**3.5**

Here is the balance sheet of Company A after completion of the deal:

Post-deal (£/000)	Equity	Proportionate
Cash	25.0	37.0
Other current assets	5.0	41.0
Non-current assets	10.0	37.0
Investment in B	24.0	–
Total assets	**64.0**	**115.0**
Current liabilities	5.0	26.0
Long-term debt	39.0	69.0
Total liabilities	**44.0**	**95.0**
Share capital	10.0	10.0
Retained earnings	10.0	10.0
Total liabilities and equity	**64.0**	**115.0**

Here is the income statement of Company A after the completion of the deal:

Post-deal (£000)	Equity	Proportionate
Revenue	40.0	79.0
Operating expenses	(25.0)	(55.0)
EBITDA	**15.0**	**24.0**
Depreciation & amortization	(10.0)	(15.3)
Operating profit	**5.0**	**8.7**
Interest charges	(2.0)	(4.3)
Profit before taxes	**3.0**	**4.4**
Income taxes	(0.9)	(1.3)
Profit after taxes	**2.1**	**3.1**
Equity income (after tax)	1.0	–
Net Income	**3.1**	**3.1**

The covenants computation is the following.

Post-deal (£/000)	Equity	Calculations	Proportionate
ICR	2.56	= 5.0 / 1.95; 8.7 / 4.3 =	2.02
Leverage	3.20	= 64 / 20; 115 / 20 =	5.75

Under the equity method, Company A would meet the covenant requirements, while under proportionate consolidation both covenants would be violated. Thus, if Company A could choose between the two methods, it would choose the equity method. This example demonstrates that due to contracting arrangements, accounting is not always neutral.
<u>**Examle ends**</u>

9.2 Changes in Purchase Price Allocation

Once an acquisition is completed, the acquirer must disclose information on the purchase price allocation (PPA). The first PPA is often preliminary and acquirers have a full year to revise it until it becomes final. The importance of the PPA is clear: it has a significant effect on post-acquisition reported income. For example, allocating less of the consideration to depreciable assets and more to goodwill decreases post-acquisition depreciation expenses, thus increasing reported income (assuming no impairment losses). Also, allocating more of the consideration to, say, accrued liabilities and more to goodwill decreases post-acquisition expenses, thus increasing income. In sum, movements in the PPA over time may not be random, and they may reflect the acquirer's intention to manage reported income subsequent to the acquisition.

Example starts

On March 26, 2018, Campbell Soup completed the acquisition of Snyder's-Lance, Inc. (Snyder's-Lance) for $50.00 per share.[5] The total consideration was $6,112 million, which included the payoff of approximately $1,100 million of Snyder's-Lance debt. The acquisition was financed through a senior unsecured term loan facility and the issuance of senior notes. The excess of the purchase price over the estimated fair values of identifiable net assets was recorded as goodwill. The goodwill, which is not deductible for tax purposes, was primarily attributable to future growth opportunities, anticipated synergies, and intangible assets that did not qualify for separate recognition.

The first PPA for this acquisition appeared in the 10-Q report for the quarter ended on April 29, 2018 (third quarter for fiscal 2018). The second one was included in the 10-K report for July 29, 2018 (Campbell's fiscal year-end is end of July). The third PPA was included in the 10-Q report for the quarter ending October 28, 2018 (first quarter for fiscal 2019), and the final one was included in the 10-Q report for the quarter ending January 27, 2019 (second quarter for fiscal 2019). Here are the PPAs:

Item ($ Millions)	29/4/18	29/7/18	Change	28/10/18	27/1/19
Cash	21	21	–	21	21
Accounts receivable	220	221	**(1)**	220	220
Inventories	219	219	–	219	219
Other current assets	35	32	–	32	32
Plant assets	699	696	–	696	696
Goodwill	2,867	2,866	**140**	3,006	3,006
Amortizable intangibles	816	816	**(52)**	764	764
Non-amortizable intangibles	2,131	2,131	**(134)**	1,997	1,997
Other assets	61	65	–	65	65
Short-term debt	(1)	(1)	–	(1)	(1)
Accounts payable	(124)	(124)	–	(124)	(124)
Accrued liabilities	(116)	(115)	–	(115)	(115)
Deferred income taxes	(637)	(640)	**43**	(597)	(597)
Other liabilities	(32)	(28)	**4**	(24)	(24)
Non-controlling interests	(47)	(47)	–	(47)	(47)
Net assets acquired	**6,112**	**6,112**	–	**6,112**	**6,112**

[5]Snyder's-Lance is a snack food company that manufactures, distributes, markets, and sells snack food products in North America and Europe. Its primary brands include Snyder's of Hanover and Lance, Kettle Brand, Cape Cod, Snack Factory Pretzel Crisps, Pop Secret, Emerald, and Late July. All the data used here are available on https://investor.campbellsoupcompany.com/financial-information.

Between the 10-K report for the year ended on July 29, 2018 and the following quarter (10-Q report for October 28, 2018), the PPA was revised (see column titled "Change" in the table above). Changes included an increase in goodwill of $140 million and a decrease in amortizable intangibles of $52 million and indefinite-life (non-amortizable) intangibles by $134 million. In addition, deferred tax liabilities increased by $43 million.

Note that a decrease in non-amortizable intangible and an increase in goodwill are income-neutral, at least in the absence of impairments. Since both assets are not amortized, there will be no effect on subsequent income. However, a decrease in amortizable intangibles is an income-increasing change in the PPA, because amortization expenses will be lower in subsequent quarters.

According to the notes to the financial statements, the average useful life of the amortizable intangibles is 18 years. Therefore, the effect of the change in the PPA on annual pretax income is approximately ($52 million / 18=) $2.9 million. Pretax income in fiscal 2018 was $272 million, so the effect of the change in the PPA is to increase pretax income by approximately 1%.

Example ends

Example starts

In 1996, Disney acquired Capital Cities ABC for $18.9 billion.[6] The first PPA for the transaction appeared in the 8-K filing with the Securities and Exchange Commission in March 1996. Another PPA was included in the 1996 annual report and a final PPA was included in the notes to the 1997 annual report. Here are the condensed PPAs.

	8-K	1996	1997
Cash	1.3	1.5	1.5
Other assets	4.2	3.3	2.5
Assets	**5.5**	**4.8**	**4.0**
Liabilities	(2.7)	(4.4)	(4.3)
Net	**2.8**	**0.4**	**(0.3)**
Other	–	0.2	0.2
Net assets	**2.8**	**0.6**	**(0.1)**
Purchase price	18.9	18.9	18.9
Goodwill	**16.1**	**18.3**	**19.0**

[6]The acquisition of Capital cities/ABC got the attention of Abraham J. Briloff, a distinguished accounting professor at Baruch College, New York. Briloff wrote an article arguing that Disney used the PPA to boost its post-acquisition income by nearly $2.5 billion. The article "Disney's Real Magic: Is the entertainment giant's accounting pure Mickey Mouse?" appeared in the Wall Street Journal on March 23, 1998.

There are two major changes in the PPA over time. The first one is the increase of $1.6 billion in liabilities (from $2.7 billion to $4.3 billion). The second one is a decrease of $1.7 billion in other assets (from $4.2 billion to $2.5 billion). Overall, these changes were offset by an increase of $2.9 billion in goodwill.

Analysing the disclosures reveals that the change in liabilities resulted from identifying onerous contracts, which were not recorded by Capital Cities/ABC prior to the acquisition. In addition, Disney reduced the accounting value of amortizable intangibles by about $700 million. Altogether, these changes in the PPA allowed Disney to increase post-acquisition profits by nearly $2.5 billion over a period of 3 years.

While this example is nearly a quarter of century old, it is still considered one of the most interesting cases of using the PPA to manage post-acquisition profits.

Example ends

9.3 Full Versus Partial Methods for Goodwill and Non-controlling Interests

As discussed in Chapters 2 and 3, there are two ways to compute goodwill and non-controlling interests: the partial method and the full (or fair value) method. Under the partial method, non-controlling interests are equal to the share of non-controlling shareholders in the fair value of net assets acquired (without goodwill); under the full method, non-controlling interests include a share in goodwill. Under the partial method, goodwill represents only the portion belonging to the controlling shareholders, while under the full method, goodwill is deemed to belong to both the controlling and non-controlling shareholders. IFRS allows companies to choose between the two methods. Under US GAAP, the full fair value method is mandatory.

Under the partial method, both goodwill and non-controlling interests are lower because no goodwill is attributed to non-controlling shareholders. Lower goodwill, in turn, will result in lower future impairment losses if a cash-generating unit (CGU) is subsequently found to be impaired. This is despite the fact that goodwill should include also the non-controlling interests portion when tested for impairment.[7] Moreover, since transactions with non-controlling interests are treated as transactions with equity holders, any subsequent acquisition of non-controlling interests at fair value will result in smaller reductions in the controlling interest's equity.

Under the full method, reported net assets are higher since both goodwill and non-controlling interests include the non-controlling interests' share of goodwill. The downside of having higher goodwill is that any impairment loss could be greater. Moreover, since net assets are higher, profitability ratios such as ROE and

[7]See IAS 36, Appendix C, § C4.

ROA are lower compared to the same ratios computed under the partial method. Lastly, though it might be difficult to measure the fair value of non-controlling interests, a company planning a cash buyout of non-controlling interests in a subsidiary may want to record them at fair value. If non-controlling interests are later acquired, there will be a lower difference between the consideration paid and the non-controlling interests' recorded value, and thus a smaller percentage reduction of equity.

Example starts

On January 1, 2019 Parent acquired 80% of Sub in exchange for Parent's shares with a fair value of €200,000. The pre-acquisition balance sheets and income statements of Parent and Sub are provided below. We will show how the consolidated financial statements of Parent change depending on how non-controlling interests and goodwill are measured. We will also compute ROE and ROA under both methods (ignoring tax effects).

Pre-acquisition (€/000)	Parent	Sub book value	Sub fair value
Cash	55	30	30
Inventory	180	85	90
Property	110	100	170
Total assets	**345**	**215**	**290**
Payables	40	50	50
Long-term debt	130	90	90
Total liabilities	**170**	**140**	**140**
Share capital	150	50	–
Retained earnings	25	25	–
Total equity	**175**	**75**	–
Total liabilities & equity	**345**	**215**	–

Pre-acquisition (€/000)	Parent	Sub
Sales	250	100
Cost of sales	(140)	(80)
Gross margin	**110**	**20**
Other operating expenses	(40)	(10)
Profit before interests	**70**	**10**
Interest charges	(15)	(5)
Net income	**55**	**5**

First, we need to compute goodwill using both the full and partial method.

Post-acquisition (€/000)	Full	Partial
Consideration	200	200
Non-controlling interests	50	30
Net assets	150	150
Goodwill	**100**	**80**

Under the full method, non-controlling interests are equal to €50 (=€200/0.8 – €200), assuming goodwill accrues proportionally to controlling and non-controlling shareholders' (that is, there is no acquisition control premium or discount). Under the partial method, non-controlling interests are equal to €30 (=€150 × 20%). Next, we construct Parent's consolidated balance sheet and income statement.

Post-acquisition (€/000)	Full	Partial
Cash	85	85
Inventory	270	270
Property	280	280
Goodwill	100	80
Total assets	**735**	**715**
Payables	90	90
Long-term debt	220	220
Total liabilities	**310**	**310**
Share capital	350	350
Retained earnings	25	25
Non-controlling interests	50	30
Total equity	**425**	**405**
Total liabilities & equity	**735**	**715**

Post-acquisition (€/000)	Full	Partial
Sales	350	350
Cost of sales	(220)	(220)
Gross Margin	**130**	**130**
Other operating expenses	(50)	(50)
Profit before interests	**80**	**80**
Interest charges	(20)	(20)
Non-controlling interests	(1)	(1)
Net income	**59**	**59**

Regardless of the method used to account for goodwill and non-controlling interests, income to Parent is €59. This is because the fair value adjustments made to Sub are allocated to non-controlling interests as well as to controlling shareholders under both the full and partial goodwill method.

Despite Parent's net income being the same under both methods, ROE and ROA are different because shareholders' equity and total assets are also different.

Post-acquisition (€000)	Full (%)	Partial (%)
Return on Equity (ROE)	13.88	14.57
Return on assets (ROA)	8.03	8.25

Both measures of profitability are lower under the full goodwill method, suggesting that companies reporting under IFRS may prefer to use the partial method.

Example ends

Example starts

The following appeared in the notes to the 2011 annual report of Nestlé Group.

On 17 November 2011, the Group acquired a 60% share in the Yinlu Foods Group (Yinlu) in China. Yinlu is a significant marketer for ready-to-drink peanut milk and ready-to-eat canned rice porridge in China. It will complement Nestlé's existing product portfolio in China. The goodwill arising on this acquisition includes elements that cannot be recognized as intangible assets such as synergies, complementary market share, and competitive position. The goodwill arising from this acquisition is expected to be deductible for tax purposes. Sales and profit for the year 2011 of Yinlu Foods Group included in the Consolidated Financial Statements amount, respectively, to CHF 123 million and CHF 13 million. The Group's total sales and profit for the year 2011 would have amounted, respectively, to CHF 84,782 million and CHF 9926 million if the acquisition had been effective on 1 January 2011. These amounts have been determined based on the assumption that the fair value adjustments at the acquisition date, determined provisionally, would have been the same at 1 January.

The PPA shown in Nestlé's annual report is the following.

CHF million	Fair values
Property, plant, and equipment	427
Intangible assets	694
Inventories and other assets	254
Financial debt	(185)
Employee benefits, deferred taxes, and provisions	(171)
Other liabilities	(250)
Net assets	**769**
Non-controlling interests (40% × 769)	308
Consideration paid	1150
Goodwill	**689**

Under the full method and assuming no control discount/premium, goodwill can be estimated to be CHF 1,148 million, based on non-controlling interests of CHF 767 million (1150/0.6 – 1,150).
Example ends

Example starts
The following appeared in the notes to the 2011 annual report of Fiat.

The acquisition of the control of Chrysler represents a business combination achieved in stages and falls under the scope of IFRS 3—Business Combinations. The accounting treatment for the business combination is as follows:

- *the previously held 30% ownership interest in Chrysler initially recognized at zero by Fiat was remeasured at fair value at the date on which control was acquired and the resulting gain of €1729 million ($2487 million) has been recognized in profit or loss under Unusual income/(expense). For the purpose of establishing the fair value of Chrysler in order to calculate that gain, given that no active market price for Chrysler shares was available, in accordance with IFRS 3 it was deemed reasonable to use the equity value of $8290 million (€5763 million) for Chrysler implied in the price agreed between Fiat and the US Treasury in early June 2011 for exercising the call option on the US Treasury's 6.031% ownership interest (on a fully diluted basis) in Chrysler…;*
- *the identifiable assets acquired and identifiable liabilities assumed (…) have been measured at their acquisition-date fair value…;*
- *noncontrolling interests of 54% on a fully diluted basis, were recognized at €3112 million ($4477 million) at the Acquisition date, based on the above-stated equity value of Chrysler of $8290 million (€5763 million)….*

The PPA shown in Fiat's annual report is the following.

€ Million	
Current assets	12,539
Non-current assets	13,794
Liabilities assumed	(29,232)
Net assets	**(2,899)**
Non-controlling interests	3,112
Fair value of previously held stake (30%)	1,729
Consideration paid (16%)	881
Goodwill	**8,621**

Under the partial method, goodwill would be estimated at €3,944 million, based on non-controlling interests of -€1,565 million (=2,899 × 54%).
Example ends

9.4 Organic Versus Acquired Growth

When companies engage in acquisitions, an important question is whether subsequent growth in sales and income originated from acquisitions or from within ("organic growth" or "like-for-like basis"). To measure organic growth, one needs to find comparable figures that are not affected by acquisitions. Two otherwise comparable companies might show very different financial statements if one of them grew through acquisitions while the other generated organic growth.[8]

Most likely, the company that grew via acquisitions will have more assets on its balance sheet because of the requirements to consolidate new subsidiaries at fair value, rather than at historical cost. Furthermore, whenever a subsidiary is acquired, the parent company is required to report on its consolidated balance sheet certain assets (e.g., internally generated intangibles and goodwill) that can be shown neither on the separate financial statements of the subsidiary nor in the parent's. For instance, one of the most highly valued brands is Coca Cola. However, this brand, which is worth billions of dollars, is not recognized on Coca-Cola's balance sheet because it was never acquired. If a company were to acquire Coca-Cola, it would certainly show the value of the acquired brand in its consolidated balance sheet.

Example starts

The Tal company reported the following information in its financial statements for the year ended as of December 31, 2019:

$ (000)	31/12/2019	31/12/2018	31/12/2017
Sales	25,000	20,000	10,000
Sales growth	25%	100%	–
Net income	5,500	5,000	2,000
Income growth	10%	250%	–

In addition, the notes to the financial statements included the following information:

On July 1, 2018, we completed the acquisition of the Galgelet Corporation for a cash consideration of $100,000. The Galgelet Corporation contributed $8,000 and $2,000 to the sales and net income for the year ended 31/12/2018, and $10,000 and $3,000 to the sales and income for the year ended 31/12/2019.

To compute Tal's organic growth, we need to remove Galgelet's contribution to sales and net income:

$ (000)	31/12/2019	31/12/2018	31/12/2017
Sales	15,000	12,000	10,000
Sales growth	25%	20%	–
Net income	2,500	3,000	2,000
Income growth	(17%)	50%	–

[8]Penman S. (2010).

Removing the effect of the new subsidiary reveals lower growth rates in sales and income. This could suggest difficulties in identifying new positive net present value projects, which can lead, as in this example, to the decision to acquire new businesses.
Example ends

Example starts
During fiscals 2018, 2017, and 2016, Campbell Soup reported the following information:

$ Million	July 29, 2018	July 30, 2017	July 31, 2016
Net sales—as reported	8,685	7,890	7,961
% change	*10.08%*	*(0.9%)*	–
Net earnings—as reported	261	887	563
% change	*(70.6%)*	*57.5%*	–
Earnings per share—as reported	0.87	2.91	1.82
% change	*(70.1%)*	*59.9%*	–
Weighted average shares—basic	301 mill	305 mill	309 mill

The figures shown above are not comparable across fiscal years due to acquisitions. Specifically, there were two major acquisitions during fiscal 2018: Snyder's-Lance, which was completed on March 26, 2018 (about 4 months before fiscal year-end) and Pacific Foods, which was completed on December 12, 2017 (about 7.5 months before fiscal year-end). These acquisitions increased sales in fiscal 2018, while at the same time reduced net income due to transaction and integration costs. To compare fiscal 2018 to fiscal 2017, we need information on the effect of these acquisitions on sales and income. Campbell Soup provides the following information in the notes to its 2018 financial statements for the year ended on July 29, 2018 (Note 3—Acquisitions):

In 2018, we recognized transaction costs and integration costs of $102, associated with the Snyder's-Lance acquisition. Approximately $53 represented transactions costs, including bridge financing costs and outside advisory costs, and were recorded in Other expenses/(income). Integration costs included the following:

- *amortization of the acquisition-date fair value adjustment to inventories of $42 that was recorded in Cost of products sold;*
- *$13 of Restructuring charges;*
- *$12 of Administrative expenses; and*
- *$18 gain in Interest expense on treasury rate lock contracts used to hedge the planned financing of the acquisition.*

The acquisition of Snyder's-Lance contributed $772 to Net sales from March 26, 2018, through July 29, 2018. The contribution to Net earnings was a loss of $84 from March 26, 2018, through July 29, 2018, including the effect of the transaction and integration costs, and interest expense on the debt to finance the acquisition.

The acquisition of Pacific Foods contributed $123 to Net sales from December 12, 2017, through July 29, 2018. The contribution to Net earnings was a loss of $13 from December 12, 2017, through July 29, 2018.

In addition, Campbell Soup included pro-forma (as if) information on what would have happened to sales and income had the acquisitions occurred in the beginning of fiscal 2017:

The following unaudited summary information is presented on a consolidated pro forma basis as if the Snyder's-Lance and Pacific Foods acquisitions had occurred on August 1, 2016:

	2018	2017
Net sales	*$10,222*	*$10,324*
Net earnings attributable to Campbell	*$371*	*$773*
Net earnings per share attributable to Campbell—basic	*$1.23*	*$2.53*
Net earnings per share attributable to Campbell—assuming dilution	*$1.23*	*$2.52*

The pro forma amounts include additional interest expense on the debt issued to finance the purchases, amortization, and depreciation expense based on the estimated fair value and useful lives of intangible assets and plant assets, and related tax effects.

The pro forma results are not necessarily indicative of the combined results had the Snyder's-Lance and Pacific Foods acquisitions been completed on August 1, 2016, nor are they indicative of future combined results. The pro forma results for 2017 include pretax transaction costs of $53, pretax amortization of the acquisition-date fair value adjustment to inventories of $42, and a pretax gain of $18 on treasury rate lock contracts. Therefore, the pro forma results for 2018 exclude these items, as they are reflected in 2017.

To estimate organic growth, we can use one of two methods:

a. eliminating the results of the acquired companies from the consolidated results for fiscals 2018 and 2017;
b. ensuring that the acquired companies are included in all reported fiscal years.

Here is an assessment of organic growth after eliminating the acquisitions effects in fiscals 2018 and 2017

$ Million	July 29, 2018	July 30, 2017	July 31, 2016
Net Sales—as reported	8,685	7,890	7,961
Contribution of Snyder's-Lance	(772)	–	–
Contribution of Pacific Foods	(123)	–	–
Adjusted sales	**7,790**	**7,890**	**7,961**

$ Million	July 29, 2018	July 30, 2017	July 31, 2016
Organic growth—sales	**(1.3%)**	**(0.9%)**	–
Net earnings—as reported	261	887	563
Contribution of Snyder's-Lance	84	–	–
Contribution of Pacific Foods	13	–	–
Adjusted net earnings	**358**	–	–
Organic growth—net earnings	**(59.6%)**	**57.5%**	–
Earnings per share—as reported	0.87	2.91	1.82
Contribution of Snyder's-Lance	0.28	–	–
Contribution of Pacific Foods	0.04	–	–
Adjusted earnings per share	**1.19**	**–**	**–**
Organic growth (EPS)	**(40.9%)**	**59.9%**	
Weighted average shares—basic	301 mill	305 mill	309 mill

Example ends

Example starts

Autonomy is a software company that has made several major acquisitions: Verity, a competitor, acquired in December 2005; Etalk acquired in June 2005; Zantaz, an email archive provider, acquired in July 2007; Interwoven, an Enterprise content management provider, acquired in March 2009. There were no acquisitions in 2006 and 2008.

Organic growth becomes an especially important factor in the presence of multiple acquisitions. Being aware of its importance, Autonomy released some useful information. However, the company did not disclose information on what would sales and income be if acquisitions occurred at the beginning of the year.

In 2010 and 2009 financial statements, the company argued that organic growth was 17% and 16%, respectively.

How is organic growth measured? Organic growth is measured as sales growth from internal sources, not from acquisitions. To measure organic growth we need to identify comparable periods without acquisitions. IFRS requires additional disclosure on acquisitions in the fiscal year in which these acquisitions were made. These disclosures allow a reasonable estimation of organic growth.

Is there organic growth in 2006? First, we need to adjust annual sales for fiscal 2005 for acquisitions. The company indicates that if the acquisitions of Verity and Etalk were made on January 1, 2005, sales would have been higher by $138.5 and $16.7 million, respectively, and net income would have been higher by $0.5 and $1.8 million, respectively. So the adjusted sales for 2005 are £251.23 million. That means that 2006 exhibits no organic growth (for the three combined companies) relative to 2005. Furthermore, the growth rate in sales was slightly negative at –0.2% ($250,682 / $251,232 – 1).

$	2005	2006
Reported sales	96,032.0	250,682.0
Verity	138,500.0	–
Etalk	16,700.0	–
Total sales	**251,232.0**	**250,682.0**

Is there organic growth in 2008? We need to adjust sales for 2007 for acquisitions. The company indicates that if the acquisitions of Zantaz and Meridio were made on January 1, 2007, group profit would have been lower by $20 million. Autonomy does not disclose the effect on sales though, which is quite suspicious. However, in the earnings presentation call/transcript for the third quarter of fiscal 2007, management identified Zantaz sales for that quarter as $18.3 million. Since the acquisition was made at the end of July, a reasonable estimate of quarterly sales would be $27.5 million. If this estimate is correct, sales for fiscal 2007 would have been ($27.5 × 2.33=) $64 million higher if Zantaz was acquired on January 1, 2007. If this estimate is correct, fiscal 2008 exhibits organic growth of ($503,229 / $407,409 – 1=) 23.5%.

$	2007	2008
Reported Sales	343,409.0	503,229.0
Zantaz third quarter 2007	64,000.0	–
Total sales	**407,409.0**	**503,229.0**

It is possible to compare figures from the fourth quarter of fiscal 2008 to those pertaining to the same quarter one year before. This is so because both quarters are recorded for a similar entity. Hence, organic growth in that period is about ($145.4/$115.1 – 1=) 26.3%. If we compare the first quarter of fiscal 2008 and 2009, the growth in sales could be attributed almost entirely to organic growth ($129.8/$105.1 – 1=) 23.5%.

Is there organic growth in 2010? The company argues that the effects of acquisitions made in 2010 are small. Suppose we ignore these acquisitions. Assume that Interwoven was fully integrated by the end of the second quarter of fiscal 2009. It is therefore possible to look at percentage change in sales for the third and fourth quarter of fiscal 2010.

Looking at percentage changes in quarterly sales, it seems that organic growth in sales is about 9.5–10%. If we look at operating cash flows, the numbers show a strong increase in quarterly cash flows from operations (CFO) except for the third quarter of fiscal 2010.

Quarter	Sales	Acquisitions	Δ Q(t)/Q(t−4) (%)	CFO	Δ Q(t)/Q(t−4) (%)
Q4-06	73.4				
Q1-07	65.5				
Q2-07	73.3				

Quarter	Sales	Acquisitions	Δ Q(t)/Q(t−4) (%)	CFO	Δ Q(t)/Q(t−4) (%)
Q3-07	89.6	Zantaz			
Q4-07	115.1	Merridio			
Q1-08	105.1			25.1	
Q2-08	125.6			36.1	
Q3-08	127.1			51.4	
Q4-08	145.4			49.4	
Q1-09	129.8	Interwoven		40.4	
Q2-09	195.2			63.0	
Q3-09	191.6			84.8	
Q4-09	223.1			61.8	
Q1-10	194.2			61.7	
Q2-10	221.1		13.28	92.3	46.38
Q3-10	210.6		**9.89**	60.7	**(28.43)**
Q4-10	244.5		**9.59**	87.7	**41.82**
Q1-11	219.8		13.19	85.7	38.87

Example ends

9.5 Balance Sheet Changes and the Cash Flow Statement

Acquisitions may have a significant and sometimes counterintuitive impact on the cash flow statement. Cash paid for business combinations, net of cash acquired, is presented among the cash flows from investing activities. However, business combinations makes the interpretation of working capital changes (e.g., inventory) more challenging. On the other hand, they make the interpretation of working capital changes (say, inventory) harder, since the changes shown on the cash flow statement, among the cash flows from operating activities, might not exactly correspond to the related changes shown on the balance sheet.[9]

Both IFRS and US GAAP require presenting cash flows from obtaining or losing control of companies as a single line item, together with a separate disclosure of the amount of assets and liabilities acquired or disposed of. This helps users of financial statements to distinguish these cash flows from the ones arising from other operating, investing, and financing activities.

Example starts

On May 1, 2019, Acquire purchased 75% of Sub for a cash consideration of $2,500. Goodwill is computed using the partial method. During the year, Acquire

[9] Libby R. et al. (2020).

issued $500 in long-term debt (to be paid back at maturity) at par value and paid dividends of $300. Below we present:

- Sub's balance sheets as of January 1, 2019, May 1, 2019 (acquisition date), and December 31, 2019. At acquisition date, Sub's book values are equal to their fair values;
- Sub's income statements for the following periods: January 1, 2019–April 30, 2019, and January 1, 2019–December 31, 2019;
- Acquire's separate balance sheets as of January 1, 2019 and December 31, 2019;
- Acquire's separate income statement for the period January 1, 2019–December 31, 2019.

Required: Prepare the consolidated cash flow statement of Acquire for the year ended on December 31, 2019.

Sub's balance sheet ($)	1.1.19	1.5.19	31.12.19
Cash	1,150	1,266	1,329
Accounts receivable	350	605	505
Inventory	400	835	875
Property, plant, and equipment	1,500	1,465	1,549
Total assets	**3,400**	**4,171**	**4,258**
Current liabilities	1,350	1,800	1,800
Long-term debt	300	300	300
Total liabilities	**1,650**	**2,100**	**2,100**
Retained earnings[a]	500	821	908
Shareholders' equity	1,250	1,250	1,250
Total liabilities and equity	**3,400**	**4,171**	**4,258**

[a]Retained earnings as of May 1, 2019 and December 31, 2019 include Sub's interim net results (respectively, $321 and $408). No dividends were distributed

Sub's income statement ($)	1.1.19–30.4.19	1.1.19–31.12.19
Sales	1120	1920
Cost of goods sold	(420)	(720)
Gross profit	**700**	**1,200**
Other operating expenses	(210)	(360)
Depreciation and amortization	(35)	(84)
Operating profit	**455**	**756**
Interest expenses	(36)	(180)
Profit before taxes	**419**	**576**
Income tax expenses	(98)	(168)
Net profit	**321**	**408**

Acquire's balance sheet ($)	1.1.19	31.12.19
Cash[a]	4,000	1,200
Accounts receivable	850	450
Inventory	1,250	850
Property, plant, and equipment	2,500	2,350
Investment in Sub	–	2,500
Total assets	**8,600**	**7,350**
Current liabilities	4,300	2,000
Long-term debt	2,000	2,500
Total liabilities	**6,300**	**4,500**
Retained earnings	800	1,350
Shareholders' equity	1,500	1,500
Total liabilities and equity	**8,600**	**7,350**

[a]Cash as of December 31, 2019 reflects both the consideration and the dividends payment ($1,200 = $4,000 – $2,500 – $300)

Acquire's income statement ($)	31.12.2019
Sales	3,000
Cost of goods sold	(1,000)
Gross profit	**2,000**
Other operating expenses	(250)
EBITDA	**1,750**
Depreciation and amortization	(150)
Operating profit	**1,600**
Interest expenses	(500)
Profit before taxes	**1,100**
Income tax expenses	(250)
Net profit	**850**

First, we compute goodwill.

$	**Fair** values
Cash	1,266
Accounts receivable	605
Inventory	835
Property, plant, and equipment	1,465
Current liabilities	(1,800)
Long-term debt	(300)
Net assets	**2,071**

$	Fair values
Non-controlling interests	518
Consideration paid	2,500
Goodwill	**947**

Now, we derive Sub's income statement for the period May 1, 2019–December 31, 2019 (from the date of acquisition to fiscal year-end). Since consolidation begins when control is obtained, Sub's results for the first four months of the year will not be included in Acquire's consolidated income statement for fiscal 2019. Therefore, we need to eliminate the first four months of fiscal 2019 from the entire year on a line-by-line basis.

Sub's income statement ($)	1.1.19–30.4.19	1.1.19–31.12.19	1.5.19–31.12.19
Sales	1,120	1,920	800
Cost of goods sold	(420)	(720)	(300)
Gross profit	**700**	**1200**	**500**
Other operating expenses	(210)	(360)	(150)
EBITDA	**490**	**840**	**350**
Depreciation and amortization	(35)	(84)	(49)
Operating profit	**455**	**756**	**301**
Interest expenses	(36)	(180)	(144)
Profit before taxes	**419**	**576**	**157**
Income tax expenses	(98)	(168)	(70)
Net profit	**321**	**408**	**87**

Next, we present Acquire's consolidated income statement by combining its separate income statement and Sub's income statement for the period May 1, 2019–December 31, 2019. We assume there were no intragroup transactions between Acquire and Sub to be eliminated.

Acquire's income statement ($)	Acquire	Sub	Consolidated
Sales	3,000	800	3,800
Cost of goods sold	(1,000)	(300)	(1,300)
Gross profit	**2,000**	**500**	**2,500**
Other operating expenses	(250)	(150)	(400)
EBITDA	**1,750**	**350**	**2,100**
Depreciation and amortization	(150)	(49)	(199)
Operating profit	**1,600**	**301**	**1,901**
Interest expenses	(500)	(144)	(644)

Acquire's income statement ($)	Acquire	Sub	Consolidated
Profit before taxes	**1,100**	**157**	**1,257**
Income tax expenses	(250)	(70)	(320)
Share of non-controlling interest[a]	–	–	(22)
Net profit	**850**	**87**	**915**

[a]Non-controlling interests are computed as $87 × 25%

In preparing Acquire's consolidated balance sheet, we need to recognize goodwill as an asset, and add Sub's assets and liabilities at fair value as of the time of acquisition. We also need to recognize non-controlling interests.

Acquire's balance sheet ($)	Acquire	Sub	Consolidated
Cash	1,200	1,329	2,529
Accounts receivable	450	505	955
Inventory	850	875	1,725
Property, plant, and equipment	2,350	1,549	3,899
Investment in Sub	2,500	–	–
Goodwill	–	–	947
Total assets	**7,350**	**4,258**	**10,055**
Current liabilities	2,000	1,800	3,800
Long-term debt	2,500	300	2,800
Total liabilities	**4,500**	**2,100**	**6,600**
Retained earnings	1,350	908	1,415
Non-controlling interests	–	–	540
Shareholders' equity	1,500	1,250	1,500
Total liabilities and equity	**7,350**	**4,258**	**10,055**

Non-controlling interests are equal to $518 (from the PPA) plus $22 (equal to $87 × 25%), that is $540. Retained earnings are equal to $800 (beginning balance) plus $915 (consolidated net income accruing to controlling investors) less $300 (dividend distribution), that is $1415.

To prepare the consolidated cash flow statement, each adjustment is derived from the consolidated income statement or changes in the Acquire's balance sheet.

Cash Flows from Operations (CFO)

To compute CFO, we begin with net income (including the non-controlling interests' share of the group profit) and we add back non-cash expenses and revenues (depreciation, amortization, gains, losses, and write-offs). In this case, the only noncash items are depreciation and amortization expenses.

Potential CFO ($)	$
Acquire's net income	915
Non-controlling interests	22
Group's net income	**937**
Depreciation and amortization	199
Total	**1,136**

Without any changes in operating working capital, cash from operations would be $1,136. However, there are changes in operating working capital, such as receivables, payables, and inventory. Therefore, we need to adjust our operating cash flows.

Working Capital ($)	Receivables	Inventory	Payables
Beginning balance Acquire	850	1,250	4,300
Ending balance Acquire	450	850	2,000
Changes Acquire	**400**	**400**	**(2,300)**
Beginning balance Sub (1.5.19)	605	835	1,800
Ending balance Sub	505	875	1,800
Changes Sub	**100**	**(40)**	**–**
Total changes	**500**	**360**	**(2,300)**

Hence, total cash from operations amounts to ($304), as shown in the following table.

Cash flow from operations ($)	Consolidated
Net income (group's share)	915
Non-controlling interests	22
Depreciation and amortization	199
Accounts receivable (net of M&A deal)	500
Inventory (net of M&A deal)	360
Account payables (net of M&A deal)	(2,300)
Cash flow	**(304)**

Cash Flows from Investing Activities (CFI)

Although Acquire purchased only a 75% stake in Sub, 100% of Sub's cash is offset against the cash price to determine the cash outflow from the M&A deal. Ownership divisions between controlling and non-controlling shareholders do not affect reporting for the entity's investing cash flows.

$	Sub's acquisition
Cash	1,266
Accounts receivable	605
Inventory	835
Property, plant, and equipment	1,465
Current liabilities	(1,800)
Long-term debt	(300)
Total cash payment	**2,500**
(Cash Acquired)	(1,266)
Net cash outflow	**1,234**

Moreover, we need to account for Sub's purchase of property, plant, and equipment during the period May 1, 19–December 31, 19.

$	PPE
Beginning balance (1.5.19)	1,465
Depreciation and amortization (1.5–31.12.19)	49
Ending balance (31.12.19)	1,549
Cash outflow	**133**

During the period, Acquire made no acquisition of property, plant, and equipment, because the change (i.e., reduction) in this item is exactly equal to the depreciation and amortization expenses. The total cash flows from investing activities is thus ($1,367), which is equal to ($1,234) plus ($133).

Cash flows from investing activities ($)	Consolidated
Acquisition of property, plant, and equipment	(133)
Acquisition of Sub (net of cash acquired)	(1,234)
Cash flow	**(1,367)**

Cash Flows from Financing Activities (CFF)

Acquire's debt issuance represents a cash inflow from financing activities. The dividend distribution, on the other hand, represents a cash outflow. The total cash flows from financing activities is thus $200, as shown in the following table.

Cash flows from financing activities ($)	Consolidated
Long-term debt	500
Dividends	(300)
Cash flow	**200**

Now we have everything we need to present Acquire's cash flows statement (see below). Comparing Acquire's separate and consolidated cash flows statements yields some interesting insights:

a. cash from operations differs across statements because in the separate statement we only account for the Acquire's results and, thus, we do not have non-controlling interests. Moreover, net income, depreciation and amortization and working capital changes come solely from Acquire's separate financial statements;
b. cash flows from investing activities (acquisitions)—The consolidated cash flow statement shows the consideration paid in cash to acquire Sub less cash acquired ($2,500 – $1,236=$1,234). The separate cash flow statement, on the other hand, shows the entire consideration paid to acquire Sub, $2,500. The reason is that cash in Sub is consolidated. Otherwise, we would be double counting it;
c. cash flows from investing activities—The separate cash flow statement shows only Acquire's capital expenditures, whereas the consolidated statement shows the combined capital expenditures of Aquire's and Sub's;
d. cash flows from financing activities—This section is the same in our example under both separate and consolidated cash flows statements, but only because Sub did not raise new debt or paid dividends to the non-controlling interests. Note that if Sub were to distribute dividends, say $100, we would see a negative cash flow of $25 ($100 × 25%) as dividend payment to the parent company is an internal transaction that is eliminated in the consolidation process;
e. total cash flows—The total cash flows differ between the separate and the consolidated balance sheets by $1,329 ($2,800 – $1,471), which is exactly equal to Sub's ending cash balance. Recall, the cash balance of Sub at the date of acquisition was subtracted from the consideration paid (included in cash flows from investing activities);
f. the last point relates to the changes in working capital accounts (accounts receivable, inventory, and accounts payable). Observe the two balance sheets below. The one on the left is Acquire's balance sheet as at 1.1.2019, prior to the acquisition of Sub. The one on the right is the consolidated balance sheet as at 31.12.2019. Focus now on the balance sheet change in inventory, which is ($1,250 – $1,725=) –$475. However, the change in inventory taken from the consolidated cash flow statement is $360. The difference between the two figures, which is ($475+$360=) $835 is exactly equal to Sub's inventory balance at 1.1.2019. Similarly, balance sheet changes for accounts receivable and accounts payable are different from the corresponding changes taken from the cash flow statement.

Acquire's Cash Flows Statement ($)	Separate	Consolidated
Net income (Group's share)	850	915
Non-controlling interests	–	22
Depreciation and amortization	150	199
Accounts receivable (net of M&A deal)	400	500
Inventory (net of M&A deal)	400	360
Accounts payable (net of M&A deal)	(2,300)	(2,300)
Cash flows from operating activities	**(500)**	**(304)**
Acquisition of property, plant, and equipment	–	(133)
Acquisition of Sub (net of cash acquired)	–	(1,234)
Investment in Sub	2,500	–
Cash flows from investing activities	**(2,500)**	**(1,367)**
Long-term debt	500	500
Dividends	(300)	(300)
Cash flow from financing activities	**200**	**200**
Total cash flow	**(2,800)**	**(1,471)**
Cash balance beginning of period (a)	**4,000**	**4,000**
Cash balance ending period (b)	**1,200**	**2,529**
Cash Flow (c = b – a)	**(2,800)**	**(1,471)**

Acquire's balance sheet ($)	1.1.19	31.12.19
Cash	4,000	2,529
Accounts receivable	850	955
Inventory	1,250	1,725
Property, plant, and equipment	2,500	3,899
Goodwill	–	947
Total assets	**8,600**	**10,055**
Current liabilities	4,300	3,800
Long-term debt	2,000	2,800
Total liabilities	**6,300**	**6,600**
Retained earnings	800	1,415
Non-controlling interests	–	540
Shareholders' equity	1,500	1,500
Total liabilities and equity	**8,600**	**10,055**

Example ends

9.6 Summary

In this final chapter, we discussed how M&A transactions affect financial statement analysis. While in the previous chapter we focused on financial and valuation ratios, here we focused on the effects of M&A deals on post-transaction financial statements. Broadly speaking, there are three methods to account for significant intercorporate investments: the equity method, the proportionate consolidation, and the full consolidation under the purchase method. The choice of an accounting method has a significant effect on financial statements, for instance, when a company has covenants on its debt. Knowing that, firms can and (sometimes) do structure transactions in ways that lead to the selection of a specific method (this practice is referred to as "real financial statement management").

Even within the same consolidation method there could be other discretionary choices that could affect reported figures. For instance, under the purchase method, firms reporting under IFRS can choose between the partial and the full methods for goodwill and non-controlling interests. Post-transaction results could be very different if there are subsequent impairment losses or transactions with non-controlling shareholders. Under US GAAP, however, such an accounting choice is unavailable.

We also tackled growth, distinguishing between acquired and organic growth. When performing financial analysis, it is important to assess whether the parent generates internal growth or it depends on acquisitions in order to grow. We emphasized that measuring organic growth requires comparable figures, which are unaffected by acquisitions or divestitures. Growing through acquisitions allows companies to increase their asset base, because consolidated financial statements include internally generated intangibles owned by the acquired company; these assets can be shown neither on the subsidiary's nor on the parent's separate financial statements.

Finally, we examined how M&A transactions affect the consolidated cash flow statement. When a parent company acquires a subsidiary, the parent's cash flows from investing activities include only the cash consideration paid net of the subsidiary's cash acquired. We also demonstrated the effect of consolidation on changes in working capital accounts reported on the cash flow statement.

References

Libby R., Libby P. A., Hodge F., *Financial Accounting*, 10th edition, 2020, McGraw Hill.
Penman S., *Accounting for Value*, 2010, Columbia University Press.

Part II
Case Studies

Kraft Group (Part I): Cadbury Acquisition—Purchase Accounting

10

Introduction

On February 2, 2010, Kraft Foods Inc. ("Kraft") announced it had acquired control of Cadbury Plc ("Cadbury"). The merger between the two companies created the second largest confectionery, food, and beverage Company in the world.

Companies

Kraft (listed on the New York Stock Exchange—NYSE) is one of the biggest food companies in the world. It reported revenues of $40.4 billion and earnings from continuing operations of $3.0 billion in fiscal year 2009 (prior to the Cadbury deal). Kraft manufactures and markets packaged food products, including snacks, beverages, cheese, convenient meals, and various packaged grocery products. In fiscal year 2009, Kraft portfolio included nine brands with annual revenues exceeding $1 billion each (Kraft, Oscar Mayer, Philadelphia, Maxwell House, Nabisco, Oreo, Milka, and LU biscuits) and approximately fifty other brands each generating annual revenues of more than $100 million.

Cadbury (listed on the London Stock Exchange—LSE) is the world's second largest confectionery company, with revenues of £5.9 billion and earnings from continuing operations of £0.5 billion in fiscal 2009 (prior to the Kraft deal). Founded 200 years ago, Cadbury's brands include Cadbury, Trident, Halls, Green & Blacks, The Natural Confectionery Co., Dentyne and Hollywood.

The Deal

On September 7, 2009, Kraft announced that it had made a proposal to the board of Cadbury to combine the two companies. Kraft offered 300 pence in cash and 0.2589 new Kraft shares per Cadbury share. This proposal valued each

This case study was originally written by Chemi Wieder and Hwangman Kim under the supervision of Professor Eli Amir, at London Business School, for class discussion in Eli Amir's financial analysis course. Eli Amir and Marco Ghitti then revised the case for this book. All market data in this case study are as of the time of the deal. They might have changed since then.

E. Amir and M. Ghitti, *Financial Analysis of Mergers and Acquisitions*,
https://doi.org/10.1007/978-3-030-61769-1_10

Cadbury share at 745 pence (based on the closing price of $28.10 for a Kraft share on September 4, 2009 and an exchange rate of 1.6346 $/£) and the entire issued share capital of Cadbury at £10.2 billion.

This announcement came as a surprise to the LSE investors. Cadbury's shares rose more than 38% in early trading to 786 pence. The news also boosted shares in other food groups across Europe, including Unilever, Nestlé, Danone, and Lindt.

On November 9, 2009, Kraft approached Cadbury's shareholders directly and launched a formal, hostile offer for Cadbury on the same terms proposed in September. Kraft shares dropped in value since September 2009. Therefore, the offer valued the entire share capital of Cadbury £9.8 billion (717 pence per share). Cadbury's board advised its shareholders to reject the offer. Cadbury's Chairman, Roger Carr, said:

> [Kraft's offer] *does not come remotely close to reflecting the true value of our company, and involves the unattractive prospect of the absorption of Cadbury into a low growth conglomerate business model.* (Reuters, November 9, 2009)

Another opponent to the offer was Warren Buffet, the single largest shareholder of Kraft, holding 9.4% of its shares through Berkshire Hathaway. Buffet said:

> *Kraft stock, at its current price of $27, is a very expensive 'currency' to be used in an acquisition. In 2007, in fact, Kraft spent $3.6 billion to repurchase shares at about $33 per share, presumably, because the directors and management thought the shares to be worth more.* (Reuters, January 5, 2010)

Responding to Buffet's criticism, Kraft decided to reduce the portion of its shares offered to Cadbury's shareholders. On January 5, 2010, Kraft updated its offer by increasing the cash portion by 60 pence per share (to 360 pence per share), and decreasing the share portion by an equivalent amount. In order to finance the extra cash needed, Kraft announced on the same day that it had sold its North American pizza business to Nestlé for a total consideration of $3.7 billion.

Kraft was expected to increase its offer, because under British takeover rules if Kraft failed to win over 50% of Cadbury's shareholders until the deadline, it would have not been able to bid again for Cadbury for a year. On the last day of the deadline, January 19, 2010, Kraft published its final offer and proposed 500 pence in cash and 0.1874 Kraft's share for each share of Cadbury. Based on Kraft's share price on that day, this offer valued the entire share capital of Cadbury £11.9 billion (840 pence per share). Cadbury's board recommended its shareholders to accept the terms of the final offer.

Cadbury's Chairman, Roger Carr, said:

> *We believe the offer represents good value for Cadbury shareholders and are pleased with the commitment that Kraft Foods has made to our heritage, values and people throughout the world.* (Kraft [final prospectus], January 29, 2010)

On February 2, 2010, Kraft announced it had acquired control of Cadbury, after receiving the acceptance of 72% of Cadbury's shareholders. On March 8, 2010,

Cadbury was delisted from the LSE, after Kraft received acceptance of more than 75% of Cadbury's shareholder. Kraft acquired the remaining shares of Cadbury by June 1, 2010, thus gaining control of 100% of Cadbury's shares.

Deal Financing Description

Kraft funded the cash portion of the deal through two sources:

- selling of the Pizza business—Net cash proceeds were $2.5 billion, after transaction costs and tax;
- debt issuance—On February 8, 2010, Kraft issued $9.5 billion of senior unsecured notes at a weighted average effective rate of 5.364% (due in 3.25, 6, 10 and 30 years) to finance the Cadbury acquisition and general corporate purposes (not all the debt financing was actually used for the transaction).

Pro-Forma Financial Statements

Following the closing of the deal, Kraft prepared a pro-forma consolidated balance sheet as of December 31, 2009 reflecting:

- its merger with Cadbury;
- the divestiture of the Pizza business;

Exhibits A and **B** present Kraft and Cadbury's balance sheets as of December 31, 2009.
(Assume that these two events occurred on that day).

Fair Value Adjustments

Based on a preliminary fair value estimation, Kraft assumed the fair value of the following Cadbury's items to exceed their book value by the associated amounts:

Assets	**$ Million**	
Inventories	58	
Property and equipment	678	Excluding land[a]
Other assets (non-current)	86	Investments in associates
Intangible assets	9,871	Definite-life assets added[b]
Total assets	**10,693**	
Liabilities		
Long-term debt	135	
Deferred tax liability (DTL):		From fair value adjustments
Current	66	
Non-current	3,373	
Total liabilities	**3,574**	

[a]$146 million with useful life of 9 years
[b]$2,400 million, with remaining useful life of 15 years

GAAP Adjustments

The following liabilities were adjusted to align Cadbury's IFRS financial information with Kraft's US GAAP accounting policies:

Liabilities ($)	Million	
Other current liabilities	(10)	Legal costs not meeting US GAAP recognition criteria
Other non-current liabilities	(26)	Same as above
DTL (non-current)	59	More rigorous requirement by US GAAP in regards to recognition of tax benefit
Accrued pension	16	Change in actuarial value
Total liabilities	**39**	

Transaction Costs

Under SFAS 141R (ASC 805) costs related to a business combination must be expensed. Future acquisition-related costs were estimated at $180 million (net of tax). These costs were recorded as a current liability in the pro-forma.

Other Adjustments

Other non-current liabilities were increased by $446 million and current liabilities were decreased by $262 million to reflect a change in the anticipated timing and amount of payments to third parties.

Selling the Pizza Business

The following table presents the gain from the sale:

	$ Million
Total consideration	3,700
Book value of net assets	(894)
Transaction costs	(10)
Pretax gain	**2,796**
Tax provision	(1,207)
Gain after tax	**1,589**

The following assets were transferred as part of the Pizza business sale, with the corresponding book value amounts:

	$ Million
Inventories	102
Property equipment	317
Goodwill	475
Total	**894**

Purchase Price Allocation

SFAS 141R (ASC 805) allows for a period of time, called the measurement period, to acquire the information required to properly ascertain fair values. The measurement period ends once the acquirer obtains the necessary information about the facts as of the acquisition date, but may not exceed one year.

On its financial statements for the first quarter of fiscal 2010, Kraft published its preliminary allocation of purchase price as of February 2, 2010, for the Cadbury acquisition.

Exhibit C presents the preliminary allocation of purchase price.

During the fourth quarter of fiscal 2010, Kraft completed the allocation process, and published the final allocation of the purchase price as of February 2, 2010 for the Cadbury acquisition. If the final allocation is different from the preliminary allocation, goodwill absorbs the difference.

Exhibit D presents the final allocation of purchase price.

Questions

If required, assume the following:

- number of Cadbury shares (fully diluted): 1,395 million;
- Kraft share price: $28.36;
- exchange rate £1 = $1.595.

For Questions 1–3 assume the following:

- the Cadbury acquisition and the Pizza business sale occurred on December 31, 2009;
- Kraft purchased 100% of Cadbury shares, under the terms of the final offer.

1. Based on Kraft's fair value adjustments, compute the goodwill in the transaction.
2. Prepare the pro-forma consolidated balance sheet as of December 31, 2009, which includes the merger with Cadbury and the divestiture of the Pizza business, based on the adjustments made by Kraft.
3. Based on the pro-forma consolidated balance sheet, what would be the effect of Cadbury consolidation on Kraft income statement for fiscal year 2010? Provide a quantitative answer.

For Questions 4–6 ignore the purchase of Cadbury shares Kraft made after February 2, 2010.

4. What were the amounts of goodwill and non-controlling interests reported by Kraft in its financial statements for the first quarter of fiscal year 2010? Kraft, which reports under US GAAP, applied the full goodwill method.

5. Assume now that Kraft reports under IFRS and applies the proportionate fair value (partial) method to compute goodwill. What would be the amounts of goodwill and non-controlling interest reported by Kraft in its financial statements for the first quarter of fiscal year 2010? Discuss briefly what Kraft should consider when deciding whether to apply the full or proportionate fair value method.
6. What were the amounts of goodwill and non-controlling interest reported by Kraft in its financial statements for the fourth quarter of fiscal year 2010? How could Kraft benefit from this change in goodwill?
7. Comment on the potential effect of Kraft's "other adjustments" on its net income for fiscal periods starting after the acquisition.

Exhibit A: Kraft's Balance Sheet as of December 31, 2009

	$ Million
Cash and cash equivalents	2,101
Receivables	5,197
Inventories	3,775
Deferred income taxes	730
Other current assets	651
Total current assets	**12,454**
Property and equipment, net	10,693
Goodwill	28,764
Intangible assets	13,429
Other assets	1,374
Total assets	**66,714**
Short-term borrowings	453
Current portion of long-term debt	513
Accounts payable	3,766
Accrued expenses & other current liabilities	6,759
Total current liabilities	**11,491**
Long-term debt	18,024
Deferred income taxes	4,508
Accrued pension & postretirement costs	4,581
Other liabilities	2,138
Total liabilities	**40,742**
Common stock, no par value	–
Additional paid-in capital	23,611

	$ Million
Retained earnings	14,636
Accumulated other comprehensive losses	(3,955)
Treasury stock, at cost	(8,416)
Total shareholders' equity	**25,876**
Non-controlling interests	96
Total liabilities and equity	**66,714**

Exhibit B: Cadbury's Balance Sheet as of December 31, 2009

	$ Million
Cash and cash equivalents	383
Receivables	1,581
Inventories	1,210
Other current assets	262
Total current assets	**3,436**
Property and equipment, net	3,022
Goodwill	3,519
Intangible assets	2,629
Other assets	538
Total assets	**13,144**
Short-term borrowings	433
Accounts payable	2,550
Other current liabilities	952
Total current liabilities	**3,935**
Long-term debt	2,183
Deferred income taxes	264
Accrued pension	815
Other liabilities	252
Total liabilities	**7,449**
Common stock, no par value	–
Additional paid-in capital	378
Retained earnings	4,227
Accumulated other comprehensive income	1,058
Total shareholders' equity	**5,663**
Non-controlling interests	32
Total liabilities and equity	**13,144**

Exhibit C: Preliminary Allocation of Purchase Price

Assets	$ Million
Cash and cash equivalents	1,061
Receivables	1,387
Inventories	1,317
Other current assets	491
Property and equipment, net	3,700
Other assets	424
Intangible assets	12,637
Total assets	**21,017**
Liabilities	
Short-term borrowings	1,206
Accounts payable	1,620
Other current liabilities	1,523
Long-term debt	2,309
Deferred income taxes	3,098
Accrued pension costs	838
Other liabilities	1,028
Total liabilities	**11,622**

Exhibit D: Final Allocation of Purchase Price

Assets	$ Million
Cash and cash equivalents	1,043
Receivables	1,333
Inventories	1,298
Other current assets	660
Property and equipment, net	3,293
Other assets	593
Intangible assets	12,905
Liabilities	
Short-term borrowings	1,206
Accounts payable	1,605
Other current liabilities	1,866
Long-term debt	2,437
Deferred income taxes	3,218
Accrued pension costs	817
Other liabilities	927
Non-controlling interests	33

References

Cadbury annual report for fiscal 2009.
Kraft annual report for fiscal 2009.
Kraft final prospectus to exchange, January 29, 2010.
Kraft form 8-K/A as of February 2, 2010.
Kraft quarterly report as of March 31, 2010.
Kraft quarterly report as of December 31, 2010.

The Bank of Hope: The Merger of Wilshire Bank and BBCN Bancorp

11

Introduction

> *LOS ANGELES, Dec. 7, 2015 -- BBCN Bancorp, Inc. (NASDAQ: BBCN) ("BBCN") and Wilshire Bancorp, Inc. (NASDAQ: WIBC) ("Wilshire") today jointly announced the signing of a definitive agreement to combine in a strategic merger of equals creating the only super regional Korean-American bank in the United States.* (Globe Newswire, December 7, 2015)

The announcement of the transaction came as a surprise to Joseph Rho, Chairman of Hanmi. On November, 23, 2015, just a couple of weeks before the news, Hanmi, a Korean-American bank with a profile similar to Wilshire and BBCN, had proposed to combine Hanmi with BBCN Bancorp. Nonetheless, the board of BBCN decided to put Hanmi's deal aside and go ahead with the Wilshire transaction, which, according to BBCN officials, was on its way before Hanmi made its initial proposal. Finally defeated, Hanmi withdrew its offer for a merger on December 17, 2015.[1]

BBCN board decided to go ahead with the merger with Wilshire, a transaction that created a new bank with major presence in the most important population centers for Asian communities in the US, with either first or second market share among Korean-American banks. The new bank would have a full range of services, including, SBA Loans (see further), contact with international commerce Korean Agencies, mortgages, and other business loans.

[1]All market data in this case study are as of the time of the deal. They might have changed since then.

E. Amir and M. Ghitti, *Financial Analysis of Mergers and Acquisitions*,
https://doi.org/10.1007/978-3-030-61769-1_11

Companies

Established in 1980 in California, by 2015 Wilshire was the second largest Korean-American bank in the US, with regional presence in California, Texas, New Jersey, and New York, among other states. By the third quarter of 2015, Wilshire had $4.74 billion in assets with $3.58 billion in loans, 70% of which were concentrated in commercial real estate. Deposits, on the other hand, totalled $3.94 billion, with 27% of those not bearing any interest. The annualized net interest margin for the first nine months of 2015 was 3.49%, which translated in a net income of $47.46 million and a return on equity of 12.34%.

Wilshire was a general commercial bank, which focussed on real estate lending, both commercial and residential, but it also provided business lending, including lending to small businesses (SBA programs), letters of credit for importers and exporters, and warehouse lines of credit to mortgage loan originators.[2]

Wilshire had six loan production offices (LPOs), of which four were used "primarily for the origination of loans under the SBA lending program"; these offices were in California, Colorado, Georgia, and Washington; the other two offices, located in Southern California, were for residential mortgages.

Founded in 1989 under the name of Nara Bank, BBCN became the biggest Korean-American bank in the US after a successful merger between Nara and Center Bank, giving birth to Business Bank of Center and Nara in 2011. Afterwards, BBCN continued to grow through the acquisition of Pacific International Bank and Foster Bank both in 2013.

BBCN and Wilshire merged on July 29, 2016, giving birth to Bank of Hope. A summary of the different M&A transactions that gave birth to the Bank of Hope can be found in **Exhibit A**.

BBCN focused its business on commercial banking loans and deposits for individuals and small and medium-sized enterprises (SMEs). Among its services, the bank offered cash management products, real estate, SBA and trade finance loans.

As of September 30, 2015, BBCN assets were $7.58 billion, of which loans constituted the 77.8%; similar to Wilshire, BBCN main loan category was commercial and industrial real estate with $4.67 billion in the books. To fund these loans, the bank had $6.03 billion in deposits, of which $1.63 billion were not bearing any interests. The net interest margin for the first nine months of 2015 was 3.89%, which allowed BBCN to generate $69.39 million of net income and a return on equity of 10.23%.

The deal

As stated by the companies involved in their press conference and 8K SEC filings on December 7, 2015, the transaction was designed to be a 100% stock-for-stock deal, with Wilshire shareholders receiving 0.7034 shares in BBCN for each share they held in Wilshire. BBCN was the surviving company (with a change of name to Bank of Hope). BBCN was identified as the acquiring firm and given

[2]Small business administration (SBA) lending programs are small business loans partially guaranteed by the government (the Small Business Administration Act).

the stock-for-stock nature of the deal, it did not issue any new debt to fund the acquisition.

From a tax perspective, the acquisition by BBCN was a tax-free reorganization for Wilshire shareholders. That is, Wilshire shareholders did not pay taxes on the transaction and there was no step up in the fair value of the acquired assets.[3] Furthermore, goodwill was not amortized for tax purposes.

After the merger, the board of the Bank of Hope would consist of 16 members, nine of which designated by BBCN (56.25% of deciding power) and the remaining seven by Wilshire (43.75%). The chairman of the board would be Mr. Steven S. Koh, Chairman of Wilshire, and the CEO would be Mr. Kevin S. Kim, chairman, president, and CEO of BBCN.

On December 7, 2015, the day of the announcement, the market reaction was a 4.8% increase in Wilshire share price and a 1.6% decrease in BBCN share price; for comparison, on that day the S&P500 decreased by 0.7%.[4] A week to the announcement, the market as a whole and both companies' share price plummeted, Wilshire by 4.7% and BBCN by 9.7%, while the market decreased by 3.8%.

The following graph shows the market reaction to both announcements (Hamni and Wilshire) on Wilshire and BBCN stock prices. Information on the prices and the shares outstanding of each company can be found on **Exhibit B** and **C**, respectively (Fig. 11.1).

The (main) reason for the transaction was to generate cost savings (i.e., synergies) by eliminating duplicates on the branches and consolidating headquarter operations. Additionally, the income potential of a bigger portfolio of services and a broader client base was increased. That said, the bigger size of the resulting bank had both benefits and drawbacks; on one hand, the bank needed to comply with further and more complex regulation, which means investments in personnel and technology, on the other hand, though, the larger size allowed the bank to be a more relevant player in the market.

All in all, the merger of Wilshire and BBCN would create the largest Korean-American bank in the US, with full banking services in all the main population centers with large Asian-American communities. Moreover, this would be the only bank with a presence in Korea (Fig. 11.2).

BBCN and Wilshire both had headquarters in the Los Angeles area, very close to each other, which eased the union of the administrative tasks, and in turn, created an even greater operational leverage. Also, on the cost side, 65.7% of Wilshire branches were less than a mile away from a BBCN branch: eliminating the duplicates would allow for greater cost savings.

---

[3]Wilshire (ex) shareholders still have to pay taxes on their holding in Bank of Hope if and when they will sell it at a gain.

[4]The share price movements of both Wilshire and BBCN are similar to those of other merger and acquisition deals. As soon as rumors of a new deal leak, the bidder's share price (BBCN) often declines reflecting investors' fear of overpayment for the target. Likewise, the target's share price (Wilshire) often increases since its shareholders may receive an acquisition premium over the current share price.

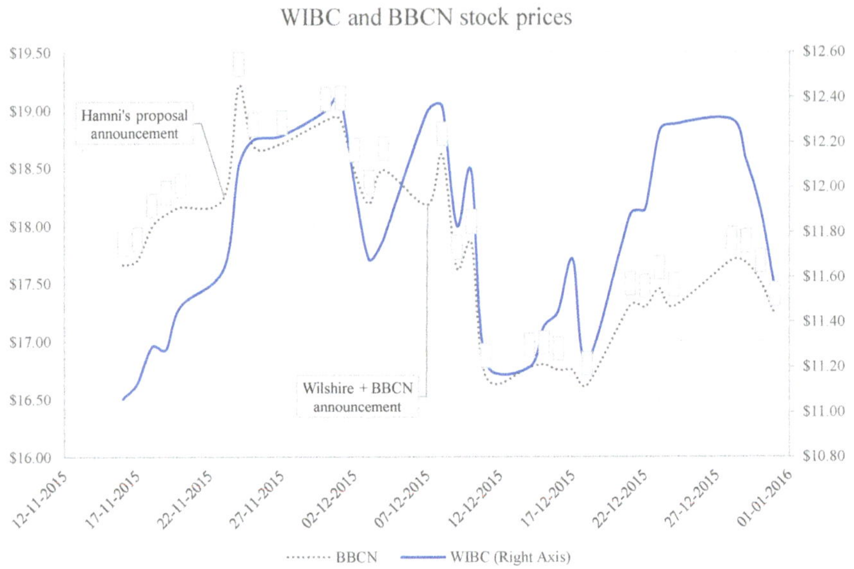

Fig. 11.1 WIBC and BBCN stock prices (*Source* Yahoo Finance)

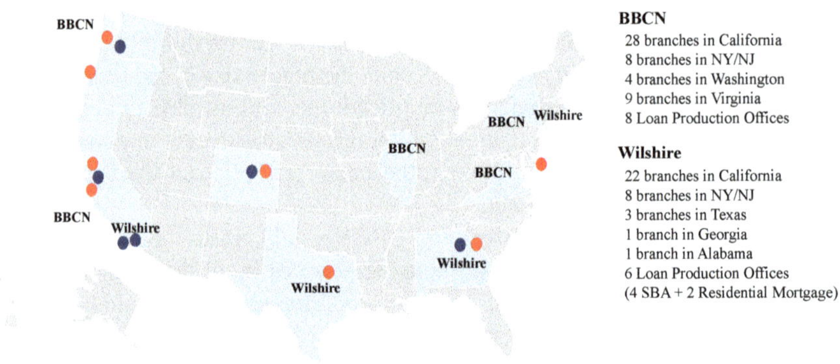

Fig. 11.2 WIBC and BBCN geographical footprint (*Source* Investor presentation, December 7, 2015)

Additionally, the merger of the two top lenders in the Korean-American spectrum would create, as a result, one of the top 10 SBA lenders in the country. It would also create a broader range of products for their customers, which would offer the possibility of increased revenue through cross-sales.

Greater value in the transaction also came from the ability of the resulting (bigger) bank to negotiate with Korean counterparts as well as with trade and development agencies to deepen trade finance relationships and increase and facilitate businesses for their customers.

As anticipated, the size of the new bank, with assets over $10 billion, meant that new regulations would apply, including the Dodd-Frank Act Stress Test (DFAST). This stress test requires banks to test the impact of three different scenarios on their business: baseline, adverse, and severe operational conditions. In order to run these scenarios, the new bank needed to invest in human and technical resources, including analytical expertise and accessible historical data, with high levels of coordination and cooperation among departments all along the organization. Another regulation that kicked-in having reached this critical size ($10 billion in balance sheet assets) was the Volcker Rule which moves from simplified to standard: this rule restricts proprietary trading and participation in most private equity and hedge funds.

According to an Independent Banker article, banks with assets over $10 billion are also subject to on-site consumer examination by the Consumer Financial Protection Bureau (CFPB), to make sure customers are treated fairly. The Durbin Amendment, which comes to function in the same threshold, means banks will lose income due to controls on how much they can charge their customers in debit card interchange or swipe fees.

In total, the new company expected to realize approximately $42.3 million in pretax cost savings between 2016 and 2017. This was a conservative estimate, which took into account potential compliance costs due to regulatory requirements that take effect for banks with more than $10 billion in assets.

Accounting

On July 29, 2016, BBCN completed the merger with Wilshire, creating Bank of Hope. As stated in the SEC filings of the company, the transaction was accounted for in accordance with ASC 805 and assets and liabilities of Wilshire were recorded at fair value at the date of acquisition.

Although the procedure that accounts for assets and liabilities of the acquired firm at fair value is the same for financial and nonfinancial firms, it is important to consider the types of assets and liabilities of a bank to understand the impact of fair value valuations. On the asset side, for example, the valuation of investments should not, for the most part, generate fair value differences, particularly when these investments are accounted for using level 1 inputs of fair value (this is because these investments should already be marketed to market on the balance sheet).

The following were the fair value adjustments made to Wilshire's financial statements to get the net assets acquired marked to fair value.

Assets	$ Thousand
Securities available for sale	(11,636)
Loans receivable	2,061
Other real estate owned ("OREO"), net	4,022
Premises and equipment	1,735
Deferred tax assets, net	(345)
Bank owned life insurance ("BOLI")	(77)

Investments in affordable housing partnerships	1,484
Servicing assets	(3,016)
Other assets[a]	(1,509)
Liabilities	
FHLB advances	6,282
Subordinated debentures	(15,197)
Other liabilities[b]	11,038

[a]Includes: accrued interest receivable, customers' liabilities on acceptances, loans held for sale, other investments, and other assets
[b]Includes: accrued interest payable, acceptances outstanding, and other liabilities

New asset identified

An additional core deposit intangible asset was identified and valued at $18,138,000.

Payment of deposits

$200 million of cash and cash equivalents were used to pay deposits. The total fair value of cash and cash equivalents after that payment was $100,127,000. The fair value of the deposits, after the $200 million, payment was $3,812,367,000.

Transaction costs

According to US GAAP for business combinations, transaction costs should be expensed immediately. In this case, the estimate of expenses was $45 million (pretax).

The definitive purchase price allocation is shown in **Exhibit D**.

Questions

1. The creation of Bank of Hope was presented as a "merger of equals." However, both US GAAP and IFRS always require designating one firm as the acquirer and the other as the acquiree. Identify the acquirer and the acquiree. Justify your answer. Is it possible to consider the transaction as a reverse acquisition?
2. What is the acquisition consideration?
3. What is the ownership structure of the new entity? What percentage of shares are held by former shareholders of BBCN and Wilshire?
4. Does goodwill emerge in the transaction? If so, how much?
5. How are new intangibles, fair value adjustments, deferred taxes, and transaction costs treated under the purchase method? Discuss in the context of the case.
6. Assume BBCN acquired only 66% of Wilshire's shares. Calculate goodwill and non-controlling interests using both the full and the partial goodwill methods. State all your assumptions.
7. Present a pro-forma consolidated balance sheet as of June 30, 2016 using information in **Exhibits E** and **F**.

Exhibit A: Mergers and Acquisitions That Made the Bank of Hope Possible

See Fig. 11.3.

Exhibit B: Stocks' Prices (Yahoo Finance)

Date	WIBC	BBCN	HOPE	S&P 500
Daily				
16/11/2015	$11.06	$17.66		$2,053.19
17/11/2015	$11.13	$17.70		$2,050.44
18/11/2015	$11.29	$17.99		$2,083.58
19/11/2015	$11.28	$18.10		$2,081.24
20/11/2015	$11.47	$18.16		$2,089.17
23/11/2015	$11.64	$18.25		$2,086.59
24/11/2015	$12.09	$19.21		$2,089.14
25/11/2015	$12.21	$18.69		$2,088.87
27/11/2015	$12.23	$18.71		$2,090.11
30/11/2015	$12.34	$18.91		$2,080.41
01/12/2015	$12.40	$18.92		$2,102.63
02/12/2015	$12.01	$18.47		$2,079.51
03/12/2015	$11.68	$18.19		$2,049.62
04/12/2015	$11.77	$18.48		$2,091.69
07/12/2015	$12.34	$18.18		$2,077.07
08/12/2015	$12.36	$18.61		$2,063.59
09/12/2015	$11.83	$17.63		$2,047.62
10/12/2015	$12.07	$17.85		$2,052.23
11/12/2015	$11.22	$16.69		$2,012.37
14/12/2015	$11.20	$16.78		$2,021.94
15/12/2015	$11.38	$16.80		$2,043.41
16/12/2015	$11.45	$16.75		$2,073.07
17/12/2015	$11.68	$16.75		$2,041.89
18/12/2015	$11.22	$16.62		$2,005.55
21/12/2015	$11.88	$17.31		$2,021.15
22/12/2015	$11.90	$17.29		$2,038.97
23/12/2015	$12.25	$17.45		$2,064.29
24/12/2015	$12.28	$17.30		$2,060.99
28/12/2015	$12.30	$17.70		$2,056.50
29/12/2015	$12.12	$17.68		$2,078.36
30/12/2015	$11.90	$17.51		$2,063.36
31/12/2015	$11.55	$17.22		$2,043.94
Weekly				
08/01/2016	$10.64	$15.67		$1,922.03

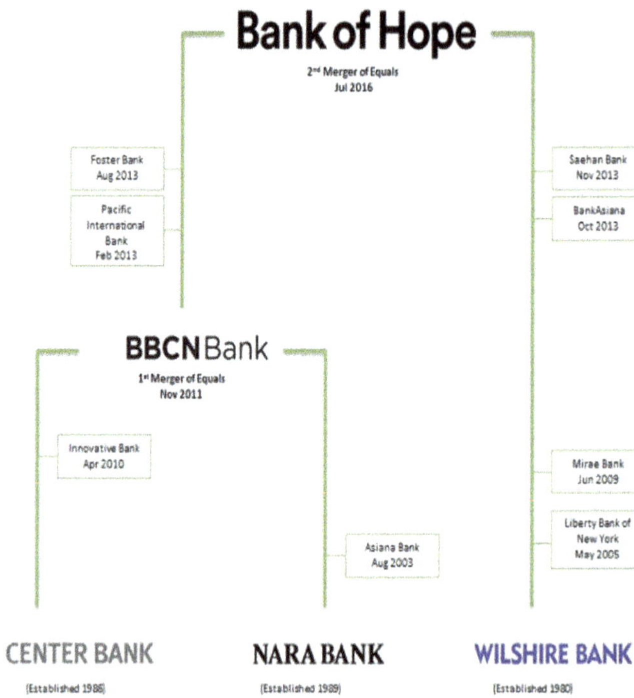

Fig. 11.3 Bank of hope structure (*Source* Bank of Hope's annual report 2016)

Date	WIBC	BBCN	HOPE	S&P 500
15/01/2016	$10.52	$15.53		$1,880.33
22/01/2016	$10.14	$14.92		$1,906.90
29/01/2016	$10.59	$15.20		$1,940.24
05/02/2016	$10.09	$14.57		$1,880.05
12/02/2016	$9.80	$14.25		$1,864.78
19/02/2016	$9.70	$13.93		$1,917.78
26/02/2016	$10.08	$14.66		$1,948.05
04/03/2016	$10.41	$15.09		$1,999.99
11/03/2016	$10.51	$15.21		$2,022.19
18/03/2016	$10.50	$15.42		$2,049.58
01/04/2016	$10.28	$15.08		$2,072.78
08/04/2016	$10.14	$14.59		$2,047.60
15/04/2016	$10.77	$15.74		$2,080.73
22/04/2016	$11.06	$16.16		$2,091.58

Date	WIBC	BBCN	HOPE	S&P 500
29/04/2016	$10.77	$15.62		$2,065.30
06/05/2016	$10.42	$15.11		$2,057.14
13/05/2016	$10.33	$14.98		$2,046.61
20/05/2016	$11.03	$15.68		$2,052.32
27/05/2016	$11.43	$16.26		$2,099.06
03/06/2016	$11.26	$16.03		$2,099.13
10/06/2016	$11.11	$15.81		$2,096.07
17/06/2016	$10.59	$15.13		$2,071.22
24/06/2016	$10.23	$14.64		$2,037.41
01/07/2016	$10.22	$14.63		$2,102.95
08/07/2016	$10.75	$15.30		$2,129.90
15/07/2016	$11.34	$16.10		$2,161.74
22/07/2016	$11.20	$15.88		$2,175.03
29/07/2016	$10.74	$15.37		$2,173.60
05/08/2016			$15.63	$2,182.87
12/08/2016			$15.36	$2,184.05
19/08/2016			$16.32	$2,183.87
26/08/2016			$16.85	$2,169.04
02/09/2016			$17.40	$2,179.98
09/09/2016			$17.21	$2,127.81
16/09/2016			$16.59	$2,139.16
23/09/2016			$17.03	$2,164.69
30/09/2016			$17.37	$2,168.27
07/10/2016			$17.58	$2,153.74
14/10/2016			$17.14	$2,132.98
21/10/2016			$16.22	$2,141.16
28/10/2016			$16.17	$2,126.41
04/11/2016			$15.45	$2,085.18
11/11/2016			$18.22	$2,164.45
18/11/2016			$19.62	$2,181.90
25/11/2016			$20.39	$2,213.35
02/12/2016			$19.99	$2,191.95
09/12/2016			$21.77	$2,259.53
16/12/2016			$21.75	$2,258.07
23/12/2016			$22.26	$2,263.79
30/12/2016			$21.89	$2,238.83

Exhibit C: Outstanding Shares and Spot Prices

	Wilshire		BBCN	
	Shares	*Spot price ($)*	*Shares*	*Spot price ($)*
09/30/2015	78,598,147	–	79,553,460	–
12/31/2015	78,643,353	11.55	79,566,356	17.22
03/31/2016	78,857,248	10.30	79,597,106	15.19
06/30/2016	78,891,607	–	79,606,821	–
07/29/2016	78,893,554	10.74	79,606,821	15.37

Exhibit D: Purchase Price Allocation

	$ Thousand
Cash and cash equivalents	100,127
Investment securities	478,938
Loans receivable	3,800,807
FRB and FHLB stock	16,539
OREO	14,866
Premises and equipment	16,812
BOLI	25,240
Servicing assets	16,203
Low income housing tax credit investments	47,111
Core deposit intangibles	18,138
Deferred tax assets, net	17,458
Other assets	76,818
Total assets	**4,629,057**
Deposits	3,812,367
Borrowings	206,282
Subordinated debentures	56,942
Other liabilities	54,751
Total liabilities	**4,130,342**

Exhibit E: Wilshire's Balance Sheet as of June 30, 2016

Assets	$ Thousand
Cash and cash equivalents	301,239
Investment securities	490,592
Total loans held for-sale	24,154
Real estate construction	50,240

Assets	$ Thousand
Residential real estate	234,979
Commercial real estate	2,719,111
Commercial and industrial	838,008
Consumer	9,590
Allowance for loan losses	(53,182)
Accrued interest receivable	8,882
Due from customers on acceptances	8,900
Other real estate owned	10,844
Premises and equipment	15,077
Federal home loan bank (FHLB) stock, at cost	16,539
Cash surrender value of life insurance	25,317
Investment in affordable housing partnerships	45,627
Deferred income taxes	17,803
Goodwill	67,473
Servicing assets	19,219
Other assets	36,373
Total assets	**4,886,785**
Noninterest-bearing demand deposits	1,134,671
Savings and interest checking	174,123
Money market deposits	1,005,142
Time deposits in denomination of $100,000 or more	1,407,025
Other time deposits	289,358
Total deposits	**4,010,319**
FHLB borrowings	200,000
Acceptance outstanding	8,900
Junior subordinated debentures	72,139
Accrued interest payable	2,417
Other liabilities	32,396
Total Liabilities	**4,326,171**
Common stock	234,917
Retained earnings	317,393
Accumulated other comprehensive income	8,304
Total shareholders' equity	**560,614**
Total liabilities and shareholders' equity	**4,886,785**

Exhibit F: BBCN's Balance Sheet as of June 30, 2016

Assets	$ Thousand
Cash and due from banks	96,814
Interest-bearing deposits in other banks	189,359
Other investments	44,465
Securities available for sale, at fair value	1,099,944
Loans held for sale, at the lower of cost or fair value	14,323
Loans receivable, net	6,507,812
Other real estate owned ("OREO"), net	16,392
Federal home loan bank ("FHLB") stock, at cost	18,964
Premises and equipment, net	37,663
Accrued interest receivable	15,787
Deferred tax assets, net	51,494
Customers' liabilities on acceptances	1,854
Bank owned life insurance ("BOLI")	47,562
Investments in affordable housing partnerships	24,029
Goodwill	105,401
Core deposit intangible assets, net	2,395
Servicing assets	12,193
Other assets	50,375
Total assets	**8,336,826**
Noninterest-bearing	1,717,045
Money market and NOW accounts	2,176,978
Savings deposits	173,549
Time deposits of $100,000 or more	1,828,649
Other time deposits	741,301
Total deposits	**6,637,522**
FHLB advances	610,398
Subordinated debentures	42,415
Accrued interest payable	7,164
Acceptances outstanding	1,854
Other liabilities	65,733
Total liabilities	**7,365,086**
Common stock, $0.001 par value; outstanding, 79,606,821	80
Additional paid-in capital	541,688
Retained earnings	418,998
Accumulated other comprehensive income (loss), net	10,974

Assets	$ Thousand
Total shareholders' equity	**971,740**
Total liabilities and shareholders' equity	**8,336,826**

References

Bank of Hope annual report 2016.
BBCN form 8-K, May 16, 2016.
BBCN Investor presentation, December 7, 2015.
BBCN quarterly report as of June 30, 2016.
Wilshire quarterly report as of June 30, 2016.

AT&T: Equity Method Investments

12

Introduction

AT&T Inc. ("AT&T" or "Company") is a holding company whose subsidiaries and affiliates operate worldwide in the telecommunications, media, and technology industries.[1] The Company has four reportable segments:

- Communications (84% of operating revenues);
- WarnerMedia (11% of operating revenues);
- Latin America (4% of operating revenues);
- Xandr, data, and advertising services (1% of operating revenues).

On June 14, 2018, the Company completed the acquisition of Time Warner Inc. ("Time Warner"), a leader in media and entertainment whose major businesses encompass an array of some of the most respected media brands. The total consideration equaled $79,358 million, excluding Time Warner's net debt at acquisition. The transaction was funded using both cash available and newly raised debt. AT&T consolidated Time Warner in its financial statements starting on June 14, 2018, in accordance with US GAAP.

The next table provides financial information on AT&T on a consolidated basis.

$ Million	2018	2017	2016
Income statement information			
Operating revenue	170,756	160,546	163,786
Operating expenses	(144,660)	(140,576)	(140,243)

[1] All market data in this case study are as of the time of the deal. They might have changed since then.

E. Amir and M. Ghitti, *Financial Analysis of Mergers and Acquisitions*,
https://doi.org/10.1007/978-3-030-61769-1_12

$ Million	2018	2017	2016
Operating income	**26,096**	**19,970**	**23,543**
Interest expense	7,957	6,300	4,910
Equity in net income (loss) of affiliates	(48)	(128)	98
Other income—net	6,782	1,597	1,081
Income tax (benefit) expense	4,920	(14,708)	6,479
Net income	**19,953**	**29,847**	**13,333**
Balance sheet information			
Total assets	531,864	444,097	403,821
Total debt (including current portion)	176,505	164,346	123,513
Shareholders' equity	193,884	142,007	124,110
Per share information			
Dividends declared per share	2.01	1.97	1.93
Book value of equity per share	26.63	23.13	20.22
Share price	28.46	38.88	42.53
Ratios			
Financial debt ratio (debt/total assets)	0.48	0.54	0.50
Earnings to fixed charges	3.42	2.63	3.59
Market-to-Book	1.07	1.68	2.10

Equity Method Investments

Following the acquisition of Time Warner, AT&T had investments in affiliates under the equity method. Equity method investments are recorded as non-current assets on the balance sheet (unless they are held for sale or distribution, in which case they are classified among current assets); the share in the net income of affiliates is presented on the income statement and increases the book value of the investment on the balance sheet (unless it is a net loss, in which case it decreases the investment's value on the balance sheet); dividends in cash received from these affiliates reduce the book value of the investment on the balance sheet and are presented in the operating section of the cash flow statement.

AT&T also acquired new investments in affiliates as part of the Time Warner acquisition. These investments include Hudson Yards, HBO Latin America Group, and Central European Media Enterprises (CME), among others. The following table presents the relevant line items for fiscals 2018 and 2017 (in $ million).

Income statements	2018	2017
Equity in net income (loss) of affiliates	(48)	(128)
Balance sheet		
Investments in and advances to Equity Affiliates	6,245	1,560
Cash flow statement		

Income statements	2018	2017
Cash flows from operating activities		
Undistributed earnings from investments in equity affiliates	292	174
Cash flows from investing activities		
Advances in and investments in equity affiliates	(1,050)	–

The large increase in the equity affiliates balance in fiscal 2018 was due primarily to the acquisition of Time Warner as outlined below.

The notes to AT&T's 2018 financial statements include the following details on equity method investments.

In the second quarter of 2018, we acquired Time Warner, which included various equity method investments. The differences between the fair value and the proportional book value of these investments' net assets were $2871. We attributed $1642 to amortizing intangibles, which will be amortized into earnings (…) over a weighted average life of 18.2 years. The earnings from these investments, subsequent to the acquisition-date, are included in the 2018 activity in the table below, as well as our consolidated statement of income for 2018 (…).

Our investments in equity affiliates at December 31, 2018 primarily include our interests in Hudson Yards [50.0%], *HBO Latin America Group* [88.2%], *Hulu* [10.0%], *Central European Media Enterprises Ltd.* [66.6%], *and SKY Mexico* [41.3%].

The following table is a reconciliation of our investments in equity affiliates as presented on our consolidated balance sheets (dollars in millions):

$ Million	2018	2017
Beginning of year	*1,560*	*1,674*
Additional investments	*237*	*51*
Time Warner investments acquired	*4,912*	–
Acquisition of remaining interests in Otter Media	*(166)*	–
Equity in net income (loss) of affiliates	*(48)*	*(128)*
Dividends and distributions received	*(243)*	*(46)*
Currency translation adjustments	*(14)*	*22*
Other adjustments	*7*	*(13)*
Total	***6,245***	***1,560***

On August 7, 2018, AT&T acquired the remaining interest in Otter Media Holdings for $157 million in cash and the conversion to equity of the $1,480 million advance made in the first quarter. At acquisition, the fair value of the total business exceeded the book value of AT&T's equity method investment and resulted in a pretax gain of $395 million. The Company consolidated that business upon close and recorded those assets at fair value, including $1,239 million of goodwill (reported in the WarnerMedia segment).

Questions

1. During fiscal 2018, AT&T purchased the remaining interests in Otter Media. Following this purchase, Otter Media became a consolidated wholly owned subsidiary of AT&T. Discuss the accounting consequences of this transaction. Be as specific as possible.
2. During fiscal 2018, AT&T acquired Time Warner. As part of the acquisition, AT&T also acquired the equity investments owned by Time Warner. Assume that all the excess of fair value over book values is attributed to CME. While AT&T holds 66.6% of CME, the company is accounted for under the equity method. Using the balance sheet and income statement of AT&T (**Exhibit A** and **B**) and CME (**Exhibit C** and **D**), present the balance sheet of AT&T as if CME is (i) fully consolidated under the purchase method, and (ii) included under the proportionate consolidation (assume a 30% tax rate).

   Note that CME did not distribute any dividends during the period. In fact, the change in the "Accumulated deficit" line item from fiscal 2017 (−$1,736 million) to fiscal 2018 (−$1,578 million) is equal to the net income generated through the year ($158 million). If needed, make additional assumptions to complete the required analysis.
3. Assume now that shortly after the date of acquisition, on July 1, 2018, CME distributed $120 million in dividends to its shareholders. These dividends came from retained earnings accumulated prior to the acquisition. Accounting rules require that such dividends should be taken into account in determining the consideration and purchase price allocation. How would your answers to question 2 change? CME has a large deficit and most likely cannot pay dividends. However, ignore that in your analysis.

Exhibit A: AT&T's Consolidated Balance Sheet as of December 31, 2018

$ Million	31.12.2018	31.12.2017
Cash and cash equivalents	5,204	50,498
Receivables	26,472	16,522
Prepaid expenses	2,047	1,369
Other current assets	17,704	10,757
Total current assets	**51,427**	**79,146**
Property and equipment, net	131,473	125,222
Goodwill	146,370	105,449
Intangible assets	163,827	114,276
Equity affiliates	6,245	1,560
Other assets	32,522	18,444
Total assets	**531,864**	**444,097**

$ Million	31.12.2018	31.12.2017
Short-term debt	10,255	38,374
Payables	43,184	34,470
Other current liabilities	10,981	8,545
Total current liabilities	**64,420**	**81,389**
Long-term debt	166,250	125,972
Deferred income taxes	57,859	43,207
Other non-current liabilities	49,451	51,522
Total liabilities	**337,980**	**302,090**
Common stock	621	6,495
Additional paid-in capital	125,525	89,563
Retained earnings	58,753	50,500
Treasury stock, at cost	(12,059)	(12,714)
Accumulated other comprehensive income	4,249	7,017
Total shareholders' equity	**184,089**	**140,861**
Non-controlling interests	9,795	1,146
Total equity	**193,884**	**142,007**
Total liabilities and equity	**531,864**	**444,097**

Exhibit B: AT&T's Consolidated Income Statement as of December 31, 2018

$ Million	31.12.2018	31.12.2017
Revenues	170,756	160,546
Cost of sales	(79,419)	(77,810)
Gross profit	**91,337**	**82,736**
SG&A expenses	(36,765)	(35,465)
Asset abandonments and impairment	(46)	(2,914)
Depreciation and amortization	(28,430)	(24,387)
Operating income	**26,096**	**19,970**
Interest expenses	(7,957)	(6,300)
Equity in net income (loss) of affiliates	(48)	(128)
Other income (expense), net	6,782	1,597
Income before taxes	**24,873**	**15,139**
Income taxes	(4920)	14,708
Net income	**19,953**	**29,847**
Non-controlling interests	(583)	(397)
Net income attributable to AT&T	**19,370**	**29,450**

Exhibit C: CME's Consolidated Balance Sheet as of December 31, 2018

$ Million	31.12.2018	31.12.2017
Cash and cash equivalents	62	59
Receivables	193	184
Prepaid expenses	–	–
Other current assets	119	178
Total current assets	**374**	**421**
Property and equipment, net	118	119
Goodwill	676	712
Intangible assets	308	358
Equity affiliates	–	–
Other assets	12	17
Total assets	**1,488**	**1,628**
Short-term debt	6	3
Payables	120	160
Other current liabilities	14	24
Total current liabilities	**140**	**187**
Long-term debt	783	1,086
Deferred income taxes	–	–
Other non-current liabilities	67	96
Total liabilities	**990**	**1,369**
Common stock	20	12
Convertible redeemable preferred stocks	269	265
Additional paid-in capital	2,004	1,906
Retained earnings	(1,578)	(1,736)
Treasury stock, at cost	–	–
Accumulated other comprehensive income	(217)	(187)
Total shareholders' equity	**498**	**259**
Non-controlling interests	–	–
Total equity	**499**	**259**
Total liabilities and equity	**1,488**	**1,628**

Exhibit D: CME's Consolidated Income Statement as of December 31, 2018

$ Million	31.12.2018	31.12.2017
Revenues	704	643
Cost of sales	(366)	(350)
Gross profit	**338**	**293**

$ Million	31.12.2018	31.12.2017
SG&A expenses	(118)	(113)
Asset abandonments and impairment	–	–
Depreciation and amortization	(42)	(40)
Operating income	**178**	**140**
Interest expenses	(50)	(83)
Equity in net income (loss) of affiliates	–	–
Other income (expense), net	(3)	17
Income before taxes	**125**	**74**
Income taxes	(28)	(23)
Income from continuing operations	**97**	**51**
Income from discontinued operations	61	(2)
Net income	**158**	**49**
Non-controlling interests	–	–
Net income attributable to CME	**158**	**50**

References

AT&T annual report 2017.
AT&T annual report 2018.
CME annual report 2018.

Nokia Siemens Networks: Purchase Accounting, Equity Method, and Proportionate Consolidation

13

Introduction

On June 19, 2006, Nokia Corporation ("Nokia") and Siemens AG ("Siemens") announced the merger of Nokia's Network Business Group and Siemens' Carrier-Related operations into a new legal entity. The newly created entity was called Nokia Siemens Networks ("NSN") and with combined pro-forma revenues for fiscal 2007 of €17 billion the merged entity was ranked among the top three industry leaders in the telecom vendor sector. **Exhibit A** contains the press release issued on June 19, 2006.

Prior to the transaction, Nokia and Siemens each owned 100% of their respective subsidiaries: Nokia's Network Manufacturing Unit and Siemens Network Manufacturing Units (**Exhibits B** and **C**). As part of the transaction, each entity relinquished control of its respective subsidiary for a 50% stake in NSN (**Exhibit D**). The economic rationale for this transaction is that Nokia (Siemens) gives up 50% stake in its subsidiary in return for 50% stake in Siemens' (Nokia's) subsidiary.

The main features of the transaction are the following:

- both Nokia and Siemens transferred to NSN total assets with a combined fair value of €13.76 billion and total liabilities with a combined fair value of €9.30 billion. The combined net book value of the new entity was about €4.46 billion with Siemens contributing €2.68 billion in fair value of net assets and Nokia €1.785 billion. The assets and liabilities transferred were measured at the lower of their carrying amount and fair value less costs to sell. These values represent fair value for the purpose of this case study. **Exhibit E** presents a pro-forma

This case study was originally written by Arik Parizer and Awais Raoof under the supervision of Professor Eli Amir, at London Business School, for class discussion in Eli Amir's financial analysis course. The case was then revised by Eli Amir and Marco Ghitti for this book. All market data in this case study are as of the time of the deal. They might have changed since then.

E. Amir and M. Ghitti, *Financial Analysis of Mergers and Acquisitions*,
https://doi.org/10.1007/978-3-030-61769-1_13

balance sheet of NSN. **Exhibit F** presents income statements for fiscal 2006 and 2007 as if NSN existed since the beginning of 2006;

- the transaction was expected to close around December 31, 2006, but, due to fraud allegations at Siemens, the transaction was delayed by several months and was finally closed in April 2007. To compensate Nokia for this delay, Siemens contributed €340 million in net cash (not included in assets transferred) to NSN without an increase in its share in the joint venture;
- DCF valuation of NSN's operations estimated the entity's enterprise value at €19.36 billion (this figure was subject to change following the purchase price allocation process during 2007). The fair value of NSN's debt was estimated at €4.47 billion (as in **Exhibit E**). So the fair value of NSN's equity was estimated at €14.90 billion (reflecting a market-to-book equity of 14.90/4.46 = 3.34). For the purpose of this case, it is assumed that, following the cash injection, the fair value of equity (net assets) is unchanged at €14.90 billion;
- Siemens and Nokia each owned an economic share of approximately 50% of NSN as a result of the deal;
- Nokia got four out of seven directors on the managing board of the joint entity; Siemens got three directors. Initially, this case assumes that the transaction is a joint venture. In practice, the ability to appoint the majority of the board indicates control;
- Nokia and Siemens expected to realize a significant non-cash gain on this transaction. Also, each company acquired a significant element of goodwill.

In its financial statements, Siemens listed the assets and liabilities that it intended to transfer to the joint venture, which were disclosed in the assets and liabilities held for disposal at the lower between cost and value-in-use rather than at fair value.

Companies

At the time of the transaction, Nokia was a manufacturer of mobile phones offering consumers a range of mobile devices. With annual sales of €41 billion, it also provided equipment, solutions, and services for network operators, service providers, and corporations. Nokia operated through four business groups: Mobile Phones, Multimedia, Enterprise Solutions, and Networks. The company was listed on both the Finnish and the New York Stock Exchanges. In 1992, Nokia decided to focus on its telecommunications business. This was the most important strategic decision in the company's history which led it to sell its billionth mobile phone business in Nigeria during 2005. **Exhibit G** presents Nokia's balance sheet for fiscal 2006 before the transaction with Siemens. **Exhibit I** presents Nokia's income statements for fiscal 2006 and 2005 prior to the transaction with Siemens.

Based in Germany, Siemens was, at the time of the transaction, a multinational company with a business portfolio in the field of electronics and electrical engineering. The company was listed on the Xetra Stock Exchange, London Stock Exchange, and the New York Stock Exchange. Annual sales were €87 billion in 2006 (**Exhibit H** and **Exhibit J**).

Exhibit K presents the income statements of Nokia and Siemens for fiscal 2006 excluding the effect of NSN.

Consolidation in the Telecom Sector

During the first decade of the twenty-first century, the telecom sector was reshaping through large mergers in response to increased competition through a similar consolidation at the operators level. In the US, SBC paid about $16 billion for AT&T, and then spent a further $67 billion to buy Bellsouth. In Europe, Telefonica, Spain's national carrier, acquired O2 from British Telecom while NTL paid £962 million for Virgin Mobile. Meanwhile the world's largest mobile operator, Vodafone, departed from its global ambitions and sold its Japanese subsidiary to Softbank for $15.4 billion.

In addition to this unprecedented wave of M&A activities, world telecom leaders were spending enormous amounts building "next-generation networks." Verizon spent $18 billion on its new network, while BT spent in excess of £10 billion on networks. Meanwhile, internet leaders such as Google, Yahoo!, and Microsoft's MSN entered the telecom business by offering free call over the internet through Voice over Internet Protocol (VOIP). For example, eBay spent $2.6 billion to acquire Skype. The aim of the Telecom leaders was to be able to offer the end-customer a quadruple play: fixed line, mobile, internet, and television, from one single provider.

The benefits to the provider were:

- reduced churn—customers who sign up for a bundle of services would not be able to defect to a rival provider of any one of the services without losing substantial discounts;
- reduced costs of acquiring new customers—providers would reduce advertising expense for customer's acquisitions and other marketing costs, because all services would be advertised together under one bundle.

The convergence into a single bundle "quadruple play" had its doubters. Mr Arun Sarin, the Chief Executive of Vodafone, had taken cautious view on this convergence, noting:

> It's very early days….it is wrong to assume that everyone wants quadruple-play. We are not saying that there are no customers who demand these services. We are only saying it's a very small fraction of customers. (*The Economist*, October 14, 2006)

In response to the increased buyer power exerted by the larger consolidated Telecom operators, also the Network Manufacturers begun to consolidate in order to increase their selling and negotiating powers while maintaining their previous margins. Some of the large consolidations in the market at that time included some telecoms giants such as: Alcatel-Lucent, Ericsson-Marconi, and Nokia Siemens.

Accounting Methods

Accounting for inter-corporate investments depends primarily on the level of ownership and control of the investor over the investee. Under IFRS, investments are recognized on the investor's financial statements as follows:

a. *Cost/Mark-to-Market:* when a company acquires a financial asset (invests in the shares or bonds of another entity without having significant influence), the initial investments is recognized at cost (which is equal to fair value at the time of the investment). Subsequently, the investment is generally treated, according to IFRS 9, as follows:

- *amortised cost*—a financial asset is measured at amortized cost if both of the following conditions are met (held-to-maturity):
  - the asset is held within a business model whose objective is to hold assets in order to collect contractual cash flows and
  - the contractual terms of the financial asset give rise on specified dates to cash flows that are solely payments of principal and interest on the principal amount outstanding;
- *fair value through other comprehensive income*—financial assets are classified and measured at fair value through other comprehensive income if they are held in a business model whose objective is achieved by both collecting contractual cash flows and selling financial assets (available for sale);
- *fair value through profit or loss*—any financial assets that are not held in one of the two business models mentioned are measured at fair value through profit or loss (trading), which is presumed to be the standard;
- *fair value option*—An entity may, at initial recognition, irrevocably designate a financial asset or liability that would otherwise have to be measured at amortized cost or fair value through other comprehensive income, to be measured at fair value through profit or loss if doing so would eliminate or significantly reduce a measurement or recognition inconsistency (sometimes referred to as an "accounting mismatch") or otherwise results in more relevant information;

b. *equity method* (IAS 28): when the investor has significant influence over the investee (usually between 20% and 50% of the voting shares), the equity method must be used. Under this method, the investment is recognized initially at cost. Subsequently, it is measured at cost plus the investor's share in changes in the net assets of the investee. The investor's share in the investee's net income is recognized on the investor's income statement. The equity method is also required in almost all joint ventures;
c. *purchase accounting* (IFRS 3 and IFRS 10, effective 2013): when the investor controls the investee (for example, it owns more than 50% of the investee's voting shares), full consolidation is required using the purchase method. This requires full consolidation of all assets and liabilities on the parent's balance sheet at fair value. That is, all assets and liabilities of the acquired company must be revalued to fair values at time of acquisition.

The excess of the acquisition consideration over the fair value of net assets acquired is recognized as goodwill on the acquirer's balance sheet. Subsequently, goodwill must be assessed at least annually for impairment and is not amortized. This accounting methodology is similar under US GAAP.

If the investor owns less than 100% of the voting shares, non-controlling interests (NCI) must be recognized. NCI represent the share of the minorities in the investee's net assets. The consolidated income statement reflects the total income of all subsidiaries less the share attributed to the non-controlling interests.

The accounting treatment of goodwill and non-controlling interests underwent serious changes with the introduction of IFRS 10 (2013):

- before IFRS 10 (2013):
  - goodwill and non-controlling interests were recognized only under the partial method;
  - goodwill was assessed multiple times in step acquisitions;
  - gains and losses were recognized (in the income statement) in disposal even if control was retained;
- after IFRS 10 (2013):
  - goodwill and non-controlling interests may be recognized under the partial or the full method;
  - goodwill is assessed only once, when control is achieved;
  - in partial disposals, gains and losses are recognized (in the income statement) only when control is relinquished;
  - in step acquisitions, gains and losses are recognized (in the income statement) on existing holdings, when control is achieved.

Questions

1. Discuss the operating strategy of Nokia and Siemens. How do joint ventures in general and this joint venture in particular fit into this strategy?
2. Discuss the advantages and disadvantages of the equity and the purchase accounting methods for Nokia and Siemens. Explain briefly which method would be most appropriate for Nokia and Siemens under IFRS.
3. Assume that both Nokia and Siemens hold equal shares in NSN, calculate the after-tax gain from disposal and the subsequent acquired goodwill on the transaction (assume a 35% tax rate). Discuss whether the gains are recognized in the income statement or not.
4. Repeat the calculations of question 3, adjusting for the additional €340 million contributed by Siemens as a compensation for the delays caused by fraud allegations at Siemens.
5. Prepare Nokia's pro-forma consolidated balance sheet and income statement as of December 31, 2006 with NSN using the equity method, the proportionate method and the purchased method. Assume that the NSN transaction was completed prior to December 31, 2006.
6. Prepare Siemens' pro-forma consolidated balance sheet and income statement as of December 31, 2006 with NSN using the equity method and the proportionate method.

7. Which method would be preferred by Nokia's management? Siemens Management? Why? Back up your answer using basic ratio analysis.

Exhibit A—Nokia AB and Siemens AG Joint Press Release, June 19, 2006

Nokia and Siemens today announced that they intend to merge the Networks Business Group of Nokia and the carrier-related operations of Siemens into a new company, to be called Nokia Siemens Networks. The 50-50 joint venture will create a global leader with strong positions in important growth segments of fixed and mobile network infrastructure and services.

The combined company is positioned to lead the development and implementation of revenue-generating and cost-saving products and services via its scale and global reach. Nokia Siemens Networks will have one of the world's best research and development teams with the ability to invest in next generation fixed and mobile product platforms and services. The new company will have a world-class fixed-mobile convergence capability, a complementary global base of customers, a deep presence in both developed and emerging markets, and one of the industry's largest and most experienced service organizations.

"We believe the partnership with Siemens is the most effective way to build the scale and broad product portfolio necessary to compete globally and create value for shareholders," said Olli-Pekka Kallasvuo, CEO of Nokia. "The communications industry is converging, and a strong and independent Nokia Siemens Networks will be ideally positioned to help customers lower costs and grow revenue while managing the challenges of converging technology" Olli-Pekka Kallasvuo will serve as chairman of Nokia Siemens Networks.

"This joint venture is an important step to strengthen our position in the market sustainably and to enable us to offer the best state of the art converged technologies and services to our customers," said Klaus Kleinfeld, CEO of Siemens. "This combination creates a leading industry player with immediate strength, excellent potential for growth and well-positioned to improve future profitability."

Strong Player with Scale and Powerful Convergence Portfolio

Based on the 2005 calendar year, the combined company had €15.8 billion in pro-forma annual revenues and is expected to start operations with 60,000 employees. Based on current market share data, it will be the second largest company in mobile infrastructure, second in services, third in fixed infrastructure, and the third largest in the overall telecommunications infrastructure market.

Nokia Siemens Networks will be able to offer its operator customers a comprehensive portfolio of fixed and mobile network products supported by a full range of professional services. The company's portfolio will include Next Generation Network convergence products like IMS, 2G GSM/EDGE access, 3G WCDMA/HSDPA access, extensive mobile core, fixed broadband, transport, IPTV, LTE, WiMAX, and low-cost mobile voice products tailored for emerging market operators.

Extensive Synergy Benefits

The estimated cost synergies of €1.5 billion annually by 2010 are expected to come primarily from the elimination of overlapping functions, consolidation and better utilization of sales and marketing organizations, reduction of overhead costs, sourcing benefits, and greater efficiencies in R&D.

A substantial portion of these synergies is expected to be realized in the first two years. These changes are expected to result in a headcount adjustment over the next four years in the range of ten to fifteen percent from the initial combined base of approximately 60,000. Detailed headcount reduction assessments will be made as part of the integration planning process and subject to required consultation with employee representatives.

Both Nokia and Siemens expect the impact of the partnership on their respective EPS, on a pro-forma basis excluding the restructuring charges, to be accretive by the end of 2007, assuming a closing by January 1, 2007.

Global Company and Leadership

Nokia Siemens Networks will have its operational headquarters in the Helsinki, Finland metropolitan area, and have strong regional headquarters in Munich, Germany, where three of the future five divisions of the new company will be based.

Simon Beresford-Wylie, currently Executive Vice President and General Manager of Networks at Nokia, will assume the position of chief executive officer immediately upon the closing of the merger. "Nokia Siemens Networks brings the two finest teams in the communications industry together at an unprecedented time of industry change," said Simon Beresford-Wylie. "I know the power of the Nokia team and have a deep appreciation for the quality and spirit of the people of Siemens. Together, the collective Nokia and Siemens teams will be a powerful force in the industry as we pursue our future goals of providing unequaled customer satisfaction and of becoming the undisputed industry champion." In addition to Simon Beresford-Wylie, Peter Schönhofer will assume the position of CFO. Schönhofer is currently a member of the executive board of Siemens AG Austria.

The transaction closing is expected to take place before January 1, 2007 and is subject to customary regulatory approvals, the completion of standard closing conditions, and the agreement of a number of detailed implementation steps. After closing, the financial results of Nokia Siemens Networks will be consolidated by Nokia and accounted for at equity by Siemens.

Exhibit B—NSN

See Fig. 13.1.

Exhibit C—Corporate Holdings Prior to the Joint Venture

See Fig. 13.2.

Exhibit D—Corporate Holdings Following the Joint Venture

See Fig. 13.3.

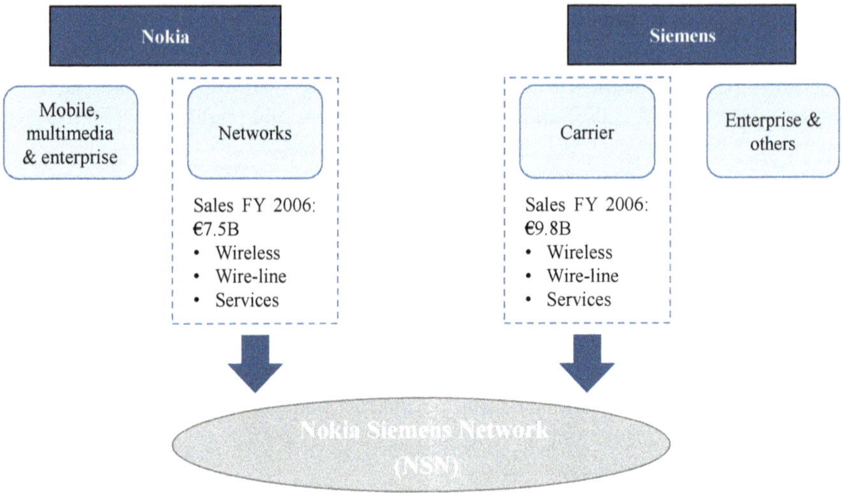

Fig. 13.1 Nokia and Siemens

Fig. 13.2 Nokia and Siemens business units

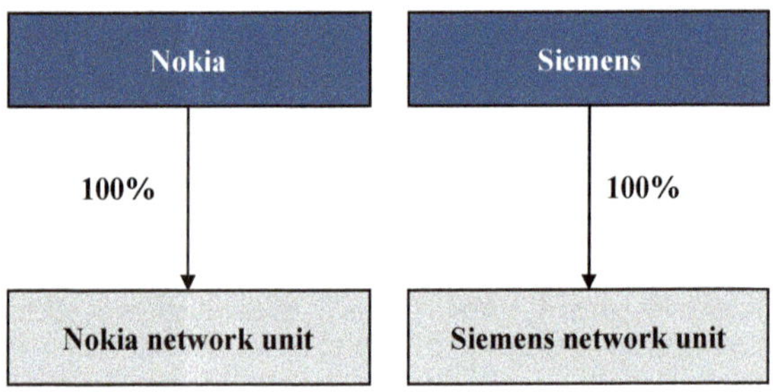

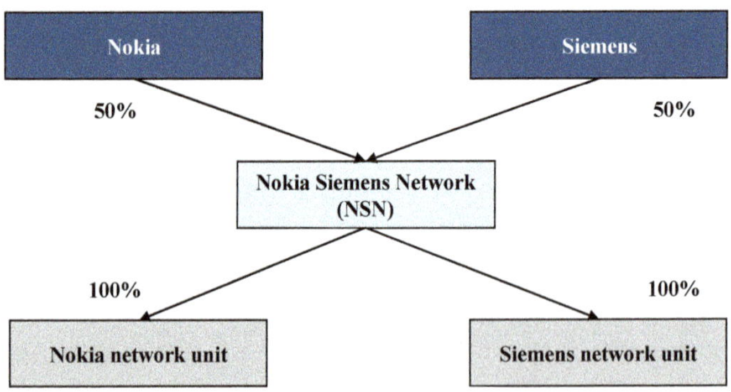

Fig. 13.3 Nokia Siemens network

Exhibit E—Balance Sheet of the Joint Venture as of December 31, 2006

€ Million	Siemens	Nokia	Combined
Cash and cash equivalents	383	255	638
Trade and other receivables	2,872	1,915	4,787
Inventories	2,219	1,479	3,698
Goodwill	392	261	653
Property, plant, and equipment	696	464	1,160
Other assets	1,696	1,131	2,827
Assets classified as held for sale	**8,258**	**5,505**	**13,763**
Trade payables	1,959	1,306	3,265
Current provisions	498	332	830
Pension plans and similar commitments	334	223	557
Non-current provisions	108	72	180
Other liabilities	2,681	1,787	4,468
Total liabilities	**5,580**	**3,720**	**9,300**
Net assets	**2,678**	**1,785**	**4,463**

Exhibit F—Pro-Forma Income Statements for NSN

€ Million	2006	2007
Sales	17,272	17,688
Operating costs	(15,372)	(15,742)
Restructuring charges	–	(700)
Depreciation	(691)	(708)
Annual synergies	–	100
Operating profits	**1,209**	**638**
Interest	(422)	(388)
Income before taxes	**787**	**250**
Taxes	(118)	(62)
Net Income	**669**	**187**

Operating costs (€15,372 + €691) breakdown:

- cost of sales, €12,326;
- R&D expenses, €1,306;
- selling and marketing expenses, €2,319;
- administrative and general expenses, €109;
- other income, €102;
- other expenses, €105.

Exhibit G—Nokia's Balance Sheet as of December 31, 2006

Assets	€ Million
Inventories	1,554
Accounts receivables	5,888
Prepaid expenses	2,496
Other financial assets	111
Available for sale investments, liquid assets	5,012
Available for sale investments, cash equivalents	2,046
Bank and cash	1,479
Total current assets	**18,586**
Capitalized development costs	251
Goodwill	532
Other intangible assets	298
Property, plant, and equipment	1,602
Investment in associated companies	224
Available for sale investments	288
Deferred tax assets	809
Long-term loans receivable	19
Other non-current assets	8
Investment in NSN	–
Total assets	**22,617**
Short-term borrowings	247
Accounts payable	3,732
Accrued expenses	3,796
Provisions, current	2,386
Total current liabilities	**10,161**
Long-term interest bearing liabilities	69
Deferred tax liabilities	205
Other long-term liabilities	122
Provisions, long-term	–
Total liabilities	**10,557**
Share capital	246
Share issue premium	2,707
Treasury shares, at cost	(2,060)
Translation differences	(34)
Fair value and other reserves	(14)
Retained earnings	11,123

Assets	€ Million
Gain due to acquisition	–
Total shareholders' equity	**11,968**
Minority interests	92
Total shareholder's equity and liabilities	**22,617**

Exhibit H—Siemens Consolidated Balance Sheet as of September 30, 2006

Assets	€ Million	Transferred
Cash and cash equivalents	10,214	
Marketable securities	596	
Accounts receivable, net	15,149	
Inventories, net	12,790	
Deferred income taxes	1,468	
Assets held for disposal	7,189	6,562
Other current assets	4,205	
Total current assets	**51,611**	
Long-term investments	3,922	
Goodwill	9,776	
Other intangible assets, net	3,243	
Property, plant and equipment, net	12,072	
Deferred income taxes	4,983	
Other assets	5,366	1,696
Total assets	**90,973**	**8,258**
Short-term debt	2,175	
Accounts payable	8,444	
Accrued liabilities	9,126	
Deferred income taxes	516	
Liabilities held for disposal	5,545	5,580
Other current liabilities	13,151	
Total current liabilities	**38,957**	
Long-term debt	13,399	
Pension plans and similar commitments	4,101	
Deferred income taxes	450	
Other accruals and provisions	4,058	
Total non-current liabilities	**22,008**	
Common stock	2,673	
Additional paid in capital	5,175	

Assets	€ Million	Transferred
Retained earnings	28,320	
Accumulated other comprehensive income	(6,862)	
Treasury stock	–	
Total equity	**29,306**	
Minority interests	702	
Total liabilities and equity	**90,973**	

Exhibit I—Nokia's Income Statement as of December 31, 2006

€ Million	2006	2005
Net sales	41,121	34,191
Cost of sales	(27,742)	(22,209)
Gross profit	**13,379**	**11,982**
R&D expenses	(3,897)	(3,825)
Selling and marketing expenses	(3,314)	(2,961)
Administrative and general expense	(666)	(609)
Other income	522	285
Other expenses	(536)	(233)
Operating Profit	**5,488**	**4,639**
Share of results of associated cos.	28	10
Financial income and expenses	207	322
Profit before taxes	**5,723**	**4,971**
Taxes	(1,357)	(1,281)
Profit before minority interests	**4,366**	**3,690**
Minority interests	(60)	(74)
Profit attributable to equity	**4,306**	**3,616**
Earnings per share		
Basic	1.06	0.83
Diluted	1.05	0.83
Average number of shares		
Basic	4,062,833	4,365,647
Diluted	4,086,529	4,371,239

Exhibit J—Siemens' Income Statement as of September 30, 2006

€ Million	2006	2005
Net sales	87,325	75,445
Cost of sales	(63,812)	(54,146)
Gross profit	**23,513**	**21,299**
R&D	(5,024)	(4,511)
Marketing, selling and general expenses	(15,470)	(13,684)
Other operating income (expense), net	205	(9)
Income from investment in other companies	647	584
Income from financial assets and marketable securities, net	337	297
Interest expense of operations, net	(39)	(32)
Other interest income (expense), net	202	241
Income from continuing operations before taxes	**4,371**	**4,185**
Income taxes	(1,078)	(979)
Minority interests	(206)	(148)
Income from continuing operations	**3,087**	**3,058**
Income (loss) from discontinued operations, net of taxes	(54)	(810)
Net income	**3,033**	**2,248**
Basic earnings per share		
Income from continuing operations	3.47	3.43
Loss from discontinued operations	(0.0606)	(0.909)
Net Income	3.40	2.52
Diluted earnings per share		
Income from continuing operations	3.29	3.27
Loss from discontinued operations	(0.058)	(0.865)
Net income	3.23	2.40
Weighted average shares outstanding-basic	890,850	890,732
Weighted average shares outstanding-diluted	937,620	936,530

Exhibit K—Nokia and Siemens Income Statements for Fiscal 2006 Excluding NSN

€ Million	Nokia	Siemens
Net sales	33,608	77,566
Cost of sales	(22,302)	(56,926)
Gross profit	**11,306**	**20,640**
R&D expenses	(3,133)	(4,482)
Selling and marketing expenses	(2,664)	(13,801)
Administrative and general expense	(535)	183
Other income	420	353
Other expenses	(431)	–
Operating Profit	**4,962**	**2,894**
Share of results of associated cos.	28	782
Financial income and expenses	391	197
Profit before taxes	**5,381**	**3,873**
Taxes	(1,306)	(1,011)
Profit before minority interests	**4,075**	**2,861**
Minority interests	(60)	(206)
Profit attributable to equity	**4,015**	**2,655**

References

Nokia and Siemens Joint Press Release, June 19, 2006.
NSN annual report 2016.
Nokia annual report 2016.
Siemens annual report 2016.

Ensign Group: The Spin-Off of CareTrust REIT

14

Introduction

The Ensign Group Inc. ("Ensign"), founded in 1999, provides assisted living and skilled nursing services in its own centers. Ensign's independent operating subsidiaries offer a broad spectrum of skilled nursing and assisted living services, physical, occupational and speech therapies, home health and hospice services, urgent care services and other rehabilitative and healthcare services at 230 facilities and 46 home health, hospice and home care agencies in California, Arizona, Texas, Washington, Utah, Idaho, Colorado, Nevada, Iowa, Oklahoma, and Oregon.

On November 7, 2013 Ensign announced the spin-off of its real estate into a real estate investment trust ("REIT") named CareTrust REIT ("CTRE") (**Exhibit A**). On June 1, 2014 the spin-off was completed (**Exhibit B** and **C**). The transaction unlocked value for the existing shareholders, and created an attractive investment for new and existing investors.[1]

The spin-off cleared Ensign's balance sheet from debt by transferring it to the spun-off entity (**Exhibit D** and **E**). This was done through financing received by CTRE and payment to Ensign. Furthermore, CTRE guaranteed a revolving credit facility of up to $150 million (with a low cost of debt), which allowed Ensign and CTRE to finance acquisitions as part of an aggressive growth strategy in a fragmented industry during a time when opportunities seemed to be plentiful.

---

[1]This case study analyzes the spin-off transaction based on the consolidated financial statements of Ensign (not its separate financial statements).

This Case Study was originally written by Joan Esteve Manasanch under the supervision of Professor Eli Amir, at London Business School, for class discussion in Eli Amir's financial analysis course. Eli Amir and Marco Ghitti then revised the case for this book. All market data in this case study are as of the time of the deal. They might have changed since then.

E. Amir and M. Ghitti, *Financial Analysis of Mergers and Acquisitions*,
https://doi.org/10.1007/978-3-030-61769-1_14

The real estate was to be leased back from CTRE to Ensign at a level of EBITDAR coverage ratio of 1.85, which is a low enough level to provide handsome margins for Ensign. The fixed rent in this case is a benefit for Ensign.

The spin-off gave Ensign the resources (clearing its debt and providing it with additional available financing) to pursue an aggressive growth strategy, and increase its profitability through effective capital allocation and business strategy focus. Coupled with the fact that Ensign was trading at depressed price levels both in absolute terms and in relation to its peers, the transaction resulted in an increased share price, unlocking approximately $200 million of shareholders' value out of a company with a market capitalization of $966 million.

REIT

A REIT is a stock-like security and, similar to stocks, it can be either publicly traded or private. The REIT invests in real estate directly, either by buying properties or mortgages. REITs receive special tax considerations and typically offer investors high yield, and a highly liquid investment in real estate. REITs both invest in and own properties (thus being responsible for the equity or value of their real estate assets). Their revenues come principally from their properties' rents.

The Spin-Off Transaction

Ensign was to separate its healthcare business and its real estate business into two separate and independent publicly traded companies, that is:

- Ensign, which would continue to provide healthcare services through its existing operations; and
- CTRE, which would own, acquire and lease real estate, serving the healthcare industry.

Ensign would accomplish the separation by distributing all of the outstanding common shares of CTRE to Ensign shareholders on a pro-rata basis. At the time of the Spin-off, CTRE, which was a wholly owned subsidiary of Ensign, held substantially all of the real estate owned by Ensign, and would operate three independent living facilities. After the spin-off, all of these properties (other than the three independent living facilities that CTRE would operate) would be leased to Ensign on a triple-net basis, under which Ensign would be responsible for all costs at the properties, including property taxes, insurance, maintenance and repair costs. CTRE intended to elect to be taxed and to qualify as a real estate investment trust for US federal income tax purposes commencing with its taxable year ending December 31, 2014.

Each Ensign shareholder would receive one ordinary share of CTRE for every share of Ensign held on May 22, 2014, the record date for the Spin-off. Following the Spin-off, shareholders would own shares in both Ensign and CTRE. The number of Ensign shares owned would not change as a result of the spin-off.

CTRE applied to list its common shares on the NASDAQ Global Select Market ("NASDAQ") under the symbol "CTRE." Ensign common shares would continue to be listed and traded on NASDAQ under the symbol "ENSG."

CTRE portfolio would consist of substantially all of the skilled nursing, assisted living, and independent living facilities owned by Ensign. CTRE expected to diversify its tenant base in the future by acquiring additional properties and leasing them to other local, regional and national healthcare providers. CTRE also expected to grow and diversify its portfolio through the acquisition of properties in different geographic markets, and in different asset classes.

Reasons for the Spin-Off

The strategic consideration and nature of Ensign's healthcare business dictated and limited the size and scope of its real estate business. After the Spin-off, CTRE would be able to make decisions regarding the real estate business irrespective of Ensign healthcare business. As a result, CTRE intended to expand into new geographic areas, acquire properties in different asset classes, diversify its tenant base and reduce its financing costs. At the same time, Ensign expected to realize benefits from being a "pure play" healthcare operator and intended to continue to pursue its historical growth practices and strategies. As such, management, regulators, market analysts, and investors would be able to focus solely on Ensign's healthcare operations.

Financing

CTRE expected to put in place a capital structure providing the flexibility to grow, and a cost of debt capital allowing it to compete for investment opportunities. Financing arrangements included bank debt, bonds, a revolving credit facility, and long-term mortgage financing.

Prior to the Spin-off, CTRE was to issue up to $260.0 million aggregate principal amount of senior unsecured notes. It would also enter into a credit agreement providing for a revolving credit facility in an aggregate principal amount of up to $150.0 million to be provided by a syndicate of banks and other financial institutions.

In connection with the Spin-off, CTRE would transfer to Ensign approximately $220.8 million of proceeds from the notes issuance in order for Ensign to repay certain debt (including trade payables) and, subject to the approval of Ensign's board of directors, pay up to eight regular quarterly dividends.

The amount of proceeds to be transferred to Ensign was determined based on the desired market capitalization of Ensign and CTRE after the Spin-off. It was not determined based on any appraisal or valuation of the CTRE properties. CTRE would use a portion of the proceeds from the notes issuance to pay the cash portion of the purging distribution, which it expected to make by December 31, 2014.

Prior to the spin-off, CTRE also intended to obtain additional mortgage indebtedness of approximately $50.5 million. After the Spin-off, the remaining proceeds from the notes issuance, the net proceeds from the additional mortgage indebtedness and borrowings under its revolving credit facility would be available for working capital purposes, to fund acquisitions and for general corporate purposes.

Accounting

The spin-off was executed via a corporate tax-free, pro-rata share distribution. The main effect of the spin-off on the financial statements of Ensign was a decrease in shareholders' equity by the book value of net assets distributed as "dividend". Net assets decreased by the same amount. Ensign did not recognize a gain or a loss from the spin-off transaction. Normally, spin-off transactions are recognized at book values under US GAAP (fair values under IFRS). If the transaction is not structured as a pro-rata distribution to existing shareholders, the transaction could result in a gain or a loss.

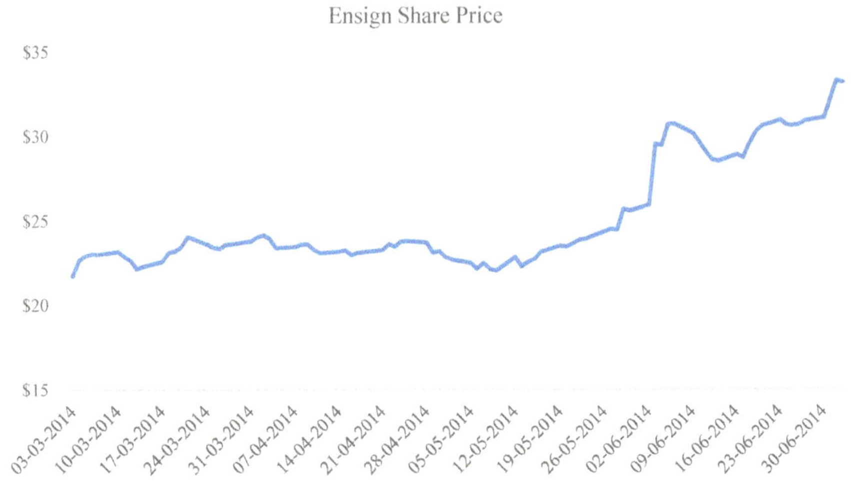

Fig. 14.1 Ensign share price (*Source* Thomson Reuters)

Evaluation of the Success of the Transaction

The spin-off appears to have been successful. By creating significant value for Ensign shareholders (which received CTRE shares). The share price increased 45% since the spin-off, and Ensign was the best performing share in its peer group during the period (see below). Additionally, the spin-off seems to have improved the value of CTRE: it started trading at $17.5 and the value increased to $19.9 (+13.7%).

Looking at the sum of both parts (Ensign+CTRE), large amount of value was created following the transaction. As of July 3, 2014, the market value of the separated entities that emerged was greater ($33.2+$19.9=$53.1, resulting in a joined market capitalization equal to $1,180 million) than the value of the combined company the first day of the spin-off ($26+$17.5=$43.5, resulting in a joined market capitalization equal to $966 million).

Ensign price chart since the spin-off was announced (March 2014, $22.5, spin-off adjusted) shows a +47% to July 3, 2014 ($33.2) and a +27% to June 1, 2014 ($26) (Fig. 14.1).

Questions

1. What are the main advantages of a spin-off transaction in general?
2. What are the main advantages of this particular spin-off?
3. In your opinion, why did not Ensign do an initial equity carve-out to maximize the spin-off value?
4. An alternative to a spin-off is a "tracking stock." Discuss the pros and cons of "tracking stock" in this particular case.
5. Describe in details the accounting entries that were recorded as a result of the spin-off in Ensign and CTRE books (consider the date provided by **Exhibits F, G, H** and **I**).

6. Suppose Ensign used the market-value method for the spin-off. Estimate the gain/loss from this transaction. On June 30, 2014, CTRE had 22,245,868 shares outstanding.

Exhibit A—Press Release—November 7, 2013

The Ensign Group, Inc. Announces REIT Spin-off; Adopts Stockholder Rights Plan

MISSION VIEJO, Calif., Nov. 7, 2013 (GLOBE NEWSWIRE)—The Ensign Group, Inc. (Nasdaq: ENSG), the parent company of the Ensign™ group of skilled nursing, rehabilitative care services, home health, hospice care, assisted living, and urgent care companies, announced today a plan to separate its healthcare business and its real estate business into two separate and independent publicly traded companies:

- The Ensign Group, Inc., which will continue to provide healthcare services through its existing operations; and
- CareTrust REIT, Inc., which will own, acquire and lease real estate serving the healthcare industry.

Ensign plans to effect the strategic separation through a spin-off in which it will distribute all of the outstanding shares of CareTrust common stock to Ensign's shareholders on a pro-rata basis. At the time of the spin-off, CareTrust, which is currently a wholly owned subsidiary of Ensign, will hold substantially all of the real property owned by Ensign, and will operate three independent living facilities. After the spin-off, these properties (other than the three independent living facilities that will be operated by CareTrust) will be leased to Ensign on a triple-net basis.

CareTrust intends to qualify and elect to be taxed as a real estate investment trust, or REIT, for U.S. federal income tax purposes, commencing with its taxable year ending December 31, 2014. The spin-off is expected to be tax-free to Ensign's shareholders, except for any cash paid in lieu of fractional shares. CareTrust has applied to list its shares on the NASDAQ stock market under the ticker symbol "CTRE."

Gregory K. Stapley, Ensign's Executive Vice President and Secretary, will become the President and Chief Executive Officer of CareTrust. Other than Mr. Stapley, Ensign's current management team will continue in place. Ensign's board of directors has appointed Chad A. Keetch, who has been working alongside Mr. Stapley for several years, to succeed Mr. Stapley as Ensign's Executive Vice President and Secretary on the effective date of the spin-off. Ensign's President and Chief Executive Officer, Christopher R. Christensen, will also serve as a CareTrust director during a transitional period.

Discussing the prospects for the two companies, Mr. Christensen said, "Our first and most pressing priority has been to ensure that the separation would result in two very healthy platforms for growth. This priority has been our guiding principle from the beginning. Unlike other separations, which on their surface may seem similar, we have taken great care to structure this in a way that safeguards our ability to provide the highest quality healthcare services and continue our successful business model, while also sharing the tremendous value we have created in our real estate with our partners and shareholders, now and over time."

Mr. Christensen also emphasized that Ensign will continue executing its existing business model and growth strategy, which will still include the purchase of real estate assets and the potential for significant value creation that comes with them, just as it always has.

Mr. Stapley reported that CareTrust, as a healthcare-oriented REIT, is expected to not only pursue skilled nursing, assisted living, and independent living properties, but also to eventually diversify into other property classes and activities, such as medical office buildings, long-term acute care hospitals and inpatient rehabilitation facilities, and the provision of some mortgage and development financing. CareTrust also expects to immediately begin pursuing growth opportunities in regions outside of its current geographic footprint.

Mr. Stapley added, "Although CareTrust will be independent and will make diversification of its tenant base a top priority, at the outset our biggest advantage will be our relationship with Ensign." He noted that Ensign has consistently been pursued by many REITs and other real estate investors looking to establish a landlord-tenant relationship with Ensign as one of the industry's premier operating companies. "We are fortunate that CareTrust will inherit, as its first tenant, the best of the best. Ensign's strong track record of operating performance and its industry-leading management team will provide CareTrust with a solid foundation on which to build into the future," he said.

Both gentlemen remarked that Ensign is pursuing the strategic transaction from a position of strength, and not one of necessity. "The health of our balance sheet, our strong cash flow, favorable market conditions, and the tax-free nature of the transaction have allowed us to establish projected capital structures for both companies that leave each not only quite healthy, but with plenty of runway for both near-term and long-term growth," added Mr. Christensen.

In connection with the proposed spin-off, Ensign's board of directors adopted a stockholder rights plan to facilitate CareTrust's REIT qualification. As a REIT, CareTrust will have to satisfy certain requirements relating to diversity of ownership, including a requirement that not more than 50% of its stock may be owned by five or fewer individuals. In order to satisfy these requirements, CareTrust's charter will include "excess share" provisions typical for REITs that will prohibit ownership of more than 9.8% of its outstanding shares. The stockholder rights plan has been adopted to discourage anyone from exceeding this ownership level at Ensign prior to the spin-off, and thereby facilitate CareTrust's REIT qualification after the spin-off. The plan is also designed to protect against coercive or abusive takeover tactics, and will help ensure that Ensign's shareholders are not deprived of the opportunity to realize the full and fair value of their investment. The plan will terminate on the first business day after the spin-off, but in any event no later than November 6, 2014.

Under the stockholder rights plan, Ensign's shareholders of record at the close of business on November 18, 2013 will receive a dividend of one right for each share of Ensign common stock held. Initially, these rights will not be exercisable and will trade with shares of Ensign common stock. These rights will generally become exercisable only if a person or group (i) acquires beneficial ownership of 9.8% or more of Ensign's common stock, (ii) that already beneficially owns 9.8% or more of Ensign's common stock acquires additional shares, or (iii) commences a tender offer or exchange offer which, if consummated, could result in a person or group owning 9.8% or more of Ensign's common stock.

If a person or group exceeds the ownership threshold, the rights will entitle each holder other than the acquiring person or group to receive, for the exercise price of $200 per right, shares of common stock (or, in certain circumstances, other consideration) having a market value equal to twice the exercise price. Ensign's board may redeem the rights at a price of $0.001 per right at any time up to ten business days after a person or group has exceeded the threshold.

Shareholders are not required to take any action to receive the rights distribution. Until the rights become exercisable, the rights will be represented by outstanding common stock certificates (or, in the case of shares of common stock reflected on the direct registration system, notations in the book-entry account system of the transfer agent). The issuance of the rights will have no dilutive effect and will not impact reported earnings per share for Ensign. The dividend should not be taxable to Ensign's shareholders. The full text of the stockholder rights plan will be filed with the Securities and Exchange Commission.

CareTrust has filed a registration statement on Form 10 relating to the spin-off with the Securities and Exchange Commission. The spin-off is subject to customary conditions, including receipt of a favorable ruling from the Internal Revenue Service that the spin-off will qualify as a tax-free transaction, receipt of a tax opinion from counsel, effectiveness of the registration statement filed with the Securities and Exchange Commission, execution of intercompany agreements, and final approval by Ensign's board of directors. Ensign anticipates that the spin-off will be completed in the first quarter of 2014, but there can be no assurances regarding the final terms and structure of the spin-off or that it will be completed. In addition, Ensign management affirmed that Ensign does not intend to "stand still" or otherwise abate its acquisition program during the pendency of the transaction, and references to the property counts, capitalization or financial condition of either Ensign or CareTrust and similar statements may change as a result of acquisitions, expenditures or other changes made prior to the effective date of the spin-off.

Citigroup Global Markets Inc. and Wells Fargo Securities, LLC are serving as financial advisors to Ensign in connection with the spin-off. Skadden, Arps, Slate, Meagher & Flom LLP is serving as legal advisor to Ensign.

Conference Call: Ensign invites investors to listen to a conference call with Ensign's senior management on November 8, 2013, at 10:00 a.m. Pacific Time (1:00 p.m. Eastern Time), to discuss the proposed spin-off. To listen to the webcast, or to view any financial or other statistical information required by SEC Regulation G, please visit the Investors section of the Ensign website at http://investor.ensigngroup.net. The webcast will be recorded, and will be available for replay via the website until 5:00 p.m. Pacific Time on Friday, November 29, 2013.

Exhibit B—Press Release—June 3, 2014

The Ensign Group, Inc. Announces Completion of Spin-off of CareTrust REIT, Inc.

MISSION VIEJO, Calif., June 3, 2014 (GLOBE NEWSWIRE)—The Ensign Group, Inc., the parent company of the Ensign™ group of skilled nursing, rehabilitative care services, home health, hospice care, assisted living, and urgent care companies, announced today the successful completion of its spin-off of CareTrust REIT, Inc. In the spin-off, Ensign stockholders received one share of CareTrust common stock for each share of Ensign common stock held at the close of business on May 22, 2014. The spin-off is effective from and after June 1, 2014, with CareTrust shares distributed on June 2, 2014. Starting today, shares of CareTrust common stock will commence trading on the NASDAQ Global Select Market on a "regular-way" market (Nasdaq: CTRE).

"With the completion of the spin-off, we look forward to continuing our pursuit of a new standard for quality healthcare services in the post-acute care industry," said Christopher Christensen, Ensign's Chief Executive Officer. Mr. Christensen also emphasized that Ensign will continue executing its existing business model and growth strategy, which will include acquiring and retaining the real estate assets for both well-performing and struggling skilled nursing and assisted living facilities across the US. As a result of the spin-off, CareTrust is now a separate and independent publicly traded, self-administered, and self-managed real estate investment trust ("REIT") primarily engaged in the ownership, acquisition and leasing of healthcare-related properties. Mr. Christensen also added, "The health of our balance sheet, our strong cash flow, favorable market conditions and the tax-free nature of the transaction have allowed us to establish capital structures for both companies that leave each not only quite healthy, but with plenty of potential for both near-term and long-term growth." Since May 20, 2014, there were two markets in Ensign common stock: a "regular-way" or "due-bills" market (Nasdaq: ENSG) in which shares of Ensign common stock traded with an entitlement to receive shares of CareTrust common stock on the distribution date; and an "ex-distribution" market (Nasdaq: ENSGV) in which shares of Ensign common stock traded without an entitlement to receive shares of CareTrust common stock on the distribution date. Starting today, all shares of Ensign common stock will trade only on a "regular-way" market without any entitlement to receive shares of CareTrust common stock.

In addition, as a result of the completion of the spin-off, Ensign's stockholder rights plan will expire by its terms at 5:00 p.m., New York City time, on June 3, 2014. Stockholders are not required to take any action as a result of this expiration. In connection with the expiration of the rights plan, Ensign will take routine actions to voluntarily deregister the related preferred stock purchase rights under the Securities Exchange Act of 1934, and to delist the preferred stock purchase rights from NASDAQ. These actions are administrative in nature and will have no effect on Ensign's common stock, which continues to be listed on NASDAQ.

Wells Fargo Securities, LLC served as lead financial advisor to Ensign in connection with the spin-off, and Citigroup Global Markets Inc. also served as a financial advisor. Skadden, Arps, Slate, Meagher & Flom LLP served as legal advisor to Ensign.

Exhibit C—Press Release—June 3, 2014

CareTrust REIT, Inc. Announces Completion of Spin-Off from the Ensign Group, Inc.

MISSION VIEJO, Calif., June 3, 2014 (GLOBE NEWSWIRE)—CareTrust REIT, Inc. (Nasdaq: CTRE) announced today the successful completion of its spin-off from The Ensign Group, Inc. (Nasdaq: ENSG). In the spin-off, Ensign stockholders received one share of CareTrust common stock for each share of Ensign common stock held at the close of business on May 22, 2014. The spin-off is effective from and after June 1, 2014, with CareTrust shares distributed on June 2, 2014.

"With the spin-off complete, we are excited to finally be a pure-play real estate business, and the newest REIT serving the growing healthcare industry," said Greg Stapley, CareTrust's Chief Executive Officer. He noted that CareTrust is seeking growth opportunities nationwide and intends to diversify its asset and tenant base.

Mr. Stapley also expressed appreciation to Ensign's officers and directors who made the spin-off possible, and especially its legal and accounting staffs and the many outside consultants who worked tirelessly to complete the complex work of spinning out the new company and executing multiple financing transactions to facilitate the spin-off simultaneously. "Ensign will always be a part of our company's heritage, and the foundation of our real estate portfolio, for which we are deeply grateful," he added.

Since May 20, 2014, shares of CareTrust common stock have traded on a "when-issued" basis (Nasdaq: CTREV). The "when-issued" trading market was a market for shares of CareTrust common stock to be distributed to Ensign stockholders on the distribution date. Starting today, shares of CareTrust common stock will commence trading on the NASDAQ Global Select Market on a "regular-way" market (Nasdaq: CTRE).

As a result of the spin-off, CareTrust is now a separate and independent publicly traded, self-administered, and self-managed real estate investment trust ("REIT") primarily engaged in the ownership, acquisition, and leasing of healthcare-related properties. CareTrust owns substantially all of the real property owned by Ensign prior to the spin-off, and leases these properties to Ensign on a triple-net basis (other than three independent living facilities which are operated by CareTrust). Ensign, through its consolidated operating subsidiaries, will continue to make acquisitions and provide healthcare services through its existing operations.

Wells Fargo Securities, LLC, and Citigroup Global Markets Inc. served as lead financial advisors to Ensign in connection with the spin-off. Skadden, Arps, Slate, Meagher & Flom LLP served as Ensign's primary legal advisor, and KPMG LLP provided tax advisory services.

Exhibit D—Excerpts from Ensign's Financial Statements as of September 30, 2014

On June 1, 2014, the Company completed the separation of its healthcare business and its real estate business into two publicly traded companies through a tax-free distribution of all of the outstanding shares of common stock of CareTrust REIT, Inc. (CareTrust) to Ensign stockholders on a pro-rata basis (the Spin-off). Ensign stockholders received one share of CareTrust common stock for each share of Ensign common stock held at the close of business on May 22, 2014, the record date for the Spin-off. The Spin-off was effective from and after June 1, 2014, with shares of CareTrust common stock distributed on June 2, 2014. CareTrust is listed on the NASDAQ Global Select Market (NASDAQ) and trades under the ticker symbol "CTRE."

The Company received a private letter ruling from the Internal Revenue Service (IRS) substantially to the effect that the Spin-off will qualify as a tax-free transaction for U.S. federal income tax purposes. The private letter ruling relies on certain facts, representations, assumptions, and undertakings. The Company also received opinions from its advisors as to the satisfaction of certain requirements for the tax-free treatment of the Spin-off, and an opinion of counsel that, commencing with CareTrust's taxable year ending on December 31, 2014, CareTrust has been organized in conformity with the requirements for qualification as a real estate investment trust ("REIT") under the Internal Revenue Code of 1986, as amended, and its proposed method of operation will enable it to meet the requirements for qualification and taxation as a REIT.

Prior to the Spin-off, the Company entered into a Separation and Distribution Agreement with CareTrust, setting forth the mechanics of the Spin-off, certain organizational matters and other ongoing obligations of the Company and CareTrust. The Company and CareTrust or their respective subsidiaries, as applicable, also entered into a number of other agreements to govern the relationship between CareTrust and the Company after the Spin-off.

Immediately before the Spin-off, on May 30, 2014, while CareTrust was a wholly owned subsidiary of the Company, CareTrust raised $260,000 of debt financing (the Bond). CareTrust also entered into the Fifth Amended and Restated Loan Agreement, with General Electric Capital Corporation (GECC), which consisted of an additional loan of $50,676 to an aggregate principal amount of $99,000 (the Ten Project Note).

The Ten Project Note and the Bond were assumed by CareTrust in connection with the Separation and Distribution Agreement. CareTrust transferred $220,752 to the Company, a portion of which the Company used to retire $208,635 of long-term debt prior to maturity. The remaining portion was used to pay prepayment penalties and other third party fees relating to the early retirement of outstanding debt. The amount retained by the Company of $8219 was recorded as restricted cash, of which $6400 is classified as current assets and $1819 is classified as non-current assets as of June 1, 2014. The amount represents a portion of the proceeds received from CareTrust in connection with the Separation and Distribution

Agreement that the Company intends to use to pay up to eight regular quarterly dividend payments. During the third quarter of 2014, the Company utilized $1567 to pay the third quarter dividend payments.

As of September 30, 2014, the Company has $6652 of restricted cash remaining, which is classified as current assets as the Company intends to utilize all the remaining amount to make dividend payments within the next twelve months. The remaining cash of $78,731 that CareTrust retained on the Spin-off date was transferred to CareTrust as part of the assets and liabilities contributed to CareTrust in connection with the Spin-off.

As of March 31, 2014, the Company operated 120 affiliated facilities. Prior to the Spin-off, the Company separated the healthcare operations from the independent living operations at two locations, resulting in a total of 122 affiliated facilities. The Company contributed to CareTrust the assets and liabilities associated with all of the 94 real property and three independent living facilities that CareTrust now operates that were previously owned by the Company.

The results of the three independent living facilities that were transferred to CareTrust in connection with the Spin-off were not material to the Company's three and nine months ended September 30, 2014 or 2013. The assets and liabilities were contributed to CareTrust based on their historical carrying values, which were as follows (in thousands):

	$ Thousand
Cash and cash equivalents	78,731
Other current assets	34
Property and equipment, net	421,846
Deferred financing costs	11,088
Accounts payable and accrued expenses	(4,971)
Current deferred tax liabilities	(125)
Deferred tax liability	(5,925)
Current maturities of long-term debt	(2,342)
Lon-term debt (less current maturities)	(357,171)
Net contribution	**141,165**

Exhibit E—Excerpts from CTRE's Financial Statements as of June 30, 2014

Separation from Ensign—Prior to June 1, 2014, CareTrust REIT, Inc. ("CareTrust" or the "Company") was a wholly owned subsidiary of The Ensign Group, Inc. ("Ensign"). On June 1, 2014, Ensign completed the separation of its healthcare business and its real estate business into two separate and independent publicly traded companies through the distribution of all of the outstanding shares of common stock of CareTrust to Ensign stockholders on a pro-rata basis ("spin-off"). Ensign stockholders received one share of CareTrust common stock for each share of Ensign common stock held at the close of business on May 22, 2014, the record date for the Spin-off. The Spin-off was effective from and after June 1, 2014, with shares of CareTrust common stock distributed by Ensign on June 2, 2014. The Company was formed on October 29, 2013 and had minimal activity prior to the Spin-off.

Prior to the Spin-off, the Company and Ensign entered into a Separation and Distribution Agreement, setting forth the mechanics of the Spin-off, certain organizational matters, and other ongoing obligations of the Company and Ensign. The Company and Ensign or their respective subsidiaries, as applicable, also entered into a number of other agreements to govern the relationship between Ensign and the Company after the Spin-off.

The Company and Ensign also entered into an Opportunities Agreement, which grants the Company the right to match any offer from a third party to finance the acquisition or development of any healthcare or senior living facility by Ensign or any of its affiliates for a period of one year following the Spin-off. In addition, this agreement grants Ensign, subject to certain exceptions, the right to either purchase and operate, or lease and operate, the facilities included in any portfolio of five or fewer healthcare or senior living facilities presented to the Company during the first year following the Spin-off; provided that the portfolio is not subject to an existing lease with an operator or manager that has a remaining term of more than one year, and is not presented to the Company by or on behalf of another operator seeking lease or other financing. If Ensign elects to lease and operate such a property or portfolio, the lease would be on substantially the same terms as the Master Leases.

In accordance with the Financial Accounting Standards Board ("FASB") Accounting Standards Codification ("ASC") 505-60, *Equity—Spinoffs and Reverse Spinoffs*, the accounting for the separation of the Company follows its legal form, with Ensign as the legal and accounting spinnor and the Company as the legal and accounting spinnee, due to the relative significance of Ensign's healthcare business, the relative fair values of the respective companies, the retention of all senior management (except Mr. Gregory K. Stapley) by Ensign, and other relevant indicators. The assets and liabilities contributed to the Company from Ensign, or incurred in connection with the Spin-off in the case of certain debt, were as follows:

	$ Thousand
Real estate investments, net	421,846
Cash and cash equivalents	78,731
Accounts receivable and prepaid assets and other current assets	1,900
Deferred financing costs, net	11,088
Debt	(359,512)
Other liabilities	(6,838)
Net contribution	**147,215**

Exhibit F—Ensign's Consolidated Balance Sheet as of September 30, 2014

$ Thousand	9.30.2014	12.31.2013
Cash and cash equivalents	39,206	65,755
Restricted cash	6,652	–
Accounts receivables	120,647	111,370
Investments	5,883	5,511
Prepaid expenses	13,510	19,128
Deferred tax assets	8,033	9,232
Total current assets	**193,931**	**210,996**
Property, and equipment, net	127,448	479,770
Insurance subsidiary deposits and investments	18,170	16,888
Escrow deposits	600	1,000
Deferred tax asset	11,493	4,464
Restricted and other assets	8,449	9,804
Intangible assets, net	6,560	5,718
Goodwill	25,719	23,935
Other indefinite-lived intangibles	10,509	7,740
Total assets	**402,879**	**760,315**
Accounts payable	27,783	23,793
Accrued expenses and related liabilities	90,552	81,252
Short-term borrowings	110	7,411
Total current liabilities	**118,445**	**112,456**
Long-term debt	3,307	251,895
Accrued self-insurance liabilities	33,658	33,642
Fair value of interest rate swap	–	1,828
Deferred rent and other long-term liabilities	3,151	3,237
Total liabilities	**158,561**	**403,058**
Common stock	23	22
Additional paid-in capital	110,090	101,364
Retained earnings	136,043	257,502
Treasury stock	(1,505)	(1,680)
Accumulated other comprehensive loss	–	(1,112)
Total shareholders' equity	**244,651**	**356,096**
Non-controlling interests	(333)	1,161
Total shareholder's equity and liabilities	**402,879**	**760,315**

Exhibit G—Ensign's Consolidated Income Statement as of September 30, 2014

	$ Thousand
Net sales	750,537
Cost of services	(601,532)
Facility rent	(30,008)
General and administrative expenses	(44,370)
Depreciation and amortization	(21,343)
Income from operations	**53,284**
Interest expenses	(12,490)
Interest income	435
Income before taxes	**41,229**
Provision for income taxes	(18,284)
Net income	**22,945**
Non-controlling interests	1,494
Net income attributable to Ensign	**24,439**

Exhibit H—Ensign's Consolidated Cash Flows Statement as of September 30, 2014

	$ Thousand
Net income	22,945
Depreciation and amortization	21,343
Amortization of deferred financing fees and debt discount	539
Deferred income taxes	(510)
Provision for doubtful accounts	9,271
Share-based compensation	3,813
Excess tax benefit from share-based compensation	(2,403)
Loss on extinguishment of debt	4,067
Loss on termination of interest rate swap	1,661
Loss on disposition of property and equipment	14
Change in operating assets and liabilities	5,947
Net cash provided by operating activities	**66,687**
Purchase of property and equipment	(42,125)
Cash payment for business acquisition	(42,968)
Cash payment for asset acquisitions	(7,939)
Escrow deposits	(600)
Escrow deposits used to fund business acquisitions	1,000

	$ Thousand
Change in restricted cash	(6,652)
Cash proceeds from the sale of property and equipment	1
Restricted and other assets	(124)
Net cash used in investing activities	**(99,407)**
Proceeds from issuance of debt	400,677
Payment on long-term debt	(301,171)
Issuance of treasury stock	175
Cash retained by CareTrust at separation	(78,731)
Issuance of common stock	2,510
Dividends paid	(4,753)
Excess tax benefit from share-based compensation	2,416
Prepayment penalties	(2,069)
Payment of deferred financing costs	(12,883)
Net cash provided by financing activities	**6,171**
Net (decrease) increase in cash and cash equivalents	**(26,549)**
Cash and cash equivalents beginning of period	65,755
Cash and cash equivalents end of period	39,206

Exhibit I—Selected Financial Data from CTRE's Financial Statement as of December 31, 2014 and June 30, 2014

Shareholder's equity as of December 31, 2014

$ Thousand	2014	2013
Common stock	313	–
Additional paid-in capital	246,041	–
Cumulative distributions in excess of earnings	(132,892)	–
Invested equity	–	164,517
Accumulated other comprehensive loss	–	(1,828)
Total shareholders' equity	**113,462**	**162,689**

Statements of equity as of December 31, 2014—*Reclassification of invested equity to common stock and additional paid-in capital in conjunction with the spin-off*

$ Thousand	2014
Common stock	222
Additional paid-in capital	146,980
Cumulative distributions in excess of earnings	–

$ Thousand	2014
Invested equity	(147,207)
Accumulated other comprehensive loss	–
Total shareholders' equity	–

Cash flows statement as of June 30, 2014—*Financing section*

$ Thousand	2014
Proceeds from the issuance of senior notes	260,000
Proceeds from the issuance of mortgage notes	50,676
Repayments of borrowings under senior credit facility	(88,701)
Payments on the mortgage notes payable	(66,856)
Payments on the senior secured term loan	(65,624)
Payments of deferred financing costs	(12,945)
Total	**76,550**

References

CTRE press release, June 3, 2014.
CTRE annual report 2014.
CTRE quarterly report as of June 30, 2014.
Ensign quarterly report as of September 30, 2014.
Ensign press release, June 3, 2014.
Ensign press release, November 7, 2013.

Altria Group: The Carve-Out and Spin-Off of Kraft

15

Introduction

Altria Group, Inc. ("Altria"), previously named Philip Morris Corporation was, at the time of the transaction, one of the world's largest tobacco companies.[1] Kraft Foods Inc. ("Kraft") is one of the world's largest food and beverage companies in the world, with products such as Kraft cheese, Ritz crackers, Maxwell House coffee, and Toblerone chocolate. Altria acquired Kraft in 1998 and subsequently combined it with other acquired businesses: General Foods and Nabisco. From 1998 to 2001, Kraft was a wholly owned subsidiary of Altria.

Carve-Out 2001

As of December 31, 2000, Kraft had:

- 275 million Class A common shares outstanding (granting one vote per share);
- 1,180 million Class B common shares outstanding (granting ten votes per share).

Both Class A and B common shares were entirely held by Altria prior to the carve-out.

On June 13, 2001, Kraft completed an initial public offering (IPO) of 280 million shares of its Class A common stock at a price of $31.00 per share.

After the completion of the IPO, Altria owned approximately 83.9% of the outstanding shares of Kraft's capital through its 49.5% stake in Kraft's Class A common stock [(275 / (275 + 280)], granting one vote each, and its 100% stake in Kraft's Class B common stock, granting ten votes each. Therefore, it held 97.7% of the combined voting power of Kraft's outstanding common stock. At the beginning of 2007, Altria owned 83.9% in Kraft.

[1]All market data in this case study are as of the time of the deal. They might have changed since then.

E. Amir and M. Ghitti, *Financial Analysis of Mergers and Acquisitions*,
https://doi.org/10.1007/978-3-030-61769-1_15

The IPO proceeds, net of underwriting discount and expenses, amounting to $8.4 billion, were used to retire a portion of the debt incurred to finance the Nabisco acquisition.

As a result of the IPO, an adjustment of $8.4 billion to the carrying amount of Altria's investment in Kraft has been reflected on Altria's consolidated balance sheet as an increase to additional paid-in capital of $4.4 billion (net of currency translation adjustments and other comprehensive losses) and minority interest of $3.7 billion.

Exhibit A and **B** shows Altria's and Kraft's consolidated balance sheet as of December 31, 2001 following the carve-out transaction.

Spin-Off 2007

As early as 2004, Altria considered to spin-off Kraft in a large restructuring plan aimed at streamlining operations and unlocking shareholder value. The spin-off was repeatedly postponed as Altria faced tobacco-related litigation, which could have made the deal difficult.

Plans were to spin-off Kraft, as well as Philip Morris International, the international arm of the tobacco business. After the Kraft spin-off, Altria could engage in an optimization of the capital structures of its local tobacco companies, raising new debt. It would also free both companies to pursue acquisition and expansion plans.

On March 30, 2007, Altria distributed all of its remaining interest in Kraft (83.9%) on a pro-rata basis to its shareholders in a tax-free distribution. The distribution ratio was established at 0.692024 Kraft's share for each outstanding share of Altria. However, since shareholders would receive cash instead of fractional shares, they would have to pay tax on any cash amount received under the arrangement.

The spin-off was valued at approximately $46.1 billion based on Kraft's closing price on March 30, 2007 ($31.66 per share and 1,455 million Kraft shares distributed by Altria) and resulted in a net decrease to Altria's stockholders' equity of $27.4 billion.

Exhibit C shows the shareholders structure of Altria and Kraft through time.

Exhibit D show Altria's consolidated cash flow statement as of December 31, 2001.

Exhibit E show Altria's and Kraft's statement of changes in equity as of December 31, 2001.

In its 2006 10-K (filed in early 2007), Kraft spin-off was presented as a post-balance-sheet event. In the 2007 10-K filing, Altria reclassified the assets and liabilities of Kraft as discontinued operations in the consolidated balance sheet for fiscal 2006 (**Exhibits F** and **G**). As such, the financial statements showed the following balances and, had the distribution been executed in 2006, it would have translated to a reduction of $27 billion in shareholders' equity.

	$ Million
Current assets of discontinued operations	7,647
Long-term assets of discontinued operations	21,767
Goodwill of discontinued operations	27,038
Current liabilities of discontinued operations	(9,866)
Long-term liabilities of discontinued operations	(16,520)
Minority interests of discontinued operations	(3,109)
Net assets/liabilities of discontinued operations	**26,957**

In 2007, Altria reflected the results of Kraft prior to the Kraft distribution date as discontinued operations on the consolidated statements of earnings and the consolidated statements of cash flows for all periods presented. There was no gain or loss recognized for the period with regard to the spin-off.

$ Thousand	2007	2006
Operating income	13,235	12,887
Interest and other debt expenses, net	215	367
Earnings from continuing operations before taxes	**13,020**	**12,520**
Pretax profit margin from continuing operations	*18%*	*19%*
Provision for income taxes	4,096	3,400
Earnings from continuing operations, net	**8,924**	**9,120**
Equity earnings and minority interest, net	237	209
Earnings from discontinued operations, net	625	2,693
Net earnings	**9,786**	**12,022**
Basic earnings per share	4.36	4.47
Earnings per share from discontinued operations	0.30	1.29
Total earnings per share	**4.66**	**5.76**
Dividends declared per share	3.05	3.32
Stockholders' equity	18,554	39,619
P/E ratio at year-end—Basic	16	15
Number of employees	84,000	175,000

Non-controlling interests from discontinued operations in fiscal 2007 were equal to $78 million.

Altria's statement of changes in shareholders' equity for 2007 (**Exhibit H**) reflects the Kraft spin-off through a negative impact of $27 billion. This was made up of a large impact on the reinvested earnings balance and some adjustments accounting for $2b.

Other Issues

Kraft was previously included in Altria's consolidated income tax return, and federal income tax contingencies were recorded as liabilities on the balance sheet of the group. After the spin-off Altria reimbursed Kraft in cash for these liabilities, which were approximately $305 million, plus pretax interest of $63 million.

Moreover, in order to make sure that shareholders received the same aggregate dividend that they would have received had they been shareholders in the group that continued to own Kraft, Altria adjusted its second quarter dividend to $0.65 per share.

Adjustments were also made to employee stock options to reflect the distribution ratio of the common stock. The new Kraft option had an exercise price equal to the Kraft market price at the time of the distribution ($31.66) multiplied by the option conversion ratio, which represented the exercise price of the original Altria option divided by Altria's market price immediately before the distribution ($87.81). The reduced exercise price of the adjusted Altria's option was determined by multiplying Altria's market price immediately following the distribution ($65.90) by the option conversion ratio.

Questions

1. What is an equity carve-out? What is a spin-off? What common objectives do they have? What are the main differences? Briefly assess their relative benefits/costs in achieving these objectives.
2. How did Altria and Kraft account for the carve-out and spin-off of Kraft in 2001 and 2007, respectively? Be as specific as possible. Use information from the relevant financial statements.
3. Why did Altria carve-out just less than 20% of its ownership of Kraft in 2001? Why did it then spin-off its remaining interest in 2007?
4. How are carve-outs accounted for under US GAAP and how are they presented in financial statements? Is there a gain/loss from the transaction? For the purpose of this computation, consider that Kraft's goodwill (as shown in Altria's 2007 financials, equal to $27,038 million) was not amortized since fiscal 2002. In fiscal 2001, Kraft's goodwill amortization amounted to $591.
5. In 1998, Ford spun-off The Associates First Capital recognizing a P&L gain of about $15 billion from the transaction. Suppose Altria could record the spin-off transaction at market value, what would be the effect on its financial statements?
6. Was the spin-off successful? Evaluate it based on Kraft's share price following the spin-off (**Exhibit I**).

Exhibit A—Altria's consolidated balance sheet as of December 31, 2001

$ Million	2001	2000
Cash and cash equivalents	453	937
Accounts receivables, net	5,148	5,019

$ Million	2001	2000
Inventories	8,923	8,765
Other current assets	2,751	2,517
Total current assets	**17,275**	**17,238**
Property, and equipment, net	15,137	15,303
Goodwill and other intangible assets	37,548	33,090
Other assets	6,144	5,034
Finance and other assets, net	8,864	8,402
Total assets	**84,968**	**79,067**
Short-term borrowings	997	3,166
Current portion of long-term debt	1,942	5,775
Accounts payable	3,600	3,787
Accrued liabilities	11,330	11,131
Income taxes	1,021	914
Dividends payable	1,251	1,176
Total current liabilities	**20,141**	**25,949**
Long-term debt	17,159	18,255
Deferred income taxes	5,238	1,827
Accrued postretirement health care costs	3,315	3,287
Minority interest	4,013	302
Other liabilities	7,796	7,015
Financial services liabilities	7,686	7,427
Total liabilities	**65,348**	**64,062**
Common stock, par value $0.33 1/3 per share	935	935
Additional paid-in capital	4,503	–
Retained earnings	37,269	33,481
Accumulated other comprehensive loss	(3,373)	(2,950)
Cost of repurchased stock	(19,714)	(16,461)
Total shareholders' equity	**19,620**	**15,005**
Total shareholder's equity and liabilities	**84,968**	**79,067**

Exhibit B—Kraft's consolidated balance sheet as of December 31, 2001

$ Million	2001	2000
Cash and cash equivalents	162	191
Accounts receivables, net	3,131	3,231
Inventories	3,026	3,041

$ Million	2001	2000
Deferred income taxes	466	504
Other current assets	221	185
Total current assets	**7,006**	**7,152**
Property, and equipment, net	9,109	9,405
Goodwill and other intangible assets	35,957	31,584
Prepaid pension assets	2,675	2,623
Other assets	1,051	1,307
Total assets	**55,798**	**52,071**
Short-term borrowings	681	146
Current portion of long-term debt	540	713
Due to parent and affiliates	1,652	865
Accounts payable	1,897	1,971
Accrued liabilities	3,877	3,637
Income taxes	228	258
Total current liabilities	**8,875**	**7,590**
Long-term debt	8,134	2,695
Deferred income taxes	5,031	1,446
Accrued postretirement health care costs	1,850	1,867
Notes payable to parent and affiliates	5,000	21,407
Other liabilities	3,430	3,018
Total liabilities	**32,320**	**38,023**
Class A common stock, no par value[a]	–	–
Class B common stock, no par value[b]	–	–
Additional paid-in capital	23,655	15,230
Retained earnings	2,391	992
Accumulated other comprehensive loss	(2,568)	(2,174)
Total shareholders' equity	**23,478**	**14,048**
Total shareholder's equity and liabilities	**55,798**	**52,071**

[a]555 million and 275 million shares issued and outstanding in 2001 and 2000
[b]1,180,000 shares issued and outstanding in 2001 and 2000

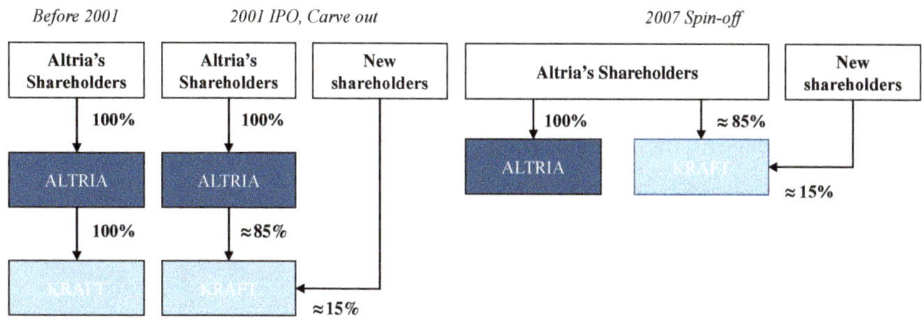

Fig. 15.1 Shareholders structure through time

Exhibit C—Altria's and Kraft's shareholders structure through time

See Fig. 15.1.

Exhibit D—Altria's consolidated cash flow statement as of December 31, 2001

$ Million	2001	2000
Net earnings	8,560	8,510
Cumulative effect of accounting change	6	–
Depreciation and amortization	2,337	1,717
Deferred income tax provision (benefit)	277	660
Loss on sale of assets and integration costs	82	–
Escrow bond for domestic tobacco litigation	(1,200)	–
Gains on sales of businesses	(8)	(274)
Other working capital changes	(1,577)	102
Financial services changes	416	329
Net cash provided (used) by operating activities	**8,893**	**11,044**
Capital expenditures	(1,922)	(1,682)
Cash payment for business acquisition, net of acquired cash	(451)	(15,576)
Cash proceeds from sales of businesses	21	433
Other	139	28
Investments in finance assets	(960)	(865)
Proceeds from finance assets	257	156
Net cash provided (used) by investing activities	**(2,916)**	**(17,506)**
Net (repayment) issuance of short-term borrowings	(5,678)	8,501
Long-term debt proceeds	4,079	3,110
Long-term debt repaid	(5,215)	(1,702)
Financial services (repayment) issuance	42	1,027

$ Million	2001	2000
Repurchase of Philip Morris common stock	(3,960)	(3,597)
Dividends paid on Philip Morris common stock	(4,769)	(4,500)
Issuance of Philip Morris common stock	779	112
Issuance of Kraft Foods Inc. common stock	8,425	–
Other	(143)	(293)
Net cash provided (used) by financing activities	**(6,440)**	**2,658**
Exchange rate changes	(21)	(359)
Net (decrease) increase in cash and cash equivalents	**(484)**	**(4,163)**
Cash and cash equivalents beginning of period	937	5,100
Cash and cash equivalents end of period	453	937

Exhibit E—Altria's consolidated statement of changes in shareholders' equity as of December 31, 2001

Altria	Common stock	APIC[a]	Retained earnings	AOCI[b]	Stock buybacks	Total equity
Balance at Dec. 31, 2000	**935**	**–**	**33,481**	**(2,950)**	**(16,461)**	**15,005**
Net (loss) income			8,560			8,560
Currency translation				(753)		(753)
Pension liability				(89)		(89)
Hedge accounting				33		33
Total OCI						**(809)**
Total earnings						**7,751**
Stock options and awards		138	70		747	955
Cash dividend			(4,842)			(4,842)
Stock repurchased					(4,000)	(4,000)
Kraft Foods Inc. sale		4,365		386		4,751
Balance at Dec. 31, 2001	**935**	**4,503**	**37,269**	**(3,373)**	**(19,714)**	**19,620**

[a]APIC—Additional paid-in capital
[b]AOCI—Accumulated other comprehensive income

Kraft	Common stock	APIC	Retained earnings	AOCI	Total equity
Balance at Dec. 31, 2000	–	**15,230**	**992**	**(2,174)**	**14,048**
Net (loss) income			1,882		1,882
Currency translation				(298)	(298)
Pension liability				(78)	(78)
Hedge accounting				(18)	(18)
Total OCI					**(394)**
Total earnings					**1,488**
Stock issuance		8,425			8,425
Cash dividend					(483)
Balance at Dec. 31, 2001	–	**23,655**	**2,391**	**(2,568)**	**23,478**

Exhibit F—Altria's consolidated balance sheet as of December 31, 2007

$ Million	2007	2006
Cash and cash equivalents	6,498	4,781
Accounts receivables, net	3,323	2,808
Inventories	10,571	8,680
Current assets of discontinued operations	–	7,647
Other current assets	2,498	2,236
Total current assets	**22,890**	**26,152**
Property, and equipment, net	8,857	7,581
Goodwill	8,001	6,197
Other intangible assets	4,953	1,908
Long-term assets of discontinued operations	–	48,805
Other assets	6,447	6,837
Finance and other assets, net	6,063	6,790
Total assets	**57,211**	**104,270**
Short-term borrowings	638	420
Current portion of long-term debt	2,445	648
Accounts payable	1,463	1,414
Accrued liabilities	11,994	10,486
Income taxes	654	782
Dividends payable	1,588	1,811
Current liabilities of discontinued operations	–	9,866
Total current liabilities	**18,782**	**25,427**

$ Million	2007	2006
Long-term debt	7,463	6,298
Deferred income taxes	2,182	1,391
Accrued postretirement costs	2,304	2,550
Long-term liabilities of discontinued operations	–	19,629
Other liabilities	2,323	2,658
Financial services liabilities	5,603	6,698
Total liabilities	**38,657**	**64,651**
Common stock, par value $0.33 1/3 per share	935	935
Additional paid-in capital	6,884	6,356
Retained earnings	34,426	59,879
Accumulated other comprehensive loss	(237)	(3,808)
Cost of repurchased stock	(23,454)	(23,743)
Total shareholders' equity	**18,554**	**39,619**
Total shareholder's equity and liabilities	**57,211**	**104,270**

Exhibit G—Kraft's consolidated balance sheet as of December 31, 2007

$ Million	2007	2006
Cash and cash equivalents	567	239
Accounts receivables, net	5,197	3,869
Inventories	4,096	3,506
Deferred income taxes	575	387
Other current assets	302	253
Total current assets	**10,737**	**8,254**
Property, and equipment, net	10,778	9,693
Goodwill	31,193	25,553
Other intangible assets	12,200	10,177
Prepaid pension assets	1,648	1,168
Other assets	1,437	729
Total assets	**67,993**	**55,574**
Short-term borrowings	7,385	1,715
Current portion of long-term debt	722	2,025
Accounts payable	4,065	2,602
Accrued liabilities	4,814	3,980
Income taxes	100	151
Total current liabilities	**17,086**	**10,473**

$ Million	2007	2006
Long-term debt	12,902	7,081
Deferred income taxes	4,876	3,930
Accrued postretirement costs	3,656	4,036
Other liabilities	2,178	1,499
Total liabilities	**40,698**	**27,019**
Class A common stock, no par value[a]	–	–
Class B common stock, no par value[b]	–	–
Additional paid-in capital	23,445	23,626
Retained earnings	12,209	11,128
Accumulated other comprehensive loss	(1,835)	(3,069)
Treasury stock, at cost	(6,524)	(3,130)
Total shareholders' equity	**27,295**	**28,555**
Total shareholder's equity and liabilities	**67,993**	**55,574**

1,735,000,000 and 555,000,000 shares issued and outstanding in 2007 and 2006
1,180,000 shares issued and outstanding in 2007 and 2006

Exhibit H—Altria's consolidated statement of changes in shareholders' equity as of December 31, 2007

	Common stock	APIC	Retained earnings	AOCI	Stock buybacks	Total equity
Balance at Dec. 31, 2006	**935**	**6,356**	**59,879**	**(3,808)**	**(23,743)**	**39,619**
Net (loss) income			9,786			9,786
Currency translation				736		736
Pension liability				744		744
Hedge accounting				(18)		(18)
Total OCI						**1,462**
Total earnings						**11,248**
FIN 48 & FAS 13-2			711			711
Stock options and awards		528			289	817
Cash dividends			(6,430)			(6,430)
Spin-off Kraft			(29,520)	2,109		(27,411)
Balance at Dec. 31, 2007	**935**	**6,884**	**34,426**	**(237)**	**(23,454)**	**18,554**

Exhibit I—Altria's post spin-off share prices (Thomson Reuters)

Date	Share price ($)
26.03.2007	$31.66
18.06.2007	$36.25
17.09.2007	$34.85
26.11.2007	$34.55
04.02.2008	$28.81

References

Altria annual report for fiscal 2001.
Altria annual report for fiscal 2007.
Altria annual report for fiscal 2008.
Kraft annual report for fiscal 2001.
Kraft annual report for fiscal 2007.
Kraft annual report for fiscal 2008.

The Sale of Coca Tea: The Impact of Taxes

16

Introduction

On January 1, 2010, Tal Corporation ("Tal") acquired all the assets and liabilities of Coca Tea Company ("Coca Tea") for $1,400,000, in a taxable stock acquisition. As a result of the acquisition, Tal had a tax basis in Coca Tea's stock of $1,400,000.

The marketing of Coca Tea in the United States did not go well and both its sales and profits were lower than expected. Nine years later, it is clear to Tal that the acquisition of Coca Tea was unsuccessful, and the value of the subsidiary decreased substantially (see below).

After lengthy negotiations, on January 1, 2019, Tal and the United Beverages Company ("UBC") reached a definitive agreement whereby UBC will buy Coca Tea for $400,000 in cash. Tal will thus recognize a loss of $1,000,000 on the initial investment.

The transaction was structured as a taxable stock acquisition, so Tal's loss on the investment was recognized as a taxable one. Given that Tal paid capital gain taxes on other transactions within the previous two years, the loss on the Coca Tea deal was carried back and Tal received a $200,000 tax refund from the government. Therefore, its total cash flow was $600,000 ($400,000, selling price + $200,000, tax refund).

Tal announced that the decision to sell Coca Tea was reached after an extensive review of several options with the assistance of external advisors. One alternative option was to restructure Coca Tea and focus on marketing it in South America. However, in this option, Coca Tea would have had to reduce workforce substantially and face lengthy negotiation with trade unions. The decision to sell the company, although at a significant loss, was probably the best option from the point of view of investors not least because Tal announced that it would be able to receive back taxes paid on previous capital gains.

Below, there are some useful information:

E. Amir and M. Ghitti, *Financial Analysis of Mergers and Acquisitions*,
https://doi.org/10.1007/978-3-030-61769-1_16

- **Exhibit A** shows the balance sheet of Coca Tea as of December 31, 2018;
- **Exhibit B** shows the balance sheet of UBC as of December 31, 2018;

Assume that the acquisition was structured and treated for tax purposes using each of the following five methods:

(a) taxable stock acquisition without S338(h)(10) election;
(b) taxable asset acquisition;
(c) taxable stock acquisition with S338(h)(10) election (consider the deal as an asset deal);
(d) tax-free stock acquisition;
(e) tax-free asset acquisition.

Here is a set of assumptions to be used in analyzing this case:

- the tax rate is 25%;
- the consideration is either cash or stock (as appropriate according to each method above);
- if the consideration is cash, $150,000 comes from cash and short-term investments and the rest comes from issuing long-term debt;
- the discount rate for future cash flows is 8%;
- under S197 of the IRC, goodwill and trademarks in a taxable asset acquisition are amortized for tax purposes over 15 year.

<u>**Questions**</u>

1. How does each of the five methods affect the taxes paid in connection with the acquisition, and who pays these taxes? What is the effect of each method on the income statement of Tal?
2. How does each method affect the way the acquisition is reflected in UBC's consolidated balance sheet as of the acquisition date? You should be able to present a consolidated balance sheet for each method. You will need to compute deferred taxes and goodwill for each method.
3. Do you think the purchase price would be the same under each method? Why? To answer this question estimate the tax basis of Coca Tea's net assets.

In your answers, consider the effect of goodwill amortization under Section 197 of the IRC, as well as other fair value adjustments, for tax purposes under each method.

Exhibit A—Coca Tea's balance sheet as of December 31, 2018 ($)

	As reported	Fair value
Receivables, net	40,000	40,000
Inventories	30,000	29,000
Prepaid expenses and other current assets	12,000	12,000
Total current assets	**82,000**	**81,000**
Properties, net	35,000	40,000
Trademarks	250,000	220,000
Other intangible assets	15,000	28,000
Total assets	**382,000**	**369,000**
Current portion of long-term debt	41,000	41,000
Accounts payable	12,000	12,000
Accrued expenses	35,000	55,000
Total current liabilities	**88,000**	**108,000**
Deferred income taxes	32,000	–
Other long-term liabilities	2,000	23,000
Total liabilities	**122,000**	**131,000**
Shareholders' equity	260,000	238,000
Total Liabilities and Equity	**382,000**	**369,000**

Trademarks and goodwill are amortized over a 15-year period.

Exhibit B—UBC's balance sheet as of December 31, 2018 ($)

	31/12/2017	31/12/2018
Cash and short-term investments	210,000	180,000
Receivables, net	80,500	85,000
Inventories	52,000	62,000
Deferred income tax benefits	14,500	18,250
Prepaid expenses and other current assets	87,250	85,250
Total current assets	**444,250**	**430,500**
Properties, net	102,500	115,000
Goodwill	220,000	205,000
Other intangible assets	95,000	120,000
Total assets	**861,750**	**870,500**
Current portion of long-term debt	90,500	102,250
Accounts payable	45,000	49,000
Accrued expenses	95,500	115,500
Total current liabilities	**231,000**	**266,750**

	31/12/2017	31/12/2018
Long-term debt	557,250	502,500
Deferred income taxes	29,000	32,000
Other liabilities	31,250	34,500
Total liabilities	**848,500**	835,**750**
Common stock ($0.01 par value)	1,000	1,000
Additional paid-in capital	125,250	122,500
Accumulated deficit	(124,750)	(101,250)
Non-controlling interests	11,750	12,500
Total shareholders' equity	**13,250**	34,750
Total liabilities and shareholders' equity	**861,750**	**870,500**

References

US Internal Revenue Service, *Amortization of goodwill and certain other intangibles*, Section 197.

US Internal Revenue Service, *Certain stock purchases treated as asset acquisitions*, Section 338.

Surgery Partners: Pushdown Accounting

17

Introduction

Surgery Partners, Inc. ("SP" or "Company") is a Delaware corporation founded on April 2015 as a holding company for facilitating an initial public offering (IPO) of common stock. SP is a fast-growing healthcare services company providing outpatient surgical services. As of December 31, 2017, the Company owned or operated a portfolio of 124 surgical facilities in the US, across 32 states, primarily in partership with physicians; SP owned a majority interest in 84 of these facilities. In addition, 77% of these facilities were multispecialty focused. During 2017, physicians provided services to patients in the Company's facilities generating $1.2 billion in revenue.[1]

Prior to September 30, 2015, the Company conducted its business through Surgery Center Holdings, Inc. ("SCH") and its subsidiaries. Surgery Center Holdings, LLC ("SH") was (and is) the sole indirect owner of the equity interests of SCH and has no other material assets. On October 1, 2015, the Company completed its IPO of 14,285,000 shares of common stock at an offering price of $19.00 per share.

On September 30, 2015, SP became the direct parent and sole member of SH ("Reorganization"). In the Reorganization, all of the equity interests held by the pre-IPO owners of SH were contributed to SP in exchange for 33,871,990 shares of common stock of the Company and certain rights to additional payments under a tax receivable agreement. After giving effect to the Reorganization, SP became a holding company, and its sole material asset is an equity interest in SH. On May 9, 2017, the Company entered into a series of transactions in which it agreed:

[1]All market data in this case study are as of the time of the deal. They might have changed since then.

E. Amir and M. Ghitti, *Financial Analysis of Mergers and Acquisitions*,
https://doi.org/10.1007/978-3-030-61769-1_17

- to acquire NSH Holdco, Inc. ("NSH"), an owner and operator of surgical facilities, for approximately $760 million through a merger of SP Merger Sub, Inc., a wholly owned subsidiary of the Company, with and into NSH ("NSH Merger"); and
- to issue to BCPE Seminole Holdings LP ("Bain Capital"), an affiliate of Bain Capital Private Equity, up to 310,000 shares of the Company's preferred stock, par value $0.01 per share, to be created out of the authorized and unissued shares of the Company's preferred stock and designated as 10.00% Series A Convertible Perpetual Participating Preferred Stock at a purchase price per share of $1,000 ("Preferred Private Placement").

In connection with the NSH Merger and the Preferred Private Placement, on May 9, 2017, the Company also entered into a Stock Purchase Agreement, by and among the Company, H.I.G. Surgery Centers, LLC ("H.I.G."), the Company's controlling stockholder, H.I.G. Bayside Debt and LBO Fund II L.P. and Bain Capital ("Common SPA"), pursuant to which H.I.G. agreed to sell all of its 26,455,651 shares of the Company's common stock to Bain Capital at a purchase price per share of $19.00 (together with the NSH Merger and the Preferred Private Placement, the "Transactions"). Following the consummation of the Transactions, NSH will be a wholly owned subsidiary of the Company, and Bain Capital will be the controlling stockholder of the Company.

Acquisition of NSH

On August 31, 2017, the Company completed its acquisition of NSH through the NSH Merger, for a total cash consideration of $711.7 million, net of cash acquired, including $19.6 million funded to an escrow account. The NSH Merger added to the Company's portfolio 22 owned or operated surgical facilities, including 7 ASCs and 15 surgical hospitals, as well as complementary ancillary services. The proceeds from the Preferred Private Placement, the 2025 Unsecured Notes and the 2017 Senior Secured Credit Facilities were used to fund the acquisition.

Fees associated with the acquisition of NSH, which includes fees incurred related to the Company's preferred equity issuances and debt financings, were approximately $82.6 million during the two and eight months ended August 31, 2017 ("Predecessor"). Approximately $45.5 million was capitalized as deferred financing costs and discount, $18.3 million was capitalized as deferred equity issuance costs, $2.4 million was expensed as merger transaction and integration costs, and $16.4 million was recorded as loss on debt refinancing costs. All capitalized costs were subsequently written off because of the application of pushdown accounting, further discussed below.

The total consideration related to the acquisition of NSH was allocated to the assets acquired and liabilities assumed based upon their respective fair values. A majority of the deferred income taxes recognized as a component of the Company's purchase price allocation is a result of the difference between the book and tax basis of the intangible assets recognized. The preliminary estimated fair value assigned to goodwill is attributable to synergies expected to arise out of the NSH Merger, by enhancing the growth profile and diversity of the Company across the healthcare continuum. The entire amount of goodwill acquired in connection with the NSH Merger was allocated to the Company's surgical facility services operating segment. The total amount of goodwill related to the NSH Merger that will be deductible for tax purposes is $153.5 million.

The amount of revenues and earnings of NSH for the one month ended September 30, 2017 ("Successor") was $34.0 million and $3.4 million, respectively, and is included in revenues and net loss attributable to SP in the condensed consolidated statement of operations.

Fair value of net assets acquired	$ Thousand
Cash consideration	762,850
Fair value of non-controlling interests	325,965
Aggregate fair value of acquisition	**1,088,815**
Cash and cash equivalents	51,159
Accounts receivable	76,101
Inventories	14,986
Prepaid expenses and other current assets	18,007
Property and equipment	174,374
Intangible assets	27,741
Goodwill	845,185
Investments in and advances to affiliates	29,737
Long-term deferred tax assets	28,182
Acquisition escrow deposit	19,600
Other long-term assets	5,309
Accounts payable	(29,652)
Accrued payroll and benefits	(27,313)
Other current liabilities	(18,355)
Current maturities of long-term debt	(16,416)
Long-term debt, less current maturities	(42,770)
Acquisition escrow liability	(19,600)
Other long-term liabilities	(47,460)
Total fair value of net assets acquired	**1,088,815**

Pushdown Accounting

On August 31, 2017, SP completed the Preferred Private Placement. In addition, Bain Capital completed the Common SPA. The purchased shares represented approximately 54.2% of the Company's outstanding common stock. As a result of the Preferred Private Placement and the Common SPA, Bain Capital became the controlling stockholder of the Company, holding Series A preferred stock and common stock that collectively represent approximately 65.7% of the voting power of all classes of capital stock of the Company as of August 31, 2017.

H.I.G. and its affiliated investment funds no longer owned any capital stock of the Company.

In connection with the change of control, the Company elected to apply "pushdown" accounting by applying the guidance in ASC 805. In accordance with ASC 805, all identifiable assets and liabilities of the Company were measured at and adjusted to fair value as of August 31, 2017, and similarly goodwill was recognized based on the terms of the transaction and the fair value of the new basis of the net assets of the Company.

During the four months ended December 31, 2017, factors became known to the Company as part of its evaluation of the assets and liabilities existing at August 31, 2017, resulting in a net increase to goodwill of $30.7 million and corresponding changes to certain classes of assets and liabilities from the preliminary allocation recorded, that are reflected in the table above. The majority of the increase to goodwill for pushdown accounting relates to the acquisition of NSH discussed above.

A majority of the deferred income taxes recognized as a component of the Company's purchase price allocation is a result of the difference between the book and tax basis of the intangible assets recognized. Goodwill recognized in connection with the application of pushdown accounting was allocated to each reportable segment as follows: $3,116 million to surgical facilities services, $151.9 million to ancillary services and $32.5 million to optical services. The total amount of the goodwill related to the application of pushdown accounting that will be deductible for tax purposes is $360.5 million.

Fair value at the time of the acquisition	$ Thousand
Equity attributable to Surgery Partners, Inc.	720,606
Redeemable preferred stocks	310,000
Fair value of non-controlling interests	957,027
Aggregate fair value	**1,987,633**
Cash and cash equivalents	214,206
Accounts receivable	253,173
Inventories	44,310
Prepaid expenses and other current assets	61,475
Property and equipment	380,085
Intangible assets	60,104
Goodwill	3,299,911
Investments in and advances to affiliates	74,722
Restricted invested assets	315
Long-term deferred tax assets	204,408
Other long-term assets	49,681
Accounts payable	(64,921)

Fair value at the time of the acquisition	$ Thousand
Accrued payroll and benefits	(54,437)
Other current liabilities	(94,740)
Current maturities of long-term debt	(49,942)
Long-term debt less current maturities	(2,142,375)
Long-term tax receivable agreement liability	(78,498)
Other long-term liabilities	(169,844)
Total fair value of net assets acquired	**1,987,633**

Questions

The acquisition of NSH and the election of pushdown accounting had a significant impact on the balance sheet of SP.

- **Exhibit A** shows the quarterly balance sheet for SP as of June 30, 2017 (Predecessor) and September 30, 2017 (Successor).
- **Exhibit B** shows the cash flow statements for SP as of August 31, 2017 and June 30, 2017 (Predecessor).
- **Exhibit C** shows the statement of changes in shareholders' equity for SP as of September 30, 2017 (Successor).

In addition, provided are the notes to SP's financial statements as of September 30, 2017 and June 30, 2017 with useful information (**Exhibit D**).

1. Using the information in the case, and provided below, construct (to the best of your ability) the balance sheet of SP as of **August 31, 2017** and **September 1, 2017**. For example, using the information in the statement of changes in shareholders' equity (below) you can construct the shareholders' equity section of the balance sheets. Guidance: Start by adding the acquisition of NSH to the balance sheet of SP as at June 30, 2017. If needed, set a plug among the "other long-term assets" line item.
2. Given the information below and your answer to question 1, assess the impact of pushdown accounting on the income statement of SP for the 4th quarter of fiscal 2017.
3. In your opinion, why did SP elect pushdown accounting?

Exhibit A—SP's consolidated balance sheets

	Successor	Predecessor
$ Thousand	30.09.2017	30.06.2017
Cash and cash equivalents	199,701	57,034
Accounts receivable	271,140	215,294

$ Thousand	Successor 30.09.2017	Predecessor 30.06.2017
Inventories	44,523	29,680
Prepaid expenses and other current assets	58,295	50,303
Total current assets	**573,659**	**352,311**
Property and equipment, net	388,697	205,744
Intangible assets, net	56,507	43,421
Goodwill	3,270,309	1,569,408
Investments in and advances to affiliates	64,427	34,488
Restricted invested assets	315	315
Long-term deferred tax assets	209,207	80,166
Financing escrow assets	–	370,000
Other long-term assets	38,733	15,634
Total assets	**4,601,854**	**2,671,487**
Accounts payable	73,251	48,210
Accrued payroll and benefits	42,439	27,437
Other current liabilities	110,850	80,436
Current maturities of long-term debt	48,472	29,919
Total current liabilities	**275,012**	**186,002**
Long-term debt less current maturities	2,144,862	1,795,265
Long-term tax receivable agreement liability	68,148	122,351
Other long-term liabilities	136,399	76,101
Non-controlling interests—redeemable	271,416	176,252
Preferred stock, $0.01 par value	326,882	–
Total Liabilities	**3,222,719**	**2,355,971**
Common stock, $0.01 par	488	488
Additional paid-in capital	704,054	324,340
Retained earnings	(9,140)	(318,576)
Total stockholders' equity	**695,402**	**6,252**
Non-controlling interests—nonredeemable	683,733	309,264
Total stockholders' equity	**1,379,135**	**315,516**
Total liabilities and stockholders' equity	**4,601,854**	**2,671,487**

Exhibit B—SP's cash flow statement from January 1, 2017 (Predecessor)

Cash flows from operating activities	31.08.2017	30.06.2017
Net (loss) income	30,418	26,049
Depreciation and amortization	30,124	22,525
Amortization of debt issuance costs, discounts and premium	5,091	3,774
Amortization of unfavorable lease liability	(217)	(162)
Equity-based compensation	3,697	2,069
Loss on disposal or impairment of long-lived assets, net	1,715	1,601
Loss on debt refinancing	18,211	–
Gain on amendment to tax receivable agreement	(15,294)	–
Deferred income taxes	(18,703)	1,894
Provisions for doubtful accost	16,297	11,463
(Income) loss from equity investments, net of distributions	489	487
Accounts receivables	8,837	(5,699)
Other operating assets and liabilities	(12,947)	(7,530)
Net cash (used in) provided by operating activities	**67,718**	**56,471**
<u>**Cash flows from investing activities**</u>		
Purchases of property and equipment, net	(18,773)	(15,102)
Payments for acquisitions, net of cash acquired	(725,853)	(14,163)
Proceeds from divestitures	70	70
Net cash used in investing activities	**(744,556)**	**(29,195)**
<u>**Cash flows from financing activities**</u>		
Principal payments on long-term debt	(1,164,237)	(113,364)
Borrowings of long-term debt	1,805,966	119,778
Payments of debt issuance costs	(58,591)	(941)
Proceeds from preferred stock issuance	310,000	–
Payments of stock issuance costs	(18,347)	–
Other financing activities	(53,446)	(45,414)
Net cash (used in) provided by financing activities	**821,345**	**(39,941)**
Net (decrease) increase in cash and cash equivalents	**144,507**	**(12,665)**
Cash and cash equivalents at beginning of period	**69,699**	**69,699**
Cash and cash equivalents at end of period	**214,206**	**57,034**

Exhibit C—SP's statement of changes in shareholders' equity

	Common Stock		APIC	Retained earnings	NCI	Total
	Shares	Amount				
Predecessor						
Balance at December 31, 2016	**48,488,616**	**485**	**320,543**	**(311,351)**	**314,997**	**324,674**
Net (loss) income	–	–	–	(11,669)	32,472	20,803
Issuance of restricted and unrestricted shares	355,607	3	(3)	–	–	–
Equity-based compensation	–	–	3,697	–	–	3,697
Cancelation of restricted shares	(33,908)	–	(790)	–	–	(790)
Acquisition of NSH	–	–	–	–	172,645	172,645
Acquisition and disposal of shares of NCI, net	–	–	3,483	–	(5,629)	(2,146)
Distributions to NCI	–	–	–	–	(38,875)	(38,875)
Balance at August 31, 2017	**48,810,315**	**488**	**326,930**	**(323,020)**	**475,610**	**480,008**
Successor						
Balance at September 1, 2017	**48,810,315**	**488**	**720,118**	**–**	**684,480**	**1405,086**
Net (loss) income	–	–	–	(9,140)	5,438	(3,702)
Issuance of restricted and unrestricted shares	–	–	–	–	–	–
Equity-based compensation	–	–	1,683	–	–	1,683
Cancellation of restricted shares	(41,019)	–	–	–	–	–
Preferred dividends	–	–	(2,633)	–	–	(2,633)
Mark to redemption adjustment	–	–	(15,566)	–	–	(15,566)
Acquisition and disposal of shares of NCI, net	–	–	452	–	(471)	(19)
Distributions to NCI	–	–	–	–	(5,714)	(5,714)
Balance at September 30, 2017	**48,769,296**	**488**	**704,054**	**(9,140)**	**683,733**	**1,379,135**

Exhibit D—SP additional information

Non-Controlling Interests—Redeemable.

A summary of activity related to the non-controlling interests—redeemable follows:

Predecessor	$(000)
Balance at December 31, 2016	**180,521**
Net income attributable to non-controlling interests—redeemable	9,615
Acquisition and disposal of shares of non-controlling interests, net—redeemable	(3,323)
Distributions to non-controlling interest—redeemable holders	(11,468)
Acquisition of NSH	153,320
Balance at August 31, 2017	**328,665**
Successor	
Balance at September 1, 2017	**271,001**
Net income attributable to non-controlling interests—redeemable	1,054
Acquisition and disposal of shares of non-controlling interests, net—redeemable	91
Distributions to non-controlling interest—redeemable holders	(730)
Balance at September 30, 2017	**271,416**

Intangible Assets: a summary of the activity related to intangible assets for the period from January 1, 2017 to August 31, 2017 (Predecessor) and the period from September 1, 2017 to September 30, 2017 (Successor) follows:

$(000)	Physician income guarantees	Management rights	Non-compete agreements	Certificates of need	Customer relation-ships	Other	Total intangi-ble assets
Predecessor							
December 31, 2016	813	21,290	16,457	3,780	3,704	1,979	48,023
Additions	445	26,900	92	745	–	130	28,312
Recr. costs	(380)	–	–	–	–	–	(380)
Amortization	–	(1,154)	(3,715)	–	(733)	(438)	(6,040)
August 31, 2017	**878**	**47,036**	**12,834**	**4,525**	**2,971**	**1,671**	**69,915**
Successor							
September 1, 2017	878	41,600	8,024	5,078	–	1,170	56,750
Additions	–	–	41	25	–	–	66
Recr. costs	(38)	–	–	–	–	–	(38)
Amortization	–	(138)	(84)	–	–	(49)	(271)
September 30, 2017	**840**	**41,462**	**7,981**	**5,103**	**-**	**1,121**	**56,507**

A summary of the activity related to intangible assets for the period from January 1, 2017 to June 30, 2017 (Predecessor) follows (in thousands):

$(000)	Physician income guarantees	Management rights	Non-compete agreements	Certificates of need	Customer relation-ships	Other	Total Intangible Assets
Predecessor							
December 31, 2016	813	21,290	16,457	3,780	3,704	1,979	48,023
Additions	175	–	92	14	–	–	281
Recr. costs	(284)	–	–	–	–	–	(284)
Amortization	–	(865)	(2,843)	–	(550)	(341)	(4,599)
June 30, 2017	**704**	**20,425**	**13,706**	**3,794**	**3,154**	**1,638**	**43,421**

Goodwill: a summary of activity related to goodwill for the period from January 1, 2017 to August 31, 2017 (Predecessor) and the period from September 1, 2017 to September 30, 2017 (Successor) follows (in thousands):

Predecessor	$(000)
Balance at December 31, 2016	**1,555,204**
Acquisitions	858,323
Divestitures	(175)
Purchase price adjustments	1,220
Balance at August 31, 2017	**2,414,572**
Successor	
Balance at September 1, 2017	**3,269,225**
Acquisitions	1,214
Divestitures	–
Purchase price adjustments	(130)
Balance at September 30, 2017	**3,270,309**

Long-Term Debt: a summary of long-term debt follows (in thousands):

$(000)	30.9.17	30.6.17
2014 revolver loan	–	91,000
2014 First Lien credit agreement	–	927,250
Term loan	1,283,626	–
Senior unsecured notes due 2021	409,821	400,000
Senior unsecured notes due 2025	370,000	370,000
Subordinated notes	–	1,000

$(000)	30.9.17	30.6.17
Notes payable and secured loans	113,547	52,793
Capital lease obligations	16,340	14,787
Less: unamortized debt issuance costs and discount	–	(31,646)
Total debt	2,193,334	1,825,184
Less: Current maturities	48,473	29,919
Total long-term debt	**2,144,862**	**1,795,265**

Long-term tax receivable agreement liabilities: on May 9, 2017, SP entered into an agreement with H.I.G. to amend an income tax receivable agreement, dated September 30, 2015 (the "TRA"). The amendment became effective on August 31, 2017. Pursuant to the amendment, SP agreed to make payments to H.I.G. pursuant to a fixed payment schedule. During the three and nine months ended September 30, 2017, SP recognized a reduction in the carrying value of the TRA liability of $43.9 million, with $15.3 million of the reduction recorded to a gain on amendment of TRA and $28.6 million recorded as a reduction to the goodwill recorded in connection with the application of pushdown accounting related to the change of control.

References

SP annual report for fiscal 2017.
SP quarterly report as of June 30, 2017 (Predecessor).
SP quarterly report as of September 30, 2017 (Successor).

Kraft Group (Part II): Cadbury Acquisition—Post-acquisition Performance

18

Introduction

On February 2, 2010, Kraft Foods Inc. ("Kraft") announced that it had acquired control of Cadbury Plc ("Cadbury"). The merger between the two companies created the second-largest confectionery, food, and beverage Company in the world.

Kraft funded the cash portion of the deal through two sources:

- selling of the Pizza business—Net cash proceeds were $2483 million, after transaction costs and tax;
- debt issuance—On February 8, 2010, Kraft issued $9.5 billion of senior unsecured notes at a weighted-average effective rate of 5.364% (due in 3.25, 6, 10 and 30 years) to finance the Cadbury acquisition and general corporate purposes (not all the debt financing was actually used for the transaction).

Pro-Forma Financial Statements

Following the finalization of the deal, Kraft prepared a pro-forma consolidated balance sheet for 31 December 2009 reflecting its merger with Cadbury and the divestiture of the Pizza business (assuming that these two events occurred on that day).

Fair Value Adjustments

Based on a preliminary fair value estimation, Kraft assumed the fair value of the following Cadbury's items to exceed their book value by the associated amounts:

This case study was originally written by Chemi Wieder under the supervision of Professor Eli Amir, at London Business School, for class discussion. Eli Amir and Marco Ghitti later revised the case for this book. All market data in this case study are as of the time of the deal. They might have changed since then.

E. Amir and M. Ghitti, *Financial Analysis of Mergers and Acquisitions*,
https://doi.org/10.1007/978-3-030-61769-1_18

Assets	$ Million	
Inventories	58	
Property and equipment	678	Excluding land
Other assets (non-current)	86	Investments in associates
Intangible assets	9,871	Definite-life assets added
Total assets	**10,693**	
Liabilities		
Long-term debt	135	
Deferred tax liability (DTL):		From fair value adjustments
Current	66	
Non-current	3,373	
Total liabilities	**3,574**	

The fair value adjustment related to:

- property and equipment is $146 million, with a useful life of 9 years;
- intangible assets is $2,400 million, with a useful life of 15 years.

GAAP Adjustments

While Cadbury uses IFRS to present its financial statements, Kraft uses US GAAP. Consequently, Kraft must adjust Cadbury's financials to US GAAP before consolidating it. The following liabilities were adjusted to align Cadbury's IFRS financial information with Kraft's US GAAP accounting policies:

Liabilities ($)	Million	
Other current liabilities	(10)	Legal costs not meeting US GAAP recognition criteria
Other non-curr. liabilities	(26)	Same as above
DTL (non-current)	59	More rigorous requirement by US GAAP in regards to recognition of tax benefit
Accrued pension	16	Change in actuarial value
Total liabilities	**39**	

Exhibit A presents Kraft's balance sheets for fiscals 2009–2011, as reported. **Exhibit B** presents the pro-forma consolidated balance sheet for December 31, 2009, as if the transaction took place on that date (see also the notes to **Exhibit B** for explanations). It was constructed based on information on Cadbury's balance sheet, fair value adjustments, and balance sheet-related GAAP adjustments.

Exhibit C presents Kraft's income statements for fiscals 2008–2011 (years ended December 31). As described earlier, Kraft sold the Pizza business in fiscal 2010; this transaction was recorded as a discontinued operation. To comply with accounting standards, and to enhance comparability, the income statements for fiscals 2008 and 2009 were adjusted to reflect the Pizza business as a discontinued operation. Therefore, **Exhibit C** also includes the income statements for fiscals 2008 and 2009 as originally reported.

Recall, that the acquisition of Cadbury's was realized in fiscal 2010. To compare fiscal 2010 with 2009, we need to prepare a pro-forma consolidated income statement for fiscal 2009. This task requires: (i) Cadbury's income statement for fiscal 2009 translated into US dollars; (ii) a separate income statement for the Pizza business for fiscal 2009; and (iii) information on differences between Cadbury's income under IFRS and its income under US GAAP.

(1) **Cadbury's income statement for fiscal 2009**

The income statement of Cadbury was issued by Kraft and is aligned with Kraft's financial reporting methods.

	$ Million	Margins
Revenues	9,326	
Cost of sales	(5,010)	
Gross profit	**4,316**	**46.3%**
SG&A expenses	(3,269)	
Asset impairment and exit costs	(256)	
Operating profit	**791**	**8.5%**
Interest and other expenses, net	(201)	
Earnings before income taxes	**590**	
Income taxes	(161)	
Net income	**429**	**4.6%**

(2) **Separate income statements for the Pizza business for fiscals 2009 and 2010**

$ Million	2009	2010
Revenues	1,632	335
Cost of sales	(968)	(202)
Gross profit	**664**	**133**
SG&A expenses	(323)	(60)
Operating profit	**341**	**73**
Income tax	(123)	(25)
Net income	**218**	**48**

(3) **Income statement GAAP adjustments**

These are the income statement items adjusted to align Cadbury's financial information under IFRS with Kraft's US GAAP accounting policies (a positive figure reflects an increase in expenses):

	$ Million	
Cost of sales	95	Actuarial losses, not recognized under IFRS
SG&A expenses	95	Actuarial losses, not recognized under IFRS
SG&A expenses	14	Periodic difference of legal expenses recognition
Interest expenses	5	Non-qualifying derivative hedging in US GAAP
Total expenses	**209**	

Exhibit D contains information retrieved from Kraft's Management Discussion and Analysis (MD&A) for fiscal 2010 (comparing operating income for fiscal 2010 with that of fiscal 2009). **Exhibit E** includes information on Kraft's acquisitions and divestitures for fiscal 2009 and fiscal 2010.

Questions

In your answers and calculations, ignore the divestitures of certain Cadbury confectionery operations in Poland and Romania (unrelated to the Pizza business).

1. Prepare a pro-forma consolidated income statement for Kraft and Cadbury for fiscal 2009. To this end, assume Kraft acquired 100% of Cadbury's shares on January 1, 2009. This pro-forma income statement will be used to analyze the post-merger financial performance of Kraft. Consequently, the pro-forma income statement should also reflect the divestiture of the Pizza business. Use a tax rate of 31.7%.
2. Companies often acquire other companies when they are unable to generate sufficient organic growth (growth from within), where growth is often measured using sales revenues. Another benefit from mergers and acquisitions is the expected synergies from the transaction. Using information in **Exhibit C**, estimate whether Kraft had organic growth in 2009, the year prior to the acquisition. Also, using information in **Exhibit C** and Cadbury's income statement for fiscal 2009, assess whether there could be potential synergies and cost savings in the acquisition. To assess synergies, examine profit margins.
3. Using all available information in the case, estimate Kraft's organic growth in fiscal 2010 (as compared to fiscal 2009) by analyzing growth in revenues, operating income, and net income.
4. Analyze the post-merger performance (2010 and 2011) of the combined company. Focus on sales growth, profit margins, return on equity, and return on assets. Use information in Note 2, fiscal 2010. To compute average figures, note that, in fiscal 2008, Kraft's shareholders' equity and total assets were $22,295 and $63,173, respectively.
5. Estimate whether Kraft was successful in materializing synergies from the merger. In your opinion, was Kraft's acquisition of Cadbury successful?

Exhibit A—Kraft's Balance Sheets for December 31, 2009–2011 ($ Million)

	31.12.2011	31.12.10	31.12.09
Cash and cash equivalents	1,974	2,481	2,101
Receivables	6,361	6,539	5,197
Inventories	5,706	5,310	3,775
Deferred income taxes	912	898	730
Other current assets	1,249	993	651
Total current assets	**16,202**	**16,221**	**12,454**
Property and equipment, net	13,813	13,792	10,693
Goodwill	37,297	37,856	28,764
Intangible assets	25,186	25,963	13,429
Prepaid pension costs	31	86	115
Other assets	1,308	1,371	1,259
Total assets	**93,837**	**95,289**	**66,714**
Short-term borrowings	182	750	453
Current portion of long-term debt	3,654	1,115	513
Accounts payable	5,525	5,409	3,766
Accrued marketing	2,863	2,515	2,181
Accrued employment costs	1,365	1,292	1,175
Other current liabilities	4,856	4,579	3,403
Total current liabilities	**18,445**	**15,660**	**11,491**
Long-term debt	23,095	26,859	18,024
Deferred income taxes	6,738	7,984	4,508
Accrued pension & postretirement costs	6,835	5,428	4,581
Other liabilities	3,396	3,416	2,138
Total liabilities	**58,509**	**59,347**	**40,742**
Common stock, no par value	–	–	–
Additional paid-in capital	31,318	31,231	23,611
Retained earnings	18,012	16,619	14,636
Accumulated other comprehensive losses	(6,637)	(3,890)	(3,955)
Treasury stock, at cost	(7,476)	(8,126)	(8,416)
Total shareholders' equity	**35,217**	**35,834**	**25,876**
Non-controlling interests	111	108	96
Total equity	**35,328**	**35,942**	**25,972**
Total liabilities and equity	**93,837**	**95,289**	**66,714**

Exhibit B—Pro-Forma Consolidated Balance Sheet for Kraft and Cadbury, as of December 31, 2009 (with Pizza Business Sale)

Notes to Exhibit B:

Kraft, Cadbury—presents the balance items of the two companies as reported in their separate annual reports as of December 31, 2009. Cadbury's reports were prepared in Pound Sterling and were translated to US dollar by Kraft, which submitted the translated reports in a filing to the SEC (Fig. 18.1).

GAAP & Other—presents the fair value, GAAP and other adjustments as estimated by Kraft.

Eliminations—The consolidation balance sheet includes only the shareholders' equity of the parent. In addition, the only goodwill recorded in an acquisition is a "new" goodwill. The identifiable assets do not include goodwill that may exist on the acquiree's books.

Goodwill—goodwill was calculated by Kraft.

Kraft Adj.—Presents the following adjustments:

- use of cash in the amount expected to be receive from the Pizza business sale;
- expense of estimated transaction costs (retained earnings) against current liabilities;
- issuance of debt to finance the acquisition which is calculated as follows (in $ million):

	$ Million
Total cash consideration	11,129
Proceeds from the Pizza business sale	(2,483)
Debt issued	**8,646**

- total value of Kraft shares issued presented in additional paid-in capital (Kraft's common stock has no par value).

Pizza—presents the divestiture of the Pizza business and includes the following:

- net proceeds from the Pizza business sale;
- reduction of the Pizza business' assets from Kraft's books. As shown in the table, these assets include inventory, property and equipment, and goodwill;
- the gain from the Pizza business sale was recorded in retained earnings.

Exhibit C—Kraft's Consolidated Statement of Earnings 2008–2011 ($ Millions)

	As reported		Reclassified	
	2011	2010	2009	2008
Revenues	54,365	49,207	38,754	40,492

	Kraft	*Cadbury*	*FV*	*GAAP*	*Other*	*Eliminations*	*Goodwill*	*Pizza*	*Kraft Adj.*	*Total*	*Pro-forma*
Cash and cash equivalents	2,101	383						2,483	(2,483)	0	2,484
Receivables	5,197	1,581									6,778
Inventories, net	3,775	1,210	58					(102)		(44)	4,941
Deferred income taxes	730	0									730
Other current assets	651	262									913
Total current assets	**12,454**	**3,436**	**58**	**0**	**0**	**0**		**2,381**	**(2,483)**	**(44)**	**15,846**
Property and equipment, net	10,693	3,022	678					(317)		361	14,076
Goodwill	28,764	3,519				(3,519)	9,506	(475)		5,512	37,795
Intangible assets, net	13,429	2,629	9,871							9,871	25,929
Other assets	1,374	538	86							86	1,998
Total assets	**66,714**	**13,144**	**10,693**	**0**	**0**	**(3,519)**	**9,506**	**1,589**	**(2,483)**	**15,786**	**95,644**
Short-term borrowings	453	433									886
Current portion of long-term debt	513	0									513
Accounts payable	3,766	2,550									6,316
Accrued expenses & other current liabilities	6,759	952	66	(10)	(262)				180	(26)	7,685
Total current liabilities	**11,491**	**3,935**	**66**	**(10)**	**(262)**	**0**		**0**	**180**	**(26)**	**15,400**
Long-term debt	18,024	2,183	135						8,646	8,781	28,988
Deferred income taxes	4,508	264	3,373	59						3,432	8,204
Accrued pension & postretirement costs	4,581	815		16						16	5,412
Other liabilities	2,138	252		(26)	446					420	2,810
Total liabilities	**40,742**	**7,449**	**3,574**	**39**	**184**	**0**		**0**	**8,826**	**12,623**	**60,814**
Common stock, no par value	0	0									
Additional paid-in capital	23,611	378				(378)			7,417	7,039	31,028
Retained earnings	14,636	4,227				(4,227)		1,589		(2,638)	16,225
Accumulated other comprehensive losses	(3,955)	1,058				(1,058)			(180)	(1,238)	(4,135)
Treasury stock, at cost	(8,416)	0									(8,416)
Total shareholders' equity	**25,876**	**5,663**	**0**	**0**	**0**	**(5,663)**	**0**	**1,589**	**7,237**	**3,163**	**34,702**
Non-controlling interests	96	32									128
Total liabilities and equity	**66,714**	**13,144**	**3,574**	**39**	**184**	**(5,663)**	**0**	**1,589**	**16,063**	**15,786**	**95,644**

Fig. 18.1 Pro-forma consolidated balance sheet

	As reported		Reclassified	
	2011	2010	2009	2008
Cost of sales	(35,350)	(31,305)	(24,819)	(27,164)
Gross profit	**19,015**	**17,902**	**13,935**	**13,328**
SG&A expenses	(12,140)	(12,001)	(8,784)	(8,613)
Asset impairment and exit costs	7	(18)	64	(1,024)
Loss on divestitures, net	–	(6)	(6)	(92)
Amortization of intangibles	(225)	(211)	(26)	(23)
Operating income	**6,657**	**5,666**	**5,183**	**3,576**
Interest and other expenses, net	(1,885)	(2,024)	(1,237)	(1,240)
Earnings from cont. operations, gross	**4,772**	**3,642**	**3,946**	**2,336**
Provision for income taxes	(1,225)	(1,147)	(1,136)	(658)
Earnings from cont. operations	**3,547**	**2,495**	**2,810**	**1,678**
Earnings from disc. operations, net	–	(1,644)	(218)	(1,215)
Net earnings	**3,547**	**4,139**	**3,028**	**2,893**
Non-controlling interests	(20)	(25)	(7)	(9)
Net earnings attributable to Kraft	**3,527**	**4,114**	**3,021**	**2,884**

The income statements for 2009 and 2008 are not as originally reported. These income statements were reclassified to reflect the discontinued operations in 2010.

	As reported	As reported	As reported
	2009	2008	2007
Revenues	40,386	41,932	35,858
Cost of sales	(25,786)	(28,088)	(23,656)
Gross profit	**14,600**	**13,844**	**12,202**
SG&A expenses	(9,108)	(8,862)	(7,587)
Asset impairment and exit costs	64	(1,024)	(440)
(Gain) loss on divestitures, net	(6)	(92)	14
Amortization of intangibles	(26)	(23)	(13)
Operating income	**5,524**	**3,843**	**4,176**
Interest and other expenses, net	(1,237)	(1,240)	(604)
Earnings before income taxes	**4,287**	**2,603**	**3,572**
Provision for income taxes	(1,259)	(755)	(1,080)
Earnings from cont. operations	**3,028**	**1,848**	**2,492**
Earnings from disc. operations, net	–	1,045	232
Net earnings	**3,028**	**2,893**	**2,724**
Non-controlling interests	(7)	(9)	(3)
Net earnings attributable to Kraft	**3,021**	**2,884**	**2,721**

Exhibit D—Analysis of Operating Income (Kraft's 2010 MD&A)

The increase in net revenues was primarily driven by the Cadbury acquisition, which added $9,143 million in net revenues during the year. Operating income increased $483 million (9.3%) to $5,666 million in 2010, due to the following:

Change in operating income	$	%
Operating income December 31, 2009 (as revised)	**5,183**	–
Higher input costs	(487)	(8.6)
Higher pricing	412	7.4
Favorable volume/mix	495	8.9
Increased operating income from Cadbury acquisition	1,139	21.8
Higher acquisition-related costs due to Cadbury	(233)	(4.3)
Integration program costs	(646)	(12.5)
Higher net asset impairment and exist costs	(82)	(1.7)
Lower other SG&A expenses	25	1.0
Change in unrealized losses on hedging activities	(136)	(2.4)
Unfavorable foreign currency	(8)	(0.1)
Other, net	4	(0.2)
Total change in op. income	**483**	**9.3**
Operating income December 31, 2010	**5,666**	–

The Cadbury acquisition, net of Integration program and higher acquisition-related costs, increased operating income by $260 million.

Exhibit E—Kraft's Acquisitions and Divestitures

Cadbury Acquisition:

Under the terms of the final offer, Kraft agreed to pay Cadbury shareholders 500 pence in cash and 0.1874 shares of Kraft common stock per Cadbury ordinary share validly tendered and 2000 pence in cash and 0.7496 shares of Kraft common stock per Cadbury ADS validly tendered. This valued Cadbury at $18.5 billion, or approximately £11.6 billion (based on the average price of $28.36 for Kraft's share on February 2, 2010, and an exchange rate of $1.595 per £1.00).

On February 2, 2010, Kraft acquired 71.73% of Cadbury shares for $13.1 billion and the value attributed to non-controlling interests was $5.4 billion. From February 2, 2010, through June 1, 2010, Kraft acquired the remaining 28.27% of Cadbury shares for $5.4 billion. Kraft had a $38 million gain on non-controlling interest acquired and recorded it within additional paid-in capital.

As part of the Cadbury acquisition, Kraft incurred and expensed transaction related fees of $218 million in 2010 and $40 million in 2009. These expenses were recorded within selling, general and administrative expenses. Acquisition financing fees of $96 million were incurred as well in 2010 (recorded within interest and other expense, net).

Cadbury contributed net revenues of $9,143 million and net earnings of $530 million from February 2, 2010, through December 31, 2010.

The following pro-forma summary presents Kraft's consolidated information as if Cadbury had been acquired on January 1, 2009.

Pro-forma December 31, 2009 ($ Million)	2010	2009
Net revenues	49,770	47,852
Net earnings attributable to Kraft	3,938	2,586

Our February 2, 2010, Cadbury acquisition was valued at $18,547 million, or $17,503 million net of cash and cash equivalents. As part of that acquisition, Kraft acquired the following assets and liabilities:

	($ Million)
Receivables[a]	1,333
Inventories	1,298
Other current assets	660
Property and equipment	3,293
Goodwill[b]	9,530
Intangible assets[c]	12,905
Other assets	593
Short-term borrowing	(1,206)
Account payable	(1,605)
Other current liabilities[d]	(1,866)
Long-term debt	(2,437)
Deferred income taxes	(3,218)
Accrued pension costs	(817)
Other liabilities	(927)
Non-controlling interests	(33)

[a]The gross amount due under the receivables Kraft acquired is $1,474 million, of which $141 million was expected to be uncollectable

[b]Goodwill will not be deductible for statutory tax purposes

[c]Kraft acquired $10.3 billion of indefinite-life intangible assets, primarily trademarks, and $2.6 billion of amortizable intangible assets, primarily customer relationships and technology. Customer relationships will be amortized over approximately 13 years and technology will be amortized over approximately 12 years

[d]Within other current liabilities, a reserve for exposures related to taxes of approximately $70 million was established within Kraft's Developing Markets segment. The cumulative exposure was approximately $150 million at December 31, 2010

Pizza Divestiture:

On March 1, 2010, Kraft completed the sale of the Pizza Business to Nestle for $3.7 billion. Accordingly, the Pizza Business results have been reflected as discontinued operations on the consolidated statement of earnings, and prior period results have been revised.

Summary results of operations for the Pizza Business through March 1, 2010, were as follows:

$ Million	2010	2009	2008
Net revenues	335	1,632	1,440
Earnings before income taxes	73	341	267
Provision for income taxes	(25)	(123)	(97)
Gain on disc. operations, net	1,596	–	–
Earnings from disc. operations, net	**1,644**	**218**	**170**

The 2010 gain on discontinued operations from the sale of Pizza Business included tax expense of $1.2 billion. The following assets of the Pizza Business were included in the Pizza Business divestiture:

	$ Million
Inventories, net	102
Property and equipment, net	317
Goodwill	475
Distributed assets of the Frozen Pizza business	**894**

LU Biscuit Acquisition:

On November 30, 2007, Kraft acquired the Groupe Danone S.A. global *LU* biscuit business ("*LU* Biscuit") for €5.1 billion (approximately $7.6 billion) in cash. *LU* Biscuit reported results from operations on a one month lag; accordingly, there was no effect on Kraft 2007 operating results. On a pro-forma basis, *LU* Biscuit would have contributed net revenues of $2.8 billion during 2007, and *LU* Biscuit's contribution to net earnings would have been insignificant to Kraft.

References

Cadbury annual report for fiscal 2009.
Kraft annual report for fiscal 2008.
Kraft annual report for fiscal 2009.
Kraft annual report for fiscal 2010.
Kraft annual report for fiscal 2011.
Kraft final prospectus to exchange, January 29, 2010.
Kraft form 8-K/A as of February 2, 2010.
Kraft quarterly report as of March 31, 2010.
Kraft quarterly report as of December 31, 2010.

Index

E. Amir and M. Ghitti, *Financial Analysis of Mergers and Acquisitions*, https://doi.org/10.1007/978-3-030-61769-1

GPSR Compliance
The European Union's (EU) General Product Safety Regulation (GPSR) is a set of rules that requires consumer products to be safe and our obligations to ensure this.

If you have any concerns about our products, you can contact us on

ProductSafety@springernature.com

In case Publisher is established outside the EU, the EU authorized representative is:

Springer Nature Customer Service Center GmbH
Europaplatz 3
69115 Heidelberg, Germany

www.ingramcontent.com/pod-product-compliance
Ingram Content Group UK Ltd.
Pitfield, Milton Keynes, MK11 3LW, UK
UKHW022226051026
15624UKWH00002B/375
9783030617684